DOUGHNUT ECONOMICS

Kate Raworth is an economist whose research focuses on the unique social and ecological challenges of the 21st century. She is a Senior Visiting Research Associate teaching at Oxford University's Environmental Change Institute, and a Senior Associate of the Cambridge Institute for Sustainability Leadership.

Over the last two decades Kate has worked as Senior Researcher at Oxfam, as a co-author of the UN's Human Development Report at the United Nations Development Programme, and as a Fellow of the Overseas Development Institute in the villages of Zanzibar.

She has been named by the *Guardian* as one of the top ten tweeters on economic transformation.

Praise for *Doughnut Economics*

'At last – an economic model that won't destroy the planet . . . I view Raworth as the John Maynard Keynes of the 21st century: by reframing the economy, she allows us to change our view of who we are, where we stand, and what we want to be.'
George Monbiot, *Guardian*

'I've never seen [these ideas] laid out so clearly, compellingly, or cheekily. Social entrepreneurs, it's doughnut time – and I strongly recommend that you take a bite.' *Forbes*

'A sharp, insightful call for a shift in thinking . . . Raworth's energetic, layperson-friendly writing makes her concept accessible as well as intriguing.' *Publishers Weekly*

'*Doughnut Economics* shows how to ensure dignity and prosperity for all people.' *Huffington Post*

'An innovative vision about how we could refocus away from growth to thriving.' This Is Money, *Daily Mail*

'Great stuff.' Caroline Lucas MP, co-leader of the Green Party

'A good starting point for a much-needed debate about economic policy priorities.' *Reuters*

'A new book you will need to know about ... Kate writes beautifully ... If only ten per cent of the ideas get implemented, the world will be a much better place.'   Duncan Green, *Oxfam Blogs*

'[*Doughnut Economics*] embeds the human economy within the natural world and within society, rather than being distinct from either.'   *The Ecologist*

'We need to fundamentally rethink the way we create and distribute wealth, and Kate Raworth's *Doughnut Economics* provides an inspiring primer as to how we must now set about that challenge.'   Jonathan Porritt

'Written in a clear and engaging style, Kate Raworth explains to the general public and students what is wrong with the standard curriculum in economics, and how to break out of that monopolised mental prison ... [*Doughnut Economics* is] a cause for celebration ... I highly recommend this book.'   Herman Daly, *Ecological Economics*

'I do not know what form a new economic technology will take ... [but] Kate Raworth's concept of "doughnut economics" as a brand new way of conceptualising economic development without being tied to infinite growth is up there as a useful idea.'   *Guardian*

'A radical viewpoint ... [Raworth's] approach centres economics on action.'   *The Hindu*

'What if it were possible to live well without trashing the planet? *Doughnut Economics* succinctly captures this tantalising possibility and takes up its challenge. Brimming with creativity, Raworth reclaims economics from the dust of academia and puts it to the service of a better world.'   Tim Jackson

'A radical and solidly-argued book ... Plausible and informative.'   *El País*

'Asks some simple and pertinent questions.'   Andrew Marr, *Spectator*

'A precious book ... State-of-the-art, unorthodox economic thinking that calls for the redistribution of wealth and resources.'   *La Repubblica*

DOUGHNUT ECONOMICS

Seven Ways to Think Like a
21st-Century Economist

Kate Raworth

17

Random House Business
20 Vauxhall Bridge Road
London SW1V 2SA

Random House Business is part of the Penguin Random House group of companies
whose addresses can be found at global.penguinrandomhouse.com.

Penguin
Random House
UK

First published by Random House Business Books in 2017
This paperback edition first published by
Random House Business Books in 2018

www.penguin.co.uk

A CIP catalogue record for this book is available from the British Library.

ISBN 9781847941398

Printed and bound in Great Britain by Clays Ltd, Elcograf S.p.A.

Penguin Random House is committed to a sustainable future
for our business, our readers and our planet. This book is made
from Forest Stewardship Council® certified paper.

The most powerful tool in economics is not money, nor even algebra. It is a pencil. Because with a pencil you can redraw the world.

Contents

CONTENTS

WHO WANTS TO BE AN ECONOMIST?

In October 2008, Yuan Yang arrived at Oxford University to study economics. Born in China and raised in Yorkshire, she had the outlook of a global citizen: passionate about current affairs, concerned about the future, and determined to make a difference in the world. And she believed that becoming an economist was the best way to equip herself to make that difference. She was eager, you could say, to become just the kind of economist that the twenty-first century needs.

But Yuan soon got frustrated. She found the theory – and the maths used to prove it – absurdly narrow in its assumptions. And since she began her studies just as the global financial system was heading into free fall, she could not help but notice it, even if her university syllabus didn't. 'The crash was a wake-up call,' she recounted. 'On the one hand we were being taught as if the financial system was not an important part of the economy. And on the other hand, its markets were clearly wreaking havoc, so we asked, "Why is there this disconnect?"' It was a disconnect, she realised, that ran far beyond the financial sector, visible in the gulf between the preoccupations of mainstream economic theory and growing real-world crises such as global inequality and climate change.

When she put her questions to her professors, they assured her that insight would come at the next level of study. So she enrolled for the next level – a Master's degree at the prestigious London School of Economics – and waited for that insight to come. Instead, the abstract theories intensified, the equations multiplied, and Yuan grew more dissatisfied. But with exams on the horizon, she faced a choice. 'At some point,' she told me, 'I realised that I just had to master this material, rather than trying to question everything. And I think that's a sad moment to have as a student.'

Many students coming to this realisation would have either walked away from economics, or swallowed its theories whole and built a lucrative career out of their qualifications. Not Yuan. She set out to find like-minded student rebels in universities worldwide and quickly discovered that, since the millennium, a growing number had publicly started to question the narrow theoretical framework that they were being taught. In 2000, economics students in Paris had sent an open letter to their professors, rejecting the dogmatic teaching of mainstream theory. 'We wish to escape from imaginary worlds!' they wrote, 'Call to teachers: wake up before it is too late!' [1] A decade later, a group of Harvard students staged a mass walk-out of a lecture by Professor Gregory Mankiw – author of the world's most widely taught economics textbooks – in protest against the narrow and biased ideological perspective that they believed his course espoused. They were, they said, 'deeply concerned that this bias affects students, the University, and our greater society'.[2]

When the financial crisis hit, it galvanised student dissent worldwide. It also spurred Yuan and her fellow rebels to launch a global network connecting over 80 student groups in more than 30 countries – from India and the US to Germany and Peru – in their demand for economics to catch up with the current generation, the century we are in, and the challenges ahead. 'It is not only the world economy that is in crisis,' they declared in an open letter in 2014:

The teaching of economics is in crisis too, and this crisis has consequences far beyond the university walls. What is taught shapes the

2

minds of the next generation of policymakers, and therefore shapes the societies we live in . . . We are dissatisfied with the dramatic narrowing of the curriculum that has taken place over the last couple of decades . . . It limits our ability to contend with the multidimensional challenges of the 21st century – from financial stability, to food security and climate change.[3]

The more radical among these student protestors have been targeting highbrow conferences with their counter-cultural critiques. In January 2015, as the American Economic Association's annual meeting got under way in Boston's Sheraton Hotel, students from the Kick It Over movement plastered accusatory posters in the hotel's corridors, elevators and toilets, projected giant subversive messages on to the conference centre's street facade, and stunned the incredulous conference-goers by occupying their sedate panel discussions

In January 2015 rebel economics students commandeered the street front of the Boston Sheraton to greet the American Economic Association's annual conference with their counter-cultural critique.

and hijacking question time.[4] 'The revolution of economics has begun,' the students' manifesto declared. 'On campus after campus we will chase you old goats out of power. Then in the months and years that follow, we will begin the work of reprogramming the doomsday machine.'[5]

It's an extraordinary situation. No other academic discipline has managed to provoke its own students – the very people who have chosen to dedicate years of their life to studying its theories – into worldwide revolt. Their rebellion has made one thing clear: the revolution in economics has indeed begun. Its success depends not only on debunking the old ideas but, more importantly, on bringing forth the new. As the ingenious twentieth-century inventor Buckminster Fuller once said, 'You never change things by fighting the existing reality. To change something, build a new model that makes the existing model obsolete.'

This book takes up his challenge, setting out seven mind-shifting ways in which we can all learn to think like twenty-first-century economists. By revealing the old ideas that have entrapped us and replacing them with new ones to inspire us, it proposes a new economic story that is told in pictures as much as in words.

The twenty-first-century challenge

The word 'economics' was coined by the philosopher Xenophon in Ancient Greece. Combining *oikos*, meaning household, with *nomos*, meaning rules or norms, he invented the art of household management, and it could not be more relevant today. This century we need some pretty insightful managers to guide our planetary household, and ones who are ready to pay attention to the needs of all of its inhabitants.

There have been extraordinary strides in human well-being over the past 60 years. The average child born on planet Earth in 1950 could expect to live just 48 years; today such a child can look forward to 71 years of life.[6] Since 1990 alone, the number of people living in extreme income poverty – on less than $1.90 a day – has fallen by more than half. Over two billion people have gained access to safe drinking water and toilets for the first time. All this while the human population has grown by almost 40%.[7]

That was the good news. The rest of the story, of course, has not turned out so well so far. Many millions of people still lead lives of extreme deprivation. Worldwide, one person in nine does not have enough to eat.[8] In 2015 six million children under the age of five died, more than half of those deaths due to easy-to-treat conditions like diarrhoea and malaria.[9] Two billion people live on less than $3 a day and over 70 million young women and men are unable to find work.[10] Deprivations such as these have been exacerbated by growing insecurities and inequalities. The 2008 financial crash sent shock waves through the global economy, robbing many millions of people of their jobs, homes, savings and security. Meanwhile, the world has become extraordinarily unequal: as of 2015 the world's richest 1% now own more wealth than all the other 99% put together.[11]

To these extremes of human circumstance, add the deepening degradation of our planetary home. Human activity is putting unprecedented stress on Earth's life-giving systems. Global average temperature has already risen by 0.8°C and we are on track for an increase of almost 4°C by 2100, threatening a scale and intensity of floods, droughts, storms and sea-level rise that humanity has never before witnessed.[12] Around 40% of the world's agricultural land is now seriously degraded and by 2025 two out of three people worldwide will live in water-stressed regions.[13] Meanwhile over 80% of the world's fisheries are fully or over-exploited and a refuse truck's worth of plastic is dumped into the ocean every minute: at this rate, by 2050 there will be more plastic than fish in the sea.[14]

These are already overwhelming facts, but growth projections add to the challenge ahead. Global population stands today at 7.3 billion and is expected to reach almost 10 billion by 2050, levelling off at around 11 billion by 2100.[15] Global economic output is – if you believe business-as-usual projections – expected to grow by 3% per year from now until 2050, doubling the global economy in size by 2037 and almost trebling it by 2050.[16] The global middle class – those spending between $10 and $100 a day – is set to expand rapidly, from 2 billion today to 5 billion by 2030, bringing a surge in demand for construction materials and consumer products.[17] These are the trends that shape humanity's prospects at the start of the twenty-first century. So what kind of thinking do we need for the journey ahead?

The authority of economics

However we tackle these interwoven challenges, one thing is clear: economic theory will play a defining role. Economics is the mother tongue of public policy, the language of public life, and the mindset that shapes society. 'In these early decades of the twenty-first century, the master story is economic: economic beliefs, values and assumptions are shaping how we think, feel and act,' writes F. S. Michaels in her book *Monoculture: How One Story is Changing Everything.*[18]

Perhaps this is why economists carry an air of authority. They take front-row seats as experts in the international policy arena – from the World Bank to the World Trade Organization – and are rarely far from the ear of power. In the US, for example, the President's Council of Economic Advisers is by far the most influential, high-profile and long-running of all the White House's advisory councils, while its sibling councils for environmental quality and science and technology are barely known beyond the Beltway. In 1968, the prestige of Nobel Prizes awarded for scientific advances in physics, chemistry and medicine was controversially extended: Sweden's central bank successfully lobbied and paid for a Nobel-Memorial prize to be awarded annually in 'Economic Sciences' too, and its laureates have become academic celebrities ever since.

Not all economists have been comfortable with this apparent authority. Back in the 1930s, John Maynard Keynes – the Englishman whose ideas would transform post-war economics – was already worrying about the role played by his profession. 'The ideas of economists and political philosophers, both when they are right and when they are wrong, are more powerful than is commonly understood. Indeed, the world is ruled by little else,' he famously wrote. 'Practical men, who believe themselves to be quite exempt from any intellectual influences, are usually the slaves of some defunct economist.'[19] The Austrian economist Friedrich von Hayek, best known as the 1940s father of neoliberalism, disagreed violently with Keynes on almost all questions of theory and policy, but on this matter they concurred. In 1974 when Hayek was awarded that Nobel-Memorial prize, he accepted it with the remark that, had he been consulted on its creation, he would have advised against it. Why? Because, he told the assembled crowd, 'the Nobel Prize confers on an individual an authority which in economics no man ought to possess', particularly, he said, because, 'the influence of the economist that mainly matters is an influence over laymen: politicians, journalists, civil servants and the public generally'.[20]

Despite such misgivings from the twentieth century's two most influential economists, the dominance of the economist's perspective on the world has only spread, even into the language of public life. In hospitals and clinics worldwide, patients and doctors have been recast as customers and service-providers. In fields and forests on every continent, economists are calculating the monetary value of 'natural capital' and 'ecosystem services', ranging from the economic worth of the world's wetlands (said to be $3.4 billion per year) to the global value of insect pollination services (equivalent to $160 billion per year).[21] Meanwhile, the financial sector's importance is constantly reinforced by media reporting, with daily radio and print headlines announcing the latest corporate quarterly results, while stock prices roll tickertape-style across the TV news.

Given the dominance of economics in public life, it is no surprise that so many university students, if given the chance, opt to study a little as part of their education. Every year, around five million college students in the United States alone graduate with at least one economics course under their belts. A standard introductory course that originated in the USA – and is widely known as Econ 101 – is now taught throughout the world, with students from China to Chile learning from translations of the very same textbooks used in Chicago and Cambridge, Massachusetts. For all of these students, Econ 101 has become a staple part of a broad education, whether they then head off to become an entrepreneur or doctor, journalist or political activist. Even for those who never study economics, the language and mindset of Econ 101 so pervades public debate that it shapes the way that we all think about the economy: what it is, how it works, and what it is for.

And here's the rub. Humanity's journey through the twenty-first century will be led by the policymakers, entrepreneurs, teachers, journalists, community organisers, activists and voters who are being educated today. But these citizens of 2050 are being taught an economic mindset that is rooted in the textbooks of 1950, which in turn are rooted in the theories of 1850. Given the fast-changing nature of the twenty-first century, this is shaping up to be a disaster. Of course the twentieth century gave rise to groundbreaking new economic thinking, most influentially in the battle of ideas between Keynes and Hayek. But though those iconic thinkers held opposing perspectives, they inherited flawed assumptions and common blind spots that lay unexamined at the root of their differences. The twenty-first-century context demands that we make those assumptions explicit and those blind spots visible so that we can, once again, rethink economics.

Walking away from economics – and back

As a teenager in the 1980s, I tried to piece together an understanding of the world by watching the evening news. The TV images that flashed daily into our living room took me far beyond my London schoolgirl life, and those images stuck. The unforgettable silent stare of pot-bellied children born into Ethiopia's famine. Lines of bodies knocked down like matchsticks by the Bhopal gas disaster. A purple-tinted hole gaping in the ozone layer. A vast oil slick swirling out of the *Exxon Valdez* into Alaska's pristine waters. By the end of the decade, I knew simply that I wanted to work for an organisation like Oxfam or Greenpeace – campaigning to end poverty and environmental destruction – and I thought that the best way to equip myself was to study economics and put its tools to work for such causes.

So I headed to Oxford University to get the skills that I believed would prepare me for the job. But the economic theory on offer left me frustrated because it made awkward assumptions about how the world worked, while glossing over the very issues I cared about most. I was lucky to have inspiring and wide-minded tutors, but they too were hemmed in by the syllabus that they were required to teach and we to master. So after four years of study, I found myself walking away from theoretical economics, too embarrassed ever to call myself 'an economist' and I immersed myself, instead, in real-world economic challenges.

I spent three years working with barefoot entrepreneurs in the villages of Zanzibar, in awe of the women who ran micro-businesses while raising their children without running water, electricity or a school in sight. I then hopped to the very different island of Manhattan, spending four years at the United Nations on the team writing the annual flagship *Human Development Report*, while witnessing barefaced power games block progress in international negotiations. I left to fulfil a long-held ambition and worked with Oxfam for over a decade. There I witnessed the precarious existences of women – from Bangladesh to Birmingham – employed at the sharp end of global supply chains. We lobbied to change the rigged rules and double standards governing international trade rules. And I explored the human-rights implications of climate change, meeting farmers from India to Zambia whose fields had been turned to bare earth because the rains had never come. Then I became a mother – of twins, to boot – and spent a year on maternity leave, immersed in the bare-bum economy of raising infants. When I returned to work, I understood the pressures on parents juggling job and family like never before.

Through all this, I gradually realised the obvious: that I could not simply walk away from economics, because it shapes the world we inhabit and its mindset had certainly shaped me, even if through my rejection of it. So I decided to walk back towards it and flip it on its head. What if we started economics not with its long-established theories, but with humanity's long-term goals, and then sought out the economic thinking that would enable us to achieve them? I tried to draw a picture of those goals and, ridiculous though it sounds, it came out looking like a doughnut – yes, the American kind with a hole in the middle. The full diagram is set out in the next chapter, but in essence it is a pair of concentric rings. Below the inner ring – the social foundation – lie critical human deprivations such as hunger and illiteracy. Beyond the outer ring – the ecological ceiling – lies critical planetary degradation such as climate change and biodiversity loss. Between those two rings is the Doughnut itself, the space in which we can meet the needs of all within the means of the planet.

Sugary, deep-fried doughnuts hardly seem a likely metaphor for humanity's aspirations but there was something about the image that struck a chord in me and in others, so it stuck. And it prompted a profoundly exciting question:

If humanity's twenty-first-century goal is to get into the Doughnut, what economic mindset will give us the best chance of getting there?

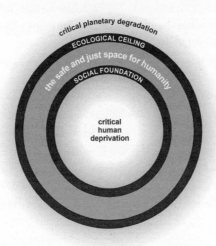

The essence of the Doughnut: a social foundation of well-being that no one should fall below, and an ecological ceiling of planetary pressure that we should not go beyond. Between the two lies a safe and just space for all.

With the Doughnut in hand, I pushed my old textbooks aside and sought out the best emerging ideas that I could find, exploring new economic thinking with open-minded university students, progressive business leaders, innovative academics and cutting-edge practitioners. This book brings together the key insights I have discovered along the way – insights into ways of thinking that I wish had crossed my path at the outset of my own economics education, and that I believe should be part of every economist's toolkit today. It draws on diverse schools of thought, such as complexity, ecological, feminist, institutional and behavioural economics. They are all rich with insight but there is still a risk that they will remain separated in silos, each school of thought nestled in its own journals, conferences, blogs, textbooks and teaching posts, cultivating its niche critique of last century's thinking. The real breakthrough lies,

11

of course, in combining what they each have to offer and to discover what happens when they dance on the same page, which is just what this book sets out to do.

Humanity faces some formidable challenges, and it is in no small part thanks to the blind spots and mistaken metaphors of outdated economic thinking that we have ended up here. But for those who are ready to rebel, look sideways, to question and think again, then these are exciting times. 'Students must learn how to discard old ideas, how and when to replace them . . . how to learn, unlearn, and relearn,' wrote the futurist Alvin Toffler.[22] This could not be more true for those seeking economic literacy: now is a great moment for unlearning and relearning the fundamentals of economics.

The power of pictures

Everybody's saying it: we need a new economic story, a narrative of our shared economic future that is fit for the twenty-first century. I agree. But let's not forget one thing: the most powerful stories throughout history have been the ones told with pictures. If we want to rewrite economics, we need to redraw its pictures too, because we stand little chance of telling a new story if we stick to the old illustrations. And if drawing new pictures sounds frivolous to you – like mere child's play – believe me it is not. Better still, let me prove it.

From prehistoric cave paintings to the map of the London Underground, images, diagrams and charts have long been at the heart of human storytelling. The reason why is simple: our brains are wired for visuals. 'Seeing comes before words. The child looks and recognizes before it speaks,' wrote the media theorist John Berger in the opening lines of his 1972 classic, *Ways of Seeing*.[23] Neuroscience has since confirmed the dominant role of visualisation in human cognition. Half of the nerve fibres in our brains are linked to our vision and, when our eyes are open, vision accounts for two-thirds of the electrical activity in the brain. It takes just 150 milliseconds for the brain to recognise an image and a mere 100 milliseconds more to attach a meaning to it.[24] Although we have blind spots in both of our eyes – where the optic nerve attaches to the retina – the brain deftly steps in to create the seamless illusion of a whole.[25]

As a result, we are born pattern-spotters, seeing faces in the clouds, ghosts in the shadows, and mythical beasts in the stars. And we learn best when there are pictures to look at. As the visual literacy expert Lynell Burmark explains, 'unless our words, concepts and ideas are hooked onto an image, they will go in one ear, sail through the brain, and go out of the other ear. Words are processed by our short-term memory where we can only retain about seven bits of information . . . Images, on the other hand, go directly into long-term memory where they are indelibly etched.'[26] With far fewer pen strokes, and without the weight of technical language, images have immediacy – and when text and image send conflicting messages, it is the visual message that most often wins.[27] So the old adage turns out to be true: a picture really is worth a thousand words.

It is hardly surprising, then, that imagery has played such a central role in the way that humans have learned to make sense of the world. In the sixth century BCE, the oldest known map of the world, the Imago Mundi, was etched into clay with a sharpened stick in Persia, showing Earth as a flat disc and with Babylon firmly at its centre. The Ancient Greek father of geometry, Euclid, mastered the analysis of circles, triangles, curves and rectangles in two-dimensional space, creating a diagrammatic convention that Isaac Newton later used to lay out his groundbreaking laws of motion, and that is still used in maths classes worldwide today. Few people have heard of the Roman architect Marcus Vitruvius Pollio but Leonardo da Vinci's visual depiction of his theory of proportion is instantly recognised the world over in the image of Vitruvian Man, standing – naked and open armed – in a circle and square simultaneously. In 1837 when Charles Darwin first drew in his field notebook an irregular little diagram of a branching tree – with the words 'I think' jotted above it – he captured the crux of an idea that would turn into *The Origin of Species*.[28]

Across cultures and time, it is clear that people have long understood the power of imagery, and its ability to overturn deeply held beliefs. Pictures stick in the mind's eye and wordlessly reshape our view of the world. No wonder Nicolaus Copernicus – who spent his life studying the motion of the planets – waited until he was on his deathbed before he dared to publish this one:

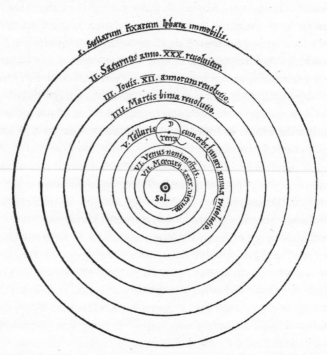

Copernicus's 1543 depiction of the universe, which showed Earth revolving around the sun.

By depicting the sun – not Earth – at the centre of our solar system, Copernicus's picture triggered an ideological revolution that would unravel church doctrine, threaten to upend papal power, and transform humanity's understanding of the cosmos and our place in it. It is extraordinary what havoc a few concentric circles can unleash.

Think, then, of the circles, parabolas, lines and curves that make up the core diagrams in economics – those seemingly innocuous pictures depicting what the economy is, how it moves, and what it is for. Never underestimate the power of such images: what we draw determines what we can and cannot see, what we notice and what we ignore, and so shapes all that follows. The images that we draw to describe the economy invoke the timeless truths of Euclid's maths and Newton's physics in their geometric simplicity. But in doing so, they slip swiftly into the back of our head, wordlessly whispering the deepest assumptions of economic theory that need never be put into words because they have been inscribed in the mind's eye. They present a very partial picture of the economy, smoothing over economic theory's own peculiar blind spots, enticing us to search for laws within their lines, and sending us in pursuit of false goals. What's more, those images linger, like graffiti on the mind, long after the words have faded; they become stowaway intellectual baggage, lodged in your visual cortex without you even realising it is there. And – just like graffiti – it is very hard to remove. So if a picture is worth a thousand words then, in economics at least, we should pay a great deal more attention to the pictures that we teach, draw and learn.

Some might dismiss this suggestion with the rebuttal that economic theory is taught not in pictures but in equations, page after page of them. Economics departments, after all, seek to recruit mathematicians, not artists, to join their ranks. But economics has in fact always been taught with both diagrams and equations, and the diagrams have played a particularly powerful role, thanks to a few maverick characters and surprise twists in the field's little-known but fascinating past.

Images in economics: a hidden history

Many of the founding fathers of economics used imagery to express their seminal ideas. When in 1758 the French economist François Quesnay published his *Tableau économique* – with its zigzagging lines depicting the flow of money as it circulated between landowners, labourers and merchants – he effectively drew up the first quantified economic model. In the 1780s the British political economist William Playfair began to invent new ways of presenting data, using what every schoolchild now knows as graphs, bar charts and pie charts. With these tools he powerfully visualised the political issues of his day, such as the sharply rising price of wheat for the day labourer, and England's shifting balance of trade with the rest of the world. A century later, the British economist William Stanley Jevons drew a picture depicting what he called 'the law of demand', plotting incremental changes in price and quantity along a curve in order to show that, as the price of a thing falls, people will want to buy more of it. Aspiring to make his theory seem as scientific as physics, he

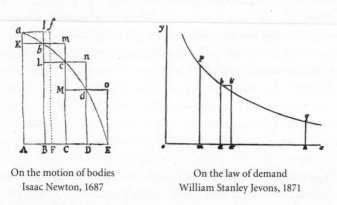

On the motion of bodies
Isaac Newton, 1687

On the law of demand
William Stanley Jevons, 1871

Aspiring to make economics seem as scientific as physics, Jevons drew his theories in the style of Newton's diagrams of the laws of motion.

16

intentionally drew it in a style that closely resembled Newton's depiction of the laws of motion. And that demand curve still features in the first diagram encountered by the novice student today.

The first half of twentieth-century economics was dominated by Alfred Marshall's 1890 book, *Principles of Economics*, the master text used to teach most students. In its preface, Marshall mused on the relative merits of using equations versus diagrams to elucidate the text. Mathematical equations, he believed, were most useful 'in helping a person to write down quickly, shortly and exactly, some of his thoughts for his own use . . . But when a great many symbols have to be used, they become very laborious to any one but the writer himself.' The value of diagrams, he believed, was far greater. 'The argument in the text is never dependent upon them; and they may be omitted,' he wrote, 'but experience seems to show that they give a firmer grasp of many important principles than can be got without their aid; and that there are many problems of pure theory, which no one who has once learnt to use diagrams will willingly handle in any other way.'[29]

It was Paul Samuelson, however, who decisively placed imagery at the heart of economic thought in the second half of the twentieth century. Known as the father of modern economics, Samuelson spent his seven-decade career at the Massachusetts Institute of Technology (MIT) and on his death in 2009 he was heralded as 'one of the giants on whose shoulders every contemporary economist stands'.[30] He was enamoured of equations and diagrams, and he profoundly influenced the use of both in economic theory and teaching. But, crucially, he believed they were suited to very different audiences: in short, equations were for the specialists; pictures for the masses.

Samuelson's first major work was the book of his doctoral dissertation, *Foundations of Economic Analysis*. Published in 1947, it was aimed at the hard-core theorist, and was unapologetically mathematical: equations, he believed, should be the mother tongue of

Paul Samuelson: the man who drew economics.

professional economists, serving to cut through muddled thinking and replace it with scientific precision. He wrote his second book, however, for an utterly different audience, and only thanks to a twist of fate.

At the end of the Second World War, US college enrolments ballooned as hundreds of thousands of ex-servicemen returned home in search of the education that they had missed and the jobs that they desperately needed. Many opted to study engineering – essential for post-war construction – and were required to learn a little economics along the way. Samuelson was, at the time, a 30-year-old professor at MIT and a self-declared 'whippersnapper go-getter in esoteric theory'. But his departmental boss, Ralph Freeman, had a problem on his hands: 800 engineering students at MIT had started a year-long compulsory course in economics and it was not going well. Samuelson recalled the conversation that took place when Freeman turned up at his office one day and closed the door behind him. 'They hate it,' Freeman confessed, 'We've tried everything. They still hate it . . . Paul, will you go on half time for a semester or two? Write a text the students will like. If they like it, yours will be good economics. Leave out whatever you like. Be as short as you wish. Whatever you come up with, that will be a vast improvement on where we are.'[31]

It was, said Samuelson, an offer he couldn't refuse and the text that he wrote over the next three years – titled simply *Economics* – became the 1948 textbook classic that shot him to lifelong fame. Fascinatingly, the strategy he chose in writing it followed right in the footsteps of the medieval Roman Catholic Church. Before the advent of the printing press, the Church had used two quite distinct methods to spread its doctrine. The learned few – monks, priests and scholars – were required to read the Bible in Latin, writing out its verses line by line. In contrast, the illiterate masses were taught the Bible's stories in pictures, painted as frescoes on church walls and illuminated in stained-glass windows. It turned out to be a highly successful mass communications strategy. Samuelson was just as smart: setting aside the specialist's equations, he fully embraced diagrams, graphs and charts to create his one-stop-shop economics course for the masses. And since his primary audience was a cohort of engineers, he adopted a visual style that they would have found familiar, drawn in the tradition of mechanical engineering and fluid mechanics. On the next page, for example, is an image from the first edition of his textbook, showing how income circulates round the economy, with new investments topping it up. It evolved to become his most famous diagram – known as the Circular Flow – and was clearly based on the metaphor of water flowing through plumbed pipes.[32]

His picture-rich textbook was a hit, and what worked for the engineers turned out to work for the rest too. *Economics* was soon adopted

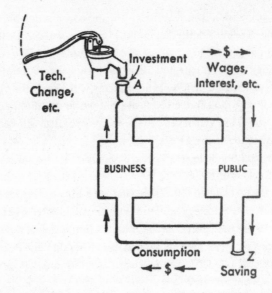

Samuelson's 1948 Circular Flow diagram, which depicted income flowing round the economy as if it were water flowing round plumbed pipes.

by university professors across the country, and then overseas. It became America's bestselling textbook – across all subjects – for nearly thirty years. Translated into more than forty languages, it sold four million copies worldwide over a span of sixty years, providing generations of students with all they needed to know about Econ 101.[33] With each new edition came more pictures: the 70 diagrams in the first edition had multiplied to almost 250 diagrams by the 11th edition in 1980. Samuelson deeply understood and relished this influence because he saw the college freshman's mind as a blank slate. 'I don't care who writes a nation's laws – or crafts its advanced treatises – so long as I can write its economics textbooks,' he declared in later years, 'The first lick is the privileged one, impinging on the beginner's tabula rasa at its most impressionable state.'[34]

A long struggle of escape

Paul Samuelson was not alone in appreciating the extraordinary influence wielded by those who determine how we begin. His teacher and mentor, Joseph Schumpeter, also realised that the ideas handed down to us can be very hard to shake off, but he was determined to do so, to make way for his own insights. As Schumpeter wrote in his 1954 *History of Economic Analysis*,

> In practice we all start our own research from the work of our predecessors, that is, we hardly ever start from scratch. But suppose we did start from scratch, what are the steps we should have to take? Obviously, in order to be able to posit to ourselves any problems at all, we should first have to visualize a distinct set of coherent phenomena as a worthwhile object of our analytic effort. In other words, analytic effort is of necessity preceded by a preanalytic cognitive act that supplies the raw material for the analytic effort. In this book, this pre-analytic cognitive act will be called Vision.

He was clear, however, that creating a new pre-analytic vision could never be an impartial process, adding:

> The first task is to verbalize the vision or to conceptualize it . . . in a more or less orderly schema or picture . . . It should be perfectly clear that there is a wide gate for ideology to enter into this process. In fact, it enters on the very ground floor, into the preanalytic cognitive act of which we have been speaking. Analytic work begins with material provided by our vision of things, and this vision is ideological almost by definition.[35]

Other thinkers have used different words to make a similar point. Schumpeter's concept of pre-analytic vision was inspired by the ideas of sociologist Karl Mannheim whose observation in the late 1920s that, 'every point of view is particular to a social situation' led him to popularise the notion that we each have a 'worldview' which acts as the lens through which we interpret the world. In the 1960s, Thomas Kuhn turned scientific research upside down by pointing out that 'scientists work from models acquired through education . . . often without quite knowing or needing to know what characteristics have given these models the status of community paradigms'.[36] In the 1970s, sociologist Erving Goffmann introduced the concept of 'framing' – in the sense that each of us views the world through a mental picture frame – to show that the way we make sense out of our jumble of experience delineates what we can then see.[37]

Pre-analytic vision. Worldview. Paradigm. Frame. These are cousin concepts. What matters more than the one you choose to use is to realise that you have one in the first place, because then you have the power to question and change it. In economics, that's an open invitation to look afresh at the mental models we employ in describing and understanding the economy. But it is no easy thing to do, as Keynes discovered. Coming up with his groundbreaking theory in the 1930s was, he admitted, 'a struggle of escape from habitual modes of thought and expression . . . The difficulty lies not in the new ideas, but in the old ones which ramify, for those of us brought up as most of us have been, into every corner of our minds.'[38]

The possibility of shaking off old mental models is enticing, but the quest for new ones comes with caveats. First, always remember that 'the map is not the territory', as the philosopher Alfred Korzybski put it: every model can only ever be a model, a necessary simplification of the world, and one that should never be mistaken for the real thing. Second, there is no correct pre-analytic vision, true paradigm or perfect frame out there to be discovered. In the deft words of the statistician George Box, 'All models are wrong, but some are useful.'[39] Rethinking economics is not about finding the correct one (because it doesn't exist), it's about choosing or creating one that best serves our purpose – reflecting the context we face, the values we hold, and the aims we have. As humanity's context, values, and aims continually evolve, so too should the way that we envision the economy.

There may be no perfect frame waiting to be found but, argues the cognitive linguist George Lakoff, it is absolutely essential to have a compelling alternative frame if the old one is ever to be debunked. Simply rebutting the dominant frame will, ironically, only serve to reinforce it. And without an alternative to offer, there is little chance of entering, let alone winning, the battle of ideas.

Lakoff has for years drawn attention to the power of verbal framing in shaping political and economic debate. He points, by way of example, to the notion of 'tax relief' widely used by US conservatives: in just two words, it frames tax as an affliction, a burden to be lifted by a heroic rescuer. How should progressives respond? Certainly not by arguing 'against tax relief' because repeating that phrase merely strengthens the frame (who could be against relief, after all?). But, says Lakoff, progressives too often try to set out their own views on tax with lengthy explanations, precisely because no concise alternative frame has been developed.[40] They desperately need an alternative two-word phrase to encapsulate their view and counter the other. In fact the frame of 'tax justice' – which instantly invokes community, fairness and accountability – has been fast gaining traction internationally as global scandals over tax havens and corporate tax avoidance have hit the headlines. Having a powerful way to frame the matter has no doubt helped to channel public outrage and mobilise widespread demand for change.[41]

Just as Lakoff's work has revealed the power of *verbal* framing in political and economic debate, this book aims to reveal the power of *visual* framing, and to use it to transform twenty-first-century economic thinking. I only realised just how powerful visual framing can be in 2011 when I first drew the Doughnut and was taken aback by the international response to it. In the arena of sustainable development, it soon became an iconic image that was used by activists, governments, corporations and academics alike to change the terms of debate. In 2015, insiders to the UN process of negotiating the Sustainable Development Goals – the 17 globally agreed goals for charting human progress – told me that, in late-night meetings to hammer out the final text, the image of the Doughnut was there on the table as a reminder of the big-picture goals they were aiming for. Many people told me that the Doughnut made visible the way that they had always thought about sustainable development; they had just never seen it drawn before. What struck me most was the impact that the image had in fostering new ways of thinking: it helped to reinvigorate old debates and instigate new ones, while offering a positive vision of an economic future worth striving for.

Visual frames, it gradually dawned on me, matter just as much as verbal ones. That realisation drove me to look back at the images that had dominated my own economic education and I saw for the first time just how powerfully they summed up and reinforced the mindset I had been taught. At the heart of mainstream economic thinking is a handful of diagrams that have wordlessly but powerfully framed the way we are taught to understand the economic world – and they are all out of date, blinkered, or downright wrong. They may lie hidden from view but they deeply frame the way we think about economics in the classroom, in government, in the boardroom, in the media, and in the street. If we want to write a new economic story, we must draw new pictures that leave the old ones lying in the pages of last century's textbooks.

What, then, if you have never studied economics, never laid your eyes on its most powerful pictures? For starters, don't kid yourself that you are immune to their influence: no one is. Those diagrams so strongly frame the way that economists, politicians and journalists talk about the economy that we all end up invoking them with our words even if we have never seen them with our eyes. But at the same time, as an economic novice, consider yourself lucky that Paul

Samuelson never got that first lick of your *tabula rasa*. The fact that you have never sat through an economics lecture may just turn out to be a distinct advantage, after all: you've less baggage to offload, less graffiti to scrub out. Every now and then, being untutored can be an intellectual asset – and this is one of those moments.

Seven ways to think like a twenty-first-century economist

Whether you consider yourself an economic veteran or novice, now is the time to uncover the economic graffiti that lingers in all of our minds and, if you don't like what you find, scrub it out; or, better still, paint it over with new images that far better serve our needs and times. The rest of this book proposes seven ways to think like a twenty-first-century economist, revealing for each of those seven ways the spurious image that has occupied our minds, how it came to be so powerful, and the damaging influence it has had. But the time for mere critique is past, which is why the focus here is on creating new images that capture the essential principles to guide us now. The diagrams in this book aim to summarise that leap from old to new economic thinking. Taken together they set out – quite literally – a new big picture for the twenty-first-century economist. So here is a whirlwind tour of the ideas and images at the heart of Doughnut Economics.

First, change the goal. For over 70 years economics has been fixated on GDP, or national output, as its primary measure of progress. That fixation has been used to justify extreme inequalities of income and wealth coupled with unprecedented destruction of the living world. For the twenty-first century a far bigger goal is needed: meeting the human rights of every person within the means of our life-giving planet. And that goal is encapsulated in the concept of the Doughnut. The challenge now is to create economies – local to

25

Seven Ways to Think:		From Twentieth-Century Economics
1. Change the Goal	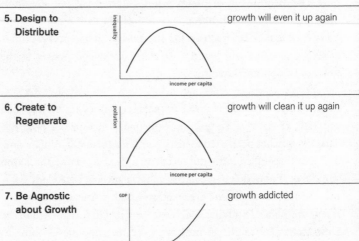	GDP
2. See the Big Picture		self-contained market
3. Nurture Human Nature		rational economic man
4. Get Savvy with Systems		mechanical equilibrium
5. Design to Distribute		growth will even it up again
6. Create to Regenerate		growth will clean it up again
7. Be Agnostic about Growth		growth addicted

the Doughnut

embedded economy

social adaptable humans

dynamic complexity

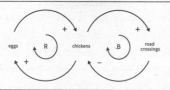

distributive by design

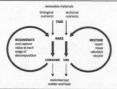

regenerative by design

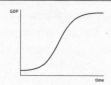

growth agnostic

global – that help to bring all of humanity into the Doughnut's safe and just space. Instead of pursuing ever-increasing GDP, it is time to discover how to thrive in balance.

Second, see the big picture. Mainstream economics depicts the whole economy with just one, extremely limited image, the Circular Flow diagram. Its limitations have, furthermore, been used to reinforce a neoliberal narrative about the efficiency of the market, the incompetence of the state, the domesticity of the household, and the tragedy of the commons. It is time to draw the economy anew, embedding it within society and within nature, and powered by the sun. This new depiction invites new narratives – about the power of the market, the partnership of the state, the core role of the household, and the creativity of the commons.

Third, nurture human nature. At the heart of twentieth-century economics stands the portrait of rational economic man: he has told us that we are self-interested, isolated, calculating, fixed in taste, and dominant over nature – and his portrait has shaped who we have become. But human nature is far richer than this, as early sketches of our new self-portrait reveal: we are social, interdependent, approximating, fluid in values, and dependent upon the living world. What's more, it is indeed possible to nurture human nature in ways that give us a far greater chance of getting into the Doughnut's safe and just space.

Fourth, get savvy with systems. The iconic criss-cross of the market's supply and demand curves is the first diagram that every economics student encounters, but it is rooted in misplaced nineteenth-century metaphors of mechanical equilibrium. A far smarter starting point for understanding the economy's dynamism is systems thinking, summed up by a simple pair of feedback loops. Putting such dynamics at the heart of economics opens up many new insights, from the boom and

28

bust of financial markets to the self-reinforcing nature of economic inequality and the tipping points of climate change. It's time to stop searching for the economy's elusive control levers and start stewarding it as an ever-evolving complex system.

Fifth, design to distribute. In the twentieth century, one simple curve – the Kuznets Curve – whispered a powerful message on inequality: it has to get worse before it can get better, and growth will (eventually) even it up. But inequality, it turns out, is not an economic necessity: it is a design failure. Twenty-first-century economists will recognise that there are many ways to design economies to be far more distributive of the value that they generate – an idea best represented as a network of flows. It means going beyond redistributing income to exploring ways of redistributing wealth, particularly the wealth that lies in controlling land, enterprise, technology, knowledge, and the power to create money.

Sixth, create to regenerate. Economic theory has long portrayed a 'clean' environment as a luxury good, affordable only for the well-off. This view was reinforced by the Environmental Kuznets Curve, which once again whispered that pollution has to get worse before it can get better, and growth will (eventually) clean it up. But there is no such law: ecological degradation is simply the result of degenerative industrial design. This century needs economic thinking that unleashes regenerative design in order to create a circular – not linear – economy, and to restore humans as full participants in Earth's cyclical processes of life.

Seventh, be agnostic about growth. One diagram in economic theory is so dangerous that it is never actually drawn: the long-term path of GDP growth. Mainstream economics views endless economic growth as a must, but nothing in nature grows for ever and the attempt to buck that trend is raising tough questions in high-income but low-growth countries. It may not be hard to give up having GDP growth as an economic goal, but it is going to be far harder to overcome our addiction to it. Today we have economies that need to grow, whether or not they make us thrive: what we need are economies that make us thrive, whether or not they grow. That radical flip in perspective invites us to become agnostic about growth, and to explore how economies that are currently financially, politically and socially addicted to growth could learn to live with or without it.

These seven ways of thinking like a twenty-first-century economist don't lay out specific policy prescriptions or institutional fixes. They promise no immediate answers for what to do next, and they are not the whole answer. But I am convinced that they are fundamental to the radically different way of thinking about economics that this century demands. Their principles and patterns will equip new economic thinkers – and the inner economist in us all – to start creating an economy that enables everyone in the house to prosper. Given the speed, scale and uncertainty of change that we face in coming years, it would be foolhardy to attempt to prescribe now all the policies and institutions that will be fit for the future: the coming generation of thinkers and doers will be far better placed to experiment and discover what works as the context continually changes. What we can do now – and must do well – is bring together the best of the emerging ideas, and so create a new economic mindset that is never set but always evolving.

The task for economic thinkers in the decades ahead will be to bring these seven ways of thinking together in practice, and to add to them many more. We have barely set out on this adventure in rethinking economics. Join the crew.

1

CHANGE THE GOAL

from GDP to the Doughnut

Once a year the leaders of the world's most powerful countries meet to discuss the global economy. In 2014, for instance, they met in Brisbane, Australia, where they discussed global trade, infrastructure, jobs and financial reform, stroked koalas for the cameras, and then rallied behind one overriding ambition. 'G20 leaders pledge to grow their economies by 2.1%' trumpeted the global news headlines – adding that this was more ambitious than the 2.0% that they had initially intended to target.[1]

How did it come to this? The G20's pledge was announced just days after the Intergovernmental Panel on Climate Change warned that the world faces 'severe, pervasive and irreversible' damage from rising greenhouse gas emissions. But the summit's Australian host, then Prime Minister Tony Abbott, had been determined to stop the meeting's agenda from being 'cluttered' by climate change and other issues that could distract from his top priority of economic growth, otherwise known as GDP growth.[2] Measured as the market value of goods and services produced within a nation's borders in a year, GDP (Gross Domestic Product) has long been used as the leading indicator of economic health. But in the context of today's social and ecological crises, how can this single, narrow metric still command such international attention?

To any ornithologist, the answer would be obvious: GDP is a cuckoo in the economic nest. And to understand why you need to know a thing or two about cuckoos, because they are wily birds. Rather than raise their own offspring, they surreptitiously lay their eggs in the unguarded nests of other birds. The unsuspecting foster parents dutifully incubate the interloper's egg along with their own. But the cuckoo chick hatches early, kicks other eggs and young out of the nest, then emits rapid calls to mimic a nest full of hungry offspring. This takeover tactic works: the foster parents busily feed their oversized tenant as it grows absurdly large, bulging out of the tiny nest it has occupied. It's a powerful warning to other birds: leave your nest unattended and it may well get hijacked.

It's a warning to economics too: lose sight of your goals and something else may well slip into their place. And that's exactly what has happened. In the twentieth century, economics lost the desire to articulate its goals: in their absence, the economic nest got hijacked by the cuckoo goal of GDP growth. It is high time for that cuckoo to fly the nest so that economics can reconnect with the purpose that it should be serving. So let's evict that cuckoo and replace it with a clear goal for twenty-first-century economics, one that ensures prosperity for all within the means of our planet. In other words, get into the Doughnut, the sweet spot for humanity.

How economics lost sight of its goal

Back in Ancient Greece, when Xenophon first came up with the term *economics* he described the practice of household management as an art. Following his lead, Aristotle distinguished *economics* from *chrematistics*, the art of acquiring wealth – in a distinction that seems to have been all but lost today. The idea of economics, and even chrematistics, as an art may have suited Xenophon, Aristotle and their time, but two thousand years later, when Isaac Newton discovered the laws of motion, the allure of scientific status became far greater. Perhaps this is why, in 1767 – just forty years after Newton's death – when the Scottish lawyer James Steuart first proposed the concept of 'political economy', he defined it no longer as an art but as 'the science of domestic policy in free nations'. But naming it as a science still didn't stop him from spelling out its purpose:

> The principal object of this science is to secure a certain fund of subsistence for all the inhabitants, to obviate every circumstance which may render it precarious; to provide every thing necessary for supplying the wants of the society, and to employ the inhabitants (supposing them to be free-men) in such a manner as naturally to create reciprocal relations and dependencies between them, so as to make their several interests lead them to supply one another with their reciprocal wants.[3]

A secure living and jobs for all in a mutually thriving community: not bad for a first stab at defining the goal (despite the tacit disregard of women and slaves that came with the times). A decade later, Adam Smith had a go at his own definition but followed Steuart's lead in considering political economy to be a goal-oriented science. It had, he wrote, 'two distinct objects: to supply a plentiful revenue or subsistence for the people, or, more properly, to enable them to provide such a revenue or subsistence for themselves; and secondly, to supply the state or commonwealth with a revenue sufficient for the public services'.[4] This definition not only defies Smith's ill-deserved modern reputation as a free-marketeer, but also keeps its eyes firmly on the prize by articulating a goal for economic thought. But it was an approach that would not last.

Seventy years after Smith, John Stuart Mill's definition of political economy started the shift in focus by recasting it as, 'a science which traces the laws of such of the phenomena of society as arise from the combined operations of mankind for the production of wealth'.[5] With this, Mill began a trend that others would further: turning attention away from naming the economy's goals and towards discovering its apparent laws. Mill's definition came to be used widely, but by no means exclusively. In fact for nearly a century the emerging science of economics was defined rather imprecisely, leading the early Chicago School economist Jacob Viner, in the 1930s, to quip simply that 'Economics is what economists do.'[6]

Not everyone found that a satisfactory answer. In 1932, Lionel Robbins of the London School of Economics stepped in with intent to clarify the matter, clearly irritated that 'We all talk about the same things, but we have not yet agreed what it is we are talking about.' He claimed to have a definitive answer. 'Economics,' he declared, 'is the science which studies human behavior as a relationship between ends and scarce means which have alternative uses.'[7] Despite its contortions, that definition seemed to close the debate, and it stuck: many mainstream textbooks still start with something very similar today. But although it frames economics as a science of human behaviour, it spends little time enquiring into those ends, let alone into the nature of the scarce means involved. In Gregory Mankiw's widely used contemporary textbook, *Principles of Economics*, the definition has become even more concise. 'Economics is the study of how society manages its scarce resources,' it declares – erasing the question of ends or goals from the page altogether.[8]

It is more than a little ironic that twentieth-century economics decided to define itself as a science of human behaviour, and then adopted a theory of behaviour – summed up in rational economic man – which, for decades, eclipsed any real study of humans, as we will see in Chapter 3. But, more crucially, during that process, the discussion of the economy's goals simply disappeared from view. Some influential economists, led by Milton Friedman and the Chicago School, claimed this was an important step forward, a demonstration that economics had become a value-free zone, shaking off any normative claims of what ought to be and emerging at last as a 'positive' science focused on describing simply what is. But this created a vacuum of goals and values, leaving an unguarded nest at the heart of the economic project. And, as every cuckoo knows, such a nest must be filled.

Cuckoo in the nest

This positive approach to economics was the textbook theory that greeted me as I arrived at university in the late 1980s. Like many novice economists, I was so busy getting to grips with the theory of demand and supply, so determined to get my head around the many definitions of money, that I did not spot the hidden values that had occupied the economic nest.

Though claiming to be value-free, conventional economic theory cannot escape the fact that value is embedded at its heart: it is wrapped up with the idea of *utility*, which is defined as a person's satisfaction or happiness gained from consuming a particular bundle of goods.[9] What's the best way to measure utility? Leave aside for a moment the catch that billions of people lack the money needed to express their wants and needs in the marketplace, and that many of the things we most value are not for sale. Economic theory is quick – too quick – in asserting that the price people are willing to pay for a product or service is a good enough marketplace proxy for calculating their utility gained. Add to this the apparently reasonable assumption that consumers always prefer more to less, and it is a short step to concluding that continual income growth (and therefore output growth) is a decent proxy for ever-improving human welfare. And with that, the cuckoo has hatched.

Like hoodwinked mother birds, we student-economists faithfully nurtured the goal of GDP growth, poring over the latest competing theories of what makes economic output grow: was it a nation's adoption of new technologies, its growing stock of machinery and factories, or even its stock of human capital? Yes, these were all fascinating questions, but not once did we seriously stop to ask whether

GDP growth was always needed, always desirable or, indeed, always possible. It was only when I opted to study what was at the time an obscure topic – the economics of developing countries – that the question of goals popped up. The very first essay question that I was set confronted me head-on: *What is the best way of assessing success in development?* I was gripped and shocked. Two years into my economic education and the question of purpose had appeared for the first time. Worse, I hadn't even realised that it had been missing.

Twenty-five years later, I wondered if the teaching of economics had moved on and recognised the need to start with a discussion of what it is all for. So, in early 2015, curiosity drew me to sit in on the opening lecture in macroeconomics – the study of the economy as a whole – for Oxford University's newest intake of economics students, many of whom were no doubt planning to be among the top policymakers and business leaders shaping the world in 2050. As his opening gambit, the senior professor put up on the screen what he called 'The Big Questions of Macroeconomics'. The top four?

1. What causes economic output to grow and to fluctuate?
2. What causes unemployment?
3. What causes inflation?
4. How are interest rates determined?

His list got longer but the questions never aimed higher, to encourage the students to consider the economy's purpose. How had the GDP growth cuckoo so successfully hijacked the economic nest? The answer can be traced back to the mid 1930s – as economists were just settling upon a goalless definition of their discipline – when the US Congress first commissioned economist Simon Kuznets to devise a measure of America's national income. The calculation he made came to be known as Gross National Product, and was based on the income generated worldwide by the nation's residents. For the first time, thanks to Kuznets, it became possible to put a dollar value on America's annual output and hence its income – and to compare it to the year before. That metric proved to be extremely useful, and it fell into welcoming hands. During the Great Depression, it enabled President Roosevelt to monitor the changing state of the US economy and so assess the impact and effectiveness of his New Deal policies. A few years later, as the country prepared to enter the Second World War, the data underlying the GNP accounts proved invaluable for converting its competitive industrial economy into a planned military one, while sustaining enough domestic consumption to keep generating further output.[10]

Other reasons were soon put forward for pursuing a growing GNP, and similar national accounts were created internationally, so that by the end of the 1950s, output growth had become the overriding policy objective in industrial countries. Eyeing the rise of the Soviet Union, the USA pursued growth for national security through military power, and the two sides became locked in a fierce ideological contest to prove whose economic ideology – the 'free market' versus central planning – could ultimately turn out more stuff. Growth appeared to offer an end to unemployment too, according to Arthur Okun, Chairman of President Johnson's Council of Economic Advisers. His analysis found that an annual 2% growth in US national output corresponded to a 1% fall in unemployment – a correlation which looked so promising that it came to be known as Okun's Law. Soon growth was portrayed as a panacea for many social, economic and political ailments: as a cure for public debt and trade imbalances, a key to national security, a means to defuse class struggle, and a route to tackling poverty without facing the politically charged issue of redistribution.

In 1960, Senator John Kennedy stood for the US presidential election on the promise of a 5% growth rate. When he won, the very first question he asked his chief economic adviser was, 'Do you think we can make good on that five per cent growth promise?'[11] That same year, the US joined other leading industrial countries to set up the Organisation for Economic Co-operation and Development (OECD), with its first priority being to achieve 'the highest sustainable economic growth' – aiming to sustain not the environment but output growth. And that ambition was soon backed up by international GNP league tables showing whose growth was in the lead.[12] In the last decades of the twentieth century, the focus shifted from measuring GNP to today's more familiar GDP, the income generated within a nation's borders. But the insistence on output growth remained. In fact it deepened, as governments, corporations and financial markets alike increasingly came to expect, demand and depend upon continual GDP growth – an addiction that lasts to this day, as we will explore in Chapter 7.

Perhaps it should be no surprise that the GDP cuckoo so deftly filled the economic nest. Why? Because the idea of ever-growing output fits snugly with the widely used metaphor of progress being a movement forwards and upwards. If you have ever watched a child learning to walk, you'll know just how thrilling that journey is. From clumsy crawling, usually backwards at first, then satisfyingly forwards, they gradually pull themselves up to standing, and take those triumphant first steps. The mastery of this movement – forwards and upwards – charts an individual child's development, but also echoes the story of progress we tell ourselves as a species. From our lolloping four-legged ancestors evolved *Homo erectus* – upright at last – who gave rise to *Homo sapiens*, always depicted mid-stride.

As George Lakoff and Mark Johnson vividly illustrate in their 1980 classic *Metaphors We Live By*, orientational metaphors such as 'good is up' and 'good is forward' are deeply embedded in Western culture, shaping the way we think and speak.[13] 'Why is she so down? Because she faced a setback then hit an all-time low,' we might say – or, 'Things are looking up: her life is moving forwards again.' No wonder we have so willingly accepted that economic success must also lie in an ever-rising national income. It fits with the deep belief, as Paul Samuelson put it in his textbook, that 'even if more material goods are not themselves most important, nevertheless, a society is happier when it is moving forward.'[14]

What would this vision of success look like if drawn on the page? Curiously, economists rarely actually draw their adopted goal of economic growth (in Chapter 7, we'll return to see why that is). But if they did, the image would be an ever-rising line of GDP: an exponential growth curve moving forwards and upwards across the page, chiming perfectly with our favourite metaphor for human and personal progress.

Kuznets himself, however, would not have chosen this as the picture of economic progress because he was well aware of the limits of his ingenious calculations from the outset. Emphasising that national income captured only the market value of goods and services produced in an economy, he pointed out that it therefore excluded the enormous value of goods and services produced by and for households, and by society in the course of daily life. In addition, he recognised that it gave no indication of how income and consumption were actually distributed between households. And since national income is a flow measure (recording only the amount of income generated each year), Kuznets saw that it needed to be complemented by a

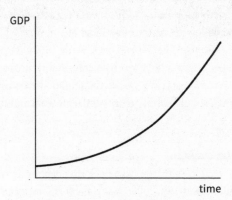

GDP growth: forwards and upwards.

stock measure, accounting for the wealth from which it was generated, and its distribution. Indeed, as GNP reached the height of its popularity in the early 1960s, Kuznets became one of its most outspoken critics, having warned from the start that 'the welfare of a nation can scarcely be inferred from a measure of national income'.[15]

The metric's creator himself may have offered up that caveat but economists and politicians alike tucked it quietly to one side: the appeal of a single year-on-year indicator for measuring economic progress had become too strong. And so over half a century, GDP growth shifted from being a policy option to a political necessity, and the de facto policy goal. To enquire whether further growth was always desirable, necessary, or indeed possible, became irrelevant, or political suicide.

One person who was willing to risk political suicide was the visionary systems thinker Donella Meadows – one of the lead authors of the 1972 *Limits to Growth* report – and she didn't mince her words. 'Growth is one of the stupidest purposes ever invented by any culture,' she declared in the late 1990s; 'we've got to have an enough.' In response to the constant call for more growth, she argued, we should always ask: 'growth of what, and why, and for whom, and who pays the cost, and how long can it last, and what's the cost to the planet, and how much is enough?'[16] For decades mainstream economists dismissed her views as foolishly radical, but they actually echo those of Kuznets, the hallowed creator of national income itself. 'Distinctions must be kept in mind,' he advised back in the 1960s, 'between quantity and quality of growth, between its costs and return, and between the short and the long term . . . Objectives should be explicit: goals for "more" growth should specify more growth of what and for what.'[17]

Evicting the cuckoo

Knocked sideways by the 2008 financial crash, alarmed by the 2011 Occupy movement's global resonance, and under growing pressure to act on climate change, it's no wonder that politicians today have started searching for words to express more inspiring visions of social and economic progress. But they seem always to revert to the same answer: growth, the ubiquitous noun, decked out in a splendid array of aspirational adjectives. In the wake of the financial crisis (while still in the midst of crises of poverty, climate change and widening inequalities), the visions offered up by political leaders started to make me feel like I had stepped into a Manhattan deli, hoping for a simple sandwich, only to be confronted by an endless choice of fillings. *What kind of growth would you like today?* Angela Merkel suggested 'sustained growth'. David Cameron proposed 'balanced growth'. Barack Obama favoured 'long-term, lasting growth'. Europe's José Manuel Barroso was backing 'smart, sustainable, inclusive, resilient growth'. The World Bank promised 'inclusive green growth'. Other flavours on offer? Perhaps you'd like it to be equitable, good, greener, low-carbon, responsible or strong. You choose – just so long as you choose growth.

Should we laugh or cry? First cry, for the lack of vision at such a critical point in human history. Then laugh. Because when politicians feel obliged to prop up GDP growth with so many qualifying terms to give it legitimacy, it's clear that this cuckoo goal is ready for booting from the nest. We evidently want something more than growth, but our politicians cannot find the words, and economists have long declined to supply them. So it's time to cry and to laugh but, most of all, it's time to talk again of what matters.

As we have seen, the founding fathers of political economy were unabashed to talk of what they thought mattered and to articulate their views on the economy's purpose. But when political economy was split up into political philosophy and economic science in the late nineteenth century, it opened up what the philosopher Michael Sandel has called a 'moral vacancy' at the heart of public policymaking. Today economists and politicians debate with confident ease in the name of economic efficiency, productivity and growth – as if those values were self-explanatory – while hesitating to speak of justice, fairness and rights. Talking about values and goals is a lost art waiting to be revived. With all the awkwardness of teenagers learning to talk about their feelings for the first time, economists and politicians – along with the rest of us – are searching for words (and of course the pictures) to articulate a greater economic purpose than growth. How can we learn to talk again of values and goals, and put them at the heart of an economic mindset that is fit for the twenty-first century?

One promising place to start is by looking to the long lineage of unsung economic thinkers whose aim was to put humanity back at the heart of economic thought. Back in 1819 the Swiss economist Jean Sismondi sought to define a new approach to political economy with human welfare, not wealth accumulation, as its goal. The English social thinker John Ruskin followed him in the 1860s, railing against the economic thinking of his day, declaring that, 'There is no wealth but life . . . That country is the richest which nourishes the greatest numbers of noble and happy human beings.'[18] When Mohandas Gandhi discovered Ruskin's book in the early 1900s, he set out to bring its ideas to life on a collective farm in India, in the name of creating an economy that elevated the moral being. In the late twentieth century, E. F. Schumacher – best known for arguing that 'small is beautiful' – sought to place ethics and the human scale at the heart of economic thought. And the Chilean economist Manfred Max-Neef proposed that development be focused on realising a set of fundamental human needs – such as sustenance, participation, creativity, and a sense of belonging – in ways that are adapted to the context and culture of each society.[19] Big-picture thinkers such as these have for centuries offered alternative visions of what the economy is for, but their ideas have been kept far from the eyes and ears of economics students, dismissed as the touchy-feely school of 'humanistic economics' (begging the question of what the rest of it has been).

Their humanistic project has, at last, gained far wider attention and credibility. You could say it began to go mainstream with the work of the economist and philosopher Amartya Sen – work for which he won a Nobel-Memorial prize. The focus of development, Sen argues, should be on 'advancing the richness of human life, rather than the richness of the economy in which human beings live'.[20] Instead of prioritising metrics like GDP, the aim should be to enlarge people's capabilities – such as to be healthy, empowered and creative – so that they can choose to be and do things in life that they value.[21] And realising those capabilities depends upon people having access to the basics of life – adapted to the context of each society – ranging from nutritious food, healthcare and education to personal security and political voice.

In 2008, the French President Nicolas Sarkozy invited twenty-five international economic thinkers, led by Sen and fellow Nobel-Memorial winner Joseph Stiglitz, to assess the measures of economic and social progress that currently guide policymaking. On surveying the state of indicators in use they came to a blunt conclusion: 'Those attempting to guide the economy and our societies,' they wrote, 'are like pilots trying to steer a course without a reliable compass.'[22] None of us want to be passengers on that directionless jet. We urgently need a way to help policymakers, activists, business leaders and citizens alike to steer a wise course through the twenty-first century. So here's a compass fit for the journey ahead.

A twenty-first-century compass

First, to get our bearings, let's put GDP growth aside and start afresh with a fundamental question: what enables human beings to thrive? A world in which every person can lead their life with dignity, opportunity and community – and where we can all do so within the means of our life-giving planet. In other words, we need to get into the

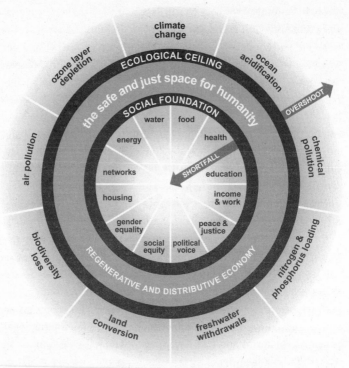

The Doughnut: a twenty-first-century compass. Between its social foundation of human well-being and ecological ceiling of planetary pressure lies the safe and just space for humanity.

Doughnut. It's the visual concept that I first drew in 2011 while working with Oxfam, and it is inspired by cutting-edge Earth-system science. Over the past five years, through conversations with scientists, activists, academics and policymakers, I have renewed and updated it to reflect the latest in both global development goals and scientific understanding. So let me introduce you to the one doughnut that might actually turn out to be good for us.

What exactly is the Doughnut? Put simply, it's a radically new compass for guiding humanity this century. And it points towards a future that can provide for every person's needs while safeguarding the living world on which we all depend. Below the Doughnut's social foundation lie shortfalls in human well-being, faced by those who lack life's essentials such as food, education and housing. Beyond the ecological ceiling lies an overshoot of pressure on Earth's life-giving systems, such as through climate change, ocean acidification and chemical pollution. But between these two sets of boundaries lies a sweet spot – shaped unmistakably like a doughnut – that is both an ecologically safe and socially just space for humanity. The twenty-first-century task is an unprecedented one: to bring all of humanity into that safe and just space.

The Doughnut's inner ring – its social foundation – sets out the basics of life on which no one should be left falling short. These twelve basics include: sufficient food; clean water and decent sanitation; access to energy and clean cooking facilities; access to education and to healthcare; decent housing; a minimum income and decent work; and access to networks of information and to networks of social support. Furthermore, it calls for achieving these with gender equality, social equity, political voice, and peace and justice. Since 1948, international human rights norms and laws have sought to establish every person's claim to the vast majority of these basics, no matter how much or how little money or power they have. Setting a target date to achieve all of them for every person alive may seem an extraordinary ambition, but it is now an official one. They are all included in the United Nation's Sustainable Development Goals – agreed by 193 member countries in 2015 – and the vast majority of these goals are to be achieved by 2030.[23]

Since the mid-twentieth century, global economic development has already helped many millions of people worldwide escape deprivation. They have become the first generations in their families to lead long, healthy and educated lives, with enough food to eat, clean water to drink, electricity in their homes, and money in their pockets – and, for many, this transformation has been accompanied by greater equality between women and men, and greater political voice. But global economic development has also fuelled a dramatic increase in humanity's use of Earth's resources, at first driven by the resource-intensive lifestyles of today's high-income countries, and more recently redoubled by the rapid growth of the global middle class. It is an economic era that has come to be known as the Great Acceleration, thanks to its extraordinary surge in human activity. Between 1950 and 2010, the global population almost trebled in size, and real World GDP increased sevenfold. Worldwide, freshwater use more than trebled, energy use increased fourfold, and fertiliser use rose over tenfold.

The effects of this dramatic intensification of human activity are clearly visible in an array of indicators that monitor Earth's living systems. Since 1950 there has been an accompanying surge in ecological impacts, from the build-up of greenhouse gases in the atmosphere to ocean acidification and biodiversity loss.[24] 'It is difficult to overestimate the scale and speed of change,' says Will Steffen, the scientist who led the study documenting these trends. 'In a single lifetime humanity has become a planetary-scale geological force . . . This is a new phenomenon and indicates that humanity has a new responsibility at a global level for the planet.'[25]

This Great Acceleration in human activity has clearly put our planet under pressure. But just how much pressure can it take before the very life-giving systems that sustain us start to break down? In other words, what determines the Doughnut's ecological ceiling? To answer that question, we have to look back over the past 100,000 years of life on Earth. For almost all of that time – as early humans trekked out of Africa and blazed a trail across continents – Earth's average temperature spiked up and down. But during just the last 12,000 years or so, it has been warmer, and far more stable too. This recent period of Earth's history is known as the Holocene. And it is a word well worth knowing because it has given us the best home we've ever had.

Agriculture was invented on many continents simultaneously during the Holocene and scientists believe that this was no coincidence. The newfound stability of Earth's climate made it possible for

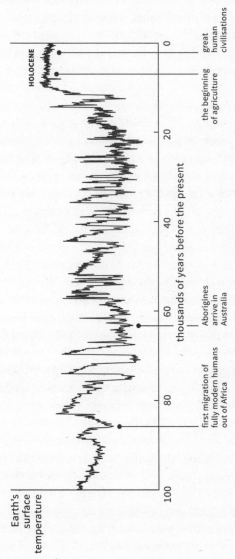

Home sweet home in the Holocene. The graph shows Earth's changing temperature over the past 100,000 years, based on data from the Greenland ice core. The last 12,000 years have been unusually stable.[26]

the descendants of hunter gatherers to settle down and live by the seasons: anticipating the rains, selecting and planting seeds, and reaping the harvest.[27] It is likewise no coincidence that all great human civilisations – from the Indus Valley, Ancient Egypt, and Shang Dynasty China to the Mayans, Greeks and Romans – emerged and flourished in this geological epoch. It is the only known phase of our planet's history in which billions of human beings can thrive.

More extraordinarily, scientists suggest that, if undisturbed, the Holocene's benevolent conditions would be likely to continue for another 50,000 years due to the unusually circular orbit that Earth is currently making of the sun – a phenomenon so rare that it last happened 400,000 years ago.[28] This is certainly something to sit back and ponder. Here we are on the only known living planet, born into its most hospitable era which, thanks to the odd way we happen to be circling the sun right now, is set to run and run. We would have to be crazy to kick ourselves out of the Holocene's sweet spot, but that is, of course, exactly what we have been doing. Our growing pressure on the planet has turned us, humanity, into the single biggest driver of planetary change. Thanks to the scale of our impact, we have now left behind the Holocene and entered uncharted territory, known as the Anthropocene: the first geological epoch to have been shaped by human activity.[29] What will it take, now that we are in the Anthropocene, to sustain the benevolent conditions that we knew in our Holocene home: its stable climate, ample fresh water, thriving biodiversity, and healthy oceans?

In 2009 an international group of Earth-system scientists, led by Johan Rockström and Will Steffen, took on this question and identified nine critical processes – such as the climate system and the freshwater cycle – that, together, regulate Earth's ability to maintain Holocene-like conditions (all nine are described more fully in the Appendix). For each of these nine processes, they asked how much pressure it can take before the stability that has allowed humanity to thrive for thousands of years is put in jeopardy, tipping Earth into an unknown state in which novel and unexpected changes are likely to happen. The catch, of course, is that it is not possible to pinpoint exactly where danger lies and, given that many of the shifts could be irreversible, we'd be wise not to find out the hard way. So the scientists proposed a set of nine boundaries, like guard-rails, where they believe each danger zone begins – equivalent to placing warning signs upstream of a river's treacherous but hidden waterfalls.

What do those warning signs say? To avoid dangerous climate change, for example, keep the concentration of carbon dioxide in the atmosphere below 350 parts per million. In terms of limiting land conversion, ensure that at least 75% of once-forested land remains forested. And when it comes to using chemical fertilisers, add at most 62 million tonnes of nitrogen and 6 million tonnes of phosphorus to Earth's soils each year. There are, of course, many uncertainties behind these top-level numbers – including questions about the regional implications of such global limits – and the science is continually evolving. But in essence, the nine planetary boundaries create the best picture we have yet seen of what it will take to hang on to the home-sweet-home of the Holocene, but to do so in the human-dominated age of the Anthropocene. And it is these nine planetary boundaries that define the Doughnut's ecological ceiling: the limits beyond which we should put no further pressure on the planet if we want to safeguard the stability of our home.

Together, the social foundation of human rights and the ecological ceiling of planetary boundaries create the inner and outer boundaries of the Doughnut. And they are, of course, deeply interconnected. If you are itching to pick up a pen and start drawing arrows on the Doughnut to explore how each of the boundaries might affect the others, you've got the idea – and the Doughnut will soon start to look more like a bowl of spaghetti.

Take, for example, what happens when hillsides are deforested. Land conversion of this kind is likely to accelerate biodiversity loss, weaken the freshwater cycle, and exacerbate climate change – and these impacts, in turn, put increased stress on remaining forests. Furthermore, the loss of forests and secure water supplies may leave local communities more vulnerable to outbreaks of disease and to lower food production, resulting in children dropping out of school. And when kids drop out of school, poverty in all its forms can have knock-on effects for generations.

Knock-on effects can, of course, be positively reinforcing, too. Reforesting hillsides tends to enrich biodiversity, increase soil fertility and water retention, and help sequester carbon dioxide. And the benefits for local communities may be many: more diverse forest food and fibre to harvest; greater security of water supply; improved nutrition and health; and more resilient livelihoods. It may be tempting, for simplicity's sake, to seek to devise policies addressing each one of the planetary and social boundaries in turn, but that simply won't work: their interconnectedness demands that they each be understood as part of a complex socio-ecological system and hence be addressed within a greater whole.[30]

Focusing on these many interconnections across the Doughnut, it becomes clear that human thriving depends upon planetary thriving. Growing sufficient, nutritious food for all requires healthy, nutrient-rich soils, ample fresh water, biodiverse crops, and a stable climate. Ensuring clean, safe water to drink depends upon the local-to-global hydrological cycle generating plentiful rainfall and continually recharging Earth's rivers and aquifers. Having clean air to breathe means halting emissions of toxic particulates that create lung-choking smog. We like to feel the warmth of the sun on our backs, but only if we are protected from its ultraviolet radiation by the ozone layer, and only if greenhouse gases in the atmosphere are not turning the sun's warmth into catastrophic global warming.

If moving into the safe and just space that lies between the Doughnut's inner and outer boundaries is our twenty-first-century challenge, the obvious question is this: how are we doing? Thanks to data advances in both human rights and Earth science, we have a

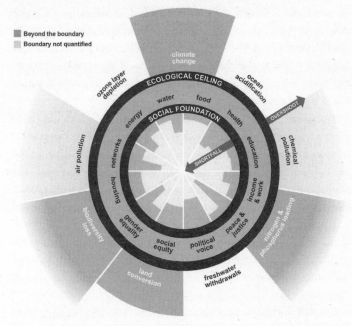

Transgressing both sides of the Doughnut's boundaries. The dark wedges below the social foundation show the proportion of people worldwide falling short on life's basics. The dark wedges radiating beyond the ecological ceiling show the overshoot of planetary boundaries (for complete data see the Appendix).

clearer picture than ever before. Despite unprecedented progress in human well-being over the past 70 years, we are far beyond the Doughnut's boundaries on both sides.

Many millions of people still live below each of the social foundation's dimensions. Worldwide, one person in nine does not have enough to eat. One in four lives on less than $3 a day, and one in eight young people cannot find work. One person in three still has no access to a toilet and one in eleven has no source of safe drinking water. One child in six aged 12–15 is not in school, the vast majority

51

of them girls. Almost 40% of people live in countries in which income is distributed highly unequally. And more than half of the world's population live in countries in which people severely lack political voice. It is extraordinary that such deprivations in life's essentials continue to limit the potential of so many people's lives in the twenty-first century.

Humanity has, at the same time, been putting Earth's life-giving systems under unprecedented stress. In fact we have transgressed at least four planetary boundaries: those of climate change, land conversion, nitrogen and phosphorus loading, and biodiversity loss. The concentration of carbon dioxide in the atmosphere now far exceeds the boundary of 350 parts per million (ppm): it is over 400ppm and still rising, pushing us towards a hotter, drier, and more hostile climate, along with a rise in sea level that threatens the future of islands and coastal cities worldwide. Synthetic fertilisers containing nitrogen and phosphorus are being added to Earth's soils at more than twice their safe levels. Their toxic run-off has already led to the collapse of aquatic life in many lakes, rivers and oceans, including a dead zone the size of Connecticut in the Gulf of Mexico. Only 62% of land that could be forested still stands as forest and even that land area continues to shrink, significantly reducing Earth's capacity to act as a carbon sink. The scale of biodiversity loss is severe: species extinction is occurring at least ten times faster than the boundary deems safe. No wonder that, since 1970, the number of mammals, birds, reptiles, amphibians and fish worldwide has fallen by half.[31] Although the global scale of chemical pollution has not yet been quantified, it is of great concern to many scientists. And human pressure on other critical Earth-system processes – such as freshwater withdrawals and ocean acidification – continues to rise towards planetary-scale danger zones, creating local and regional ecological crises in the process.

This stark picture of humanity and our planetary home at the start of the twenty-first century is a powerful indictment of the path of global economic development that has been pursued to date.

Billions of people still fall far short of their most basic needs, but we have already crossed into global ecological danger zones that profoundly risk undermining Earth's benevolent stability. In this context, what could progress possibly look like?

From endless growth to thriving in balance

'Onwards and upwards' may be a deeply familiar metaphor for progress but, in terms of the economy that we know, it has taken us into dangerous terrain. 'Humanity can affect the functioning of its own life-support systems,' says the ocean scientist Katherine Richardson. 'There are tipping points we are pushing on. How does this change our definition of progress?'[32]

For over 60 years, economic thinking told us that GDP growth was a good enough proxy for progress, and that it looked like an ever-rising line. But this century calls for quite a different shape and direction of progress. At this point in human history, the movement that best describes the progress we need is *coming into dynamic balance*, by moving into the Doughnut's safe and just space, eliminating both its shortfall and overshoot at the same time. That calls for a profound shift in our metaphors: from 'good is forward-and-up' to 'good is in-balance'. And it shifts the image of economic progress from endless GDP growth to thriving-in-balance in the Doughnut.

The image of the Doughnut, and the science behind it, may be new but the sense of dynamic balance that it invokes resonates with decades of thinking about sustainable development. The idea of Earth as a spaceship – a self-contained living capsule – gained popularity in the 1960s, prompting the economist Robert Heilbroner to point out that, 'As in all spaceships, sustained life requires that a meticulous balance be maintained between the capability of the vehicle to support life and the demands made by the inhabitants of the craft.'[33] In the 1970s, the economist Barbara Ward – a pioneer of sustainable development – called for global action to tackle both the 'inner limits' of human needs and rights and the 'outer limits' of the environmental stress that Earth can endure: she was effectively drawing the Doughnut with words rather than with a pen.[34] Later, in the 1990s, the campaigning organisation Friends of the Earth advocated the concept of 'environmental space', arguing that all people have the right to an equitable share of water, food, air, land, and other resources within the carrying capacity of the Earth.[35]

In some cultures, the idea of thriving in balance goes back much further. *Pan metron ariston* said the Ancient Greeks: 'all things in good measure is best'. In Maori culture, the concept of well-being combines spiritual, ecological, kinship and economic well-being, interwoven as interdependent dimensions. In Andean cultures, *buen vivir* – literally 'living well' – is a worldview that values 'a fullness of life in a community with others and with Nature'.[36] In recent years, Bolivia has incorporated *buen vivir* into its constitution as an ethical principle to guide the state, while Ecuador's constitution became the world's first, in 2008, to recognise that Nature, or Pachamama, 'has the right to exist, persist, maintain and regenerate its vital cycles'.[37] Such holistic and balanced conceptions of well-being are reflected in the traditional symbols of many ancient cultures, too. From Taoism's yin yang and the Maori takarangi to Buddhism's endless knot and the Celtic double spiral, each design invokes a continual dynamic dance between complementary forces.

Western cultures seeking to oust the cuckoo goal of GDP growth cannot simply put an Andean or Maori worldview in its place, but

Ancient symbols of dynamic balance: the Taoist yin yang, Maori takarangi, Buddhist endless knot, and Celtic double spiral.

must find new words and pictures to articulate an equivalent vision. What might the words for that new vision be? A first suggestion: *human prosperity in a flourishing web of life*. Yes, that is a mouthful to say – and it's telling that we lack more concise ways of expressing something so fundamental to our well-being. As for the new picture? The Doughnut, I discovered, has a role to play.

In late 2011, in the run-up to a major United Nations conference on sustainable development, I headed to the UN in New York in order to present the Doughnut to representatives from a wide range of countries, to gauge their reaction to it. I met first with the Argentinians since they were, at the time, chairing the Group of 77, the largest negotiating bloc of developing countries at the UN. As I explained the Doughnut to the Argentine negotiator, she tapped the picture firmly with her finger and said, 'I have always thought of sustainable development like this. If only you could get the Europeans to see it this way too.' So the following day I went, with curiosity, to present the Doughnut to a roomful of European officials. Once I had projected the Doughnut on to the screen and explained its core idea, the British representative spoke up. 'This is interesting,' he said. 'We hear the Latin Americans talk of "Pachamama" and find it all a bit fluffy' – waggling his hands in the air as if to illustrate – 'but I can see that this is a science-based way of saying something that's actually not so different.' Sometimes pictures can bridge a divide that words cannot cross.

Given just how far out of balance we currently are – transgressing both sides of the Doughnut – the task of coming into balance is daunting. 'We are the first generation to know that we're undermining the ability of the Earth system to support human development,' says Johan Rockström. 'This is a profound new insight and it is potentially very, very scary ... It is also an enormous privilege because it means that we are the first generation to know that we now need to navigate a transformation to a globally sustainable future.'[38]

Imagine, then, if ours could be the turnaround generation that started putting humanity on track for that future. What if we each were to mentally map our own lives on to the Doughnut, asking ourselves: how does the way that I shop, eat, travel, earn a living, bank, vote and volunteer affect my personal impact on social and planetary boundaries? What if every company strategised around a Doughnut table, asking itself: is our brand a Doughnut brand, whose core business helps to bring humanity into that safe and just space? Imagine if the G20 finance ministers – representing the world's most powerful economies – met around a Doughnut-shaped conference table to discuss how to design a global financial system that served to bring humanity into that sweet spot. These would be world-changing conversations.

In some countries, companies and communities, such conversations are actually under way. From the UK to South Africa, Oxfam has published national Doughnut reports, revealing how far each nation is from living within a nationally defined safe and just space.[39] In Yunnan Province, China, research scientists have made a Doughnut analysis of the social and ecological impacts of industry and farming around Lake Erhai, the region's key source of water.[40] Companies ranging from Patagonia, the US-based outdoor clothing manufacturer, to Sainsbury's supermarkets in the UK, have used the Doughnut to help rethink their corporate strategies. And in Kokstad, South Africa – the fastest-growing town in KwaZulu Natal – the local municipality has teamed up with urban planners and community groups in using the Doughnut to envision a sustainable and equitable future for the town.[41]

Initiatives like these are ambitious experiments in reorienting economic development, but is the Doughnut's planetary scale simply too ambitious for economics to handle? Not at all: it is a scale whose time has come. Back in Ancient Greece when Xenophon first posed the economic question, 'How should a household best manage its resources?' he was literally thinking about a single household.

Towards the end of his life he turned his attention to the next level up, the economics of the city state, and proposed a set of trade, tax and public investment policies for his home town of Athens. Jump forward almost two thousand years to Scotland, where Adam Smith decisively raised the focus of economics to the next level up again, the nation state, asking why some nations' economies thrived while others stagnated. Smith's nation-state economic lens has gripped policy attention for over two hundred and fifty years, and is entrenched by those yearly statistical comparisons of national GDP. But now faced with a globally connected economy, it is time for this generation of thinkers to take the inevitable next step. Ours is the era of the planetary household – and the art of household management is needed more than ever for our common home.

Can we live within the Doughnut?

The Doughnut provides us with a twenty-first-century compass but what determines whether or not we can actually move into its safe and just space? Five factors certainly play key roles: population, distribution, aspiration, technology and governance.

Population matters, and in an obvious way: the more of us there are, the more resources it takes to meet the needs and rights of all, and that is why it is essential for the size of the human population to stabilise. But here's the good news: although the global population is still growing, since 1971 its growth rate has been falling sharply. What's more, for the first time in human history, its fall has been due not to famine, disease or war, but to success.[42] Decades of public investment in infant and child health, in girls' education, in women's reproductive healthcare, and in women's empowerment have at last enabled women to manage the size of their families. Seen through the lens of the Doughnut, the message is clear: the most effective way to stabilise the size of the human population is to ensure that every person can lead a life free of deprivation, above the social foundation.

If population matters, distribution matters just as much because extremes of inequality push humanity beyond both sides of the Doughnut's boundaries. Thanks to the scale of global income inequality, responsibility for global greenhouse gas emissions is highly skewed: the top 10% of emitters – think of them as the global carbonistas living on every continent – generate around 45% of global emissions, while the bottom 50% of people contribute only 13%.[43] Food consumption is deeply skewed too. Around 13% of people worldwide are malnourished. How much food would it take to meet their caloric needs? Just 3% of the global food supply. To put that in context, 30%–50% of the world's food gets lost post-harvest, wasted in global supply chains, or scraped off dinner plates and into kitchen bins.[44] Hunger could, in effect, be ended with just 10% of the food that never gets eaten. From these examples it is clear that getting into the Doughnut calls for a far more equitable distribution of humanity's use of resources.

A third factor is aspiration: whatever people consider necessary for a good life. And one of the biggest influences on our aspirations is how and where we live. In 2009, humanity went urban, with over half of us living in cities and towns for the first time in history, and 70% of us are expected to be urbanites by 2050. City living tends to amplify the influence of surrounding crowds and of advertising billboards whose images promise that a better life is just a purchase away, stoking up desire for faster cars and slimmer laptops, for exotic holidays and the latest-craze gadgets. As economist Tim Jackson deftly put it, we are 'persuaded to spend money we don't have on things we don't need to make impressions that won't last on people we don't care about'.[45] Given a fast-growing global middle class, the lifestyles that people aspire to will have clear ramifications for our collective pressure on planetary boundaries.

Urbanisation may fuel consumerism but it also offers an

opportunity to meet many of people's needs – such as for housing, transport, water, sanitation, food and energy – in far more effective ways. Around 60% of the area expected to be urban by 2030 has yet to be built so the technologies used to create that infrastructure will have far-reaching social and ecological implications.[46] Can new transport systems replace traffic queues of private cars with fast and affordable public transport? Can modern urban energy systems replace fossil-fuel power with rooftop networks of solar power? Can buildings be designed to be largely self-heating and self-cooling? Can food for the city be produced in ways that help to store more carbon in the soil, and provide good jobs at the same time? It depends a great deal upon the technological choices that are made.

Governance also plays a pivotal role, from local and city scales to the national, regional and global. Designing governance that is suited to the challenges we face raises deep political issues that confront the long-standing interests and expectations of countries, corporations and communities alike. The global scale, for example, needs governance structures that can reduce humanity's pressure on planetary boundaries in ways that are equitable with respect to the distribution of their regional and national impacts. At the same time, they must be able to take account of complex interactions such as the inextricable linkages between the food, water and energy sectors. And they must be able to respond far more effectively to unexpected events, such as global food price crises, while steering a wise course on emergent technologies. Much will depend upon the twenty-first century creating far more effective forms of governance, on every scale, than have been seen before.

All five of these factors – population, distribution, aspiration, technology and governance – will significantly shape humanity's prospects for getting into the Doughnut's safe and just space, which is why they are all at the heart of ongoing policy debates. But they cannot bring about the scale of transformation required unless we also transform the economic thinking that we bring to bear. We have left this transformation late in the day – some would say too late. But today's economics students could well be the last generation with a chance of achieving our twenty-first-century goal. They deserve, at the very least, to be equipped with an economic mindset that gives them the best possible chance of succeeding. And so do we all.

The cuckoo goal of GDP growth emerged from an era of economic depression, world war, and cold war rivalry, but it dominated economic thinking for over 70 years. In a few decades' time we will look back, no doubt, and consider it bizarre that we once attempted to monitor and manage our complex planetary household with a metric so fickle, partial and superficial as GDP. The crises of our own times demand a very different goal and we are still in the early days of reimagining and renaming just what that goal should be.

If the goal is to achieve *human prosperity in a flourishing web of life* – and it looks rather like a doughnut – then how can we best think of (and draw) the economy in relation to the whole? As we will discover, the way that economists have traditionally drawn the economy – determining what's included and what's left out of the economic story – has had profound consequences for all that follows.

SEE THE BIG PICTURE

from self-contained market
to embedded economy

For four hundred years, William Shakespeare's plays have captivated theatre-goers worldwide, thanks to their unforgettable characters, gripping plots and poetic verse. To keep his actors on their toes, Shakespeare handed each member of the troupe only their own lines and cues to learn, intentionally leaving them in the dark about the unfolding plot.[1] Soon after his death, however, over-zealous editors added in complete lists of characters and, in plays such as *The Tempest*, introduced many parts along with their telltale traits:[2]

PROSPERO, the right Duke of Milan
ANTONIO, his brother, the usurping Duke of Milan
GONZALO, an honest old counsellor
CALIBAN, a savage and deformed slave
STEFANO, a drunken butler
MIRANDA, daughter to Prospero
ARIEL, an airy spirit

Describe a character as an 'usurping duke' and the actors already suspect that past wrongs are waiting to be righted. Name another as 'an honest old counsellor' and they know his word is to be trusted.

Introduce a third as a 'drunken butler' and they are waiting for the slapstick comedy. With such a character list, the play is pregnant with plot and the story ahead almost self-fulfilling.

What does this have to do with economics? Everything. 'All the world's a stage,' Shakespeare famously wrote, 'And all the men and women merely players.' He had that right: today's economic actors play out their roles on the international stage, and so enact the economic drama of our times. But who got to set that stage, who defined the telltale traits of the leading roles – and how can we now rewrite the story?

This chapter reveals the cast of characters, the script, and the playwrights behind the economic story that came to dominate the twentieth century – the one that has pushed us to the brink of collapse. But it also sets the stage for a twenty-first-century economic play – one whose characters and script can help bring us back, and into a thriving balance.

Economics may be theatre, but the play's leading roles are never explicitly spelled out in the opening pages of the textbooks. Instead, the key characters are tacitly named through the most iconic diagram in macroeconomics, the Circular Flow. First drawn by Paul Samuelson, it was originally devised simply to illustrate how income flows round the economy. But it quickly came to define the economy itself, determining which economic actors were placed centre stage and which were shunted to the wings. Intentionally or not, Samuelson drew up the twentieth-century cast list. But it was his neoliberal rivals Friedrich Hayek and Milton Friedman who – just like Shakespeare's editors – imbued each part with such telltale traits that the rest of the script almost wrote itself. In their resulting laissez-faire story of who the economy's actors are and how best to let them work, the plot was loaded from the very start.

We are all well versed in its line-up of characters, having been told that the market is efficient, that trade is win–win, and that the commons are a tragedy. Given such a cast, the triumph of the market seems almost inevitable in the unfolding plot. However, we were all also told that finance is infallible – but that part of the story unravelled so publicly during the 2008 financial crash that even the scriptwriters had to admit it rang false. It has become increasingly clear that the neoliberal economic plot – in an ironic echo of *The Tempest* itself – has whipped us into a perfect storm of extreme inequality, climate change and financial crash.

These global crises have opened up a rare chance to rewrite the entire script and perform a new economic play. The place to begin is by revisiting the cast of characters who feature in the Circular Flow. It's time to shake up macroeconomics – armed with nothing more than a pencil – by redrawing its most prized picture.

Setting the stage

When Samuelson launched his 1948 classic *Economics*, one of its many novel contributions was the Circular Flow diagram, which turned out to be a hit for teaching the masses. No wonder it has since spawned a million imitations, with a variation of it in almost every economics textbook.

As the first model of the macroeconomy that every economics student meets, this diagram gets the privileged 'first lick' of the beginner's *tabula rasa*, as Samuelson so gleefully put it. So what message does this model convey about which actors count and which to ignore when it comes to economic analysis? Centre stage is the market relationship between households and business. Households supply their labour and capital in return for wages and profits, and then spend that income buying goods and services from firms. It is this interdependence of production and consumption that creates income's circular flow. And that flow would be uninterrupted if it were not for three outer loops – involving commercial banks, government and trade – that divert some income for other uses. The model shows

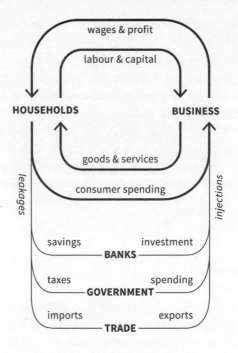

The Circular Flow diagram, which for 70 years was the defining depiction of the macroeconomy.

banks siphoning off income as savings and then returning it as investment. Government extracts income as taxes but re-injects it as public spending. Overseas traders need to be paid for the nation's imports but in turn pay out for its exports. All three of these diversions create leakages from and injections into the market's circular flow but, taken as a whole, the system is closed and complete – not unlike a circular set of plumbed pipes with water flowing round and round, as Samuelson first depicted it.

In fact the very year after Samuelson's textbook was published, that likeness inspired an ingenious engineer-turned-economist, Bill Phillips, to construct such a hydraulic machine for real. His

Bill Phillips and the MONIAC.

machine, known as the MONIAC (that's short for Monetary National Income Analogue Computer), was made up of a set of see-through water tanks connected together by tubes flowing with pink water. Designed to bring the Circular Flow diagram to life, the MONIAC's tanks and tubes represented the flow of income through the UK economy. It was the first computer model of an economy ever made and it was utterly brilliant, earning Phillips a teaching post at the London School of Economics.[3] But as a model it was also utterly flawed, as will become clear.

The engineers may have got carried away with the plumbed pipes, but the Circular Flow diagram deserves its credit because there are good reasons why it became a classic. The diagram was, for starters, the first attempt to depict the economy as a whole, and so helped to establish the field of macroeconomic modelling. Samuelson intended the diagram to illustrate Keynes's insight into how economies can spiral into recession: if household spending starts to fall (say, due to fear of hard times ahead), then firms need fewer workers: as they lay staff off, they cut the nation's take-home pay, so reducing demand even further. The result is a self-fulfilling recession, which – Keynes argued – could best be averted by boosting government spending until things got moving again and confidence was restored. What's more, the diagram also provides the basis for different ways of measuring national income in an accounting framework that is still used worldwide. It is, evidently, a handy picture, making visible many key macroeconomic ideas.

The trouble, however, lies in what it leaves invisible. In the words of the systems thinker John Sterman, 'The most important assumptions of a model are not in the equations, but what's not in them; not in the documentation, but unstated; not in the variables on the computer screen, but in the blank spaces around them.'[4] The Circular Flow diagram certainly needs to be introduced with this caveat. It makes no mention of the energy and materials on which economic activity depends, nor of the society within which those activities take place: they are simply missing from its cast of characters. Did Samuelson omit them on purpose? Unlikely: he was, after all, merely intent on illustrating the flow of income, and so they literally didn't come into the picture. But with that, the stage was set.

Scripting the play

In 1947, the year before Samuelson published his iconic Circular Flow diagram, a small laissez-faire band of wannabe economic scriptwriters – including Friedrich Hayek, Milton Friedman, Ludwig von Mises and Frank Knight – gathered in the Swiss resort of Mont

Pèlerin to start drafting what they hoped would one day become the dominant economic story. Inspired by the pro-market writings of classical liberals such as Adam Smith and David Ricardo they established what they called a 'neoliberal' agenda. Its aim, they said, was to push back hard against the threat of state totalitarianism, which was spreading fast thanks to the growing reach of the Soviet Union. But that aim gradually morphed into a hard push for market fundamentalism, and the meaning of 'neoliberal' morphed along with it. What's more, when Paul Samuelson's diagram appeared – depicting which actors were at the heart of the economy and which were pushed into the wings – it provided the perfect setting for their play.

Scriptwriting began in the late 1940s with the launch of the Mont Pelerin Society, which lives on to this day.[5] But Friedman, Hayek and the other hopeful playwrights knew they might have to wait some decades before their play could be performed. They took the long view: with backing from business and billionaires, they funded university professorships and scholarships, and built an international network of 'free market' think tanks, including the American Enterprise Institute and the Cato Institute in Washington, DC, and the Institute of Economic Affairs in London.[6]

The big time came at last in 1980 when Margaret Thatcher and Ronald Reagan teamed up to bring the neoliberal script to the international stage. Both newly elected, they were surrounded by Mont Pelerin insiders: Reagan's election team included more than twenty members of the Society, and Thatcher's first Chancellor of the Exchequer, Geoffrey Howe, was a member too. Like the longest-running of Broadway shows, the neoliberal show has been playing ever since, powerfully framing the economic debate of the past thirty years.[7] It is high time we met the cast of characters that star in its story, each accompanied here by a biographical note and a one-line character summary that – in true Shakespearean style – loads the plot from the get-go.

Economics: the twentieth-century neoliberal story
(in which we go to the brink of collapse)

Staging by Paul Samuelson
Script by the Mont Pelerin Society

Cast, in order of appearance:

THE MARKET, which is efficient – so give it free rein. As Adam Smith famously wrote, 'It is not from the benevolence of the butcher, the brewer, or the baker that we expect our dinner, but from their regard to their own interest.'[8] When the market's invisible hand is set free to work its magic of allocative efficiency, it harnesses the self-interest of every household and business to provide all the goods and jobs that are wanted.

BUSINESS, which is innovative – so let it lead. 'The business of business is business' summed up Milton Friedman's influential philosophy in the 1970s. Firms bring together labour and capital to produce novel goods and services and to maximise their profits. There is no need to look at what goes on in their factories and farms, so long as they play within the legal rules of the game.

FINANCE, which is infallible – so trust in its ways. Banks take people's savings and dutifully turn them into profitable investments. Furthermore, according to Eugene Fama's influential 'efficient-market hypothesis' of 1970, the price of financial assets always fully reflects all relevant information.[9] Hence financial markets are ever adjusting but always 'right' – and their smooth operation should not be distorted by regulation.

TRADE, which is win–win – so open your borders. David Ricardo's nineteenth-century theory of comparative advantage demonstrates that countries should focus on what they are relatively good at doing and then trade: if they do, both parties will gain from it, no matter how unequal they are.[10] Hence trade barriers should be dismantled because they only distort the efficient workings of the international market.

THE STATE, which is incompetent – so don't let it meddle. When government tries to intervene in the market, it usually makes things worse, distorting incentives and picking white elephants instead of winners. If it tries to smooth the business cycle, in classic Keynesian style, its timing will inevitably be off, and the market will pre-empt its effects.[11] Beyond defending the nation's borders and its citizens' private property, it is quite simply best for the state to leave things to the market.

Other characters not required on stage:

THE HOUSEHOLD, which is domestic – so leave it to the women. The household supplies labour and capital to the market, but there's no need to lift the roof and ask what goes on within its four walls: wives and daughters kindly take care of domestic affairs and they belong in the home, as does this matter.

THE COMMONS, which are tragic – so sell them off. In the 1960s, Garrett Hardin described 'the tragedy of the commons' in which shared resources – such as grazing land and fish stocks – tend to be over-exploited by individual users and so are depleted for all.[12] Managing such resources sustainably therefore calls for government regulation or, better still, private ownership.

SOCIETY, which is non-existent – so ignore it. 'There is no such thing as society,' Margaret Thatcher famously declared in the 1980s. 'There are individual men and women and there are families.'[13] And it is, of course, the market that connects them, as workers and as consumers.

EARTH, which is inexhaustible – so take all you want. There will be no shortage of Earth's resources, claimed the laissez-faire economist Julian Simon in the 1980s, if markets are permitted to do their job. A shortage of, say, copper or oil will raise its price, spurring people to use it more sparingly, search for new sources, and discover substitutes.[14]

POWER, which is irrelevant – so don't mention it. The only economic power to be worried about, argued Friedman, is monopoly power granted by the state when it meddles in the market, and the distortionary power of trade unions. The single best way to combat it is (no surprise) free markets and free trade.[15]

It was, undeniably, a brilliant line-up – and almost a stitch-up. The market, promised the neoliberal script, is the road to freedom, and who could be against that? But putting blind faith in markets – while ignoring the living world, society, and the runaway power of banks – has taken us to the brink of ecological, social and financial collapse. It is time for the neoliberal show to leave the stage: a very different story is emerging.

A new century, a new show

To tell a new story let's start with a new picture of the whole economy. Samuelson drew his iconic diagram in the late 1940s – in the wake of the Great Depression and the Second World War – and so was understandably focused on the question of how to get income flowing around the economy again. No wonder his diagram defined the economy in terms of its monetary flows alone.

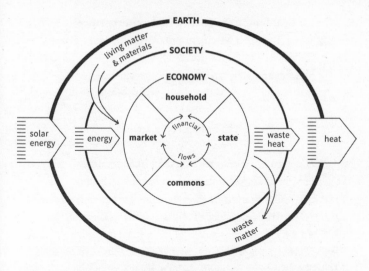

The Embedded Economy, which nests the economy within society and within the living world, while recognising the diverse ways in which it can meet people's needs and wants.

In doing so, however, it offered an extremely small stage for economic thinking, along with a stripped-down cast of characters. So let's start afresh with an economic question better suited to our own times: what do we depend upon to provision for our needs? Here's a visual answer to that question, summed up in a diagram that I have called The Embedded Economy, which brings into one picture important insights from diverse schools of economic thought.[16]

What does it show? First Earth – the living world – powered by energy from the sun. Within Earth is human society and, within that, economic activity, in which the household, the market, the commons and the state are all important realms of provisioning for human wants and needs, and are enabled by financial flows. If this diagram sets a new stage, then here is the cast of characters that it calls forth.

Economics: the twenty-first-century story
(in which we create a thriving balance)

Staging and script: a work in progress by economic
re-thinkers everywhere

Cast in order of appearance:

EARTH, which is life-giving – so respect its boundaries
SOCIETY, which is foundational – so nurture its connections
THE ECONOMY, which is diverse – so support all of its systems
THE HOUSEHOLD, which is core – so value its contribution
THE MARKET, which is powerful – so embed it wisely
THE COMMONS, which are creative – so unleash their potential
THE STATE, which is essential – so make it accountable
FINANCE, which is in service – so make it serve society
BUSINESS, which is innovative – so give it purpose
TRADE, which is double-edged – so make it fair
POWER, which is pervasive – so check its abuse

What follows is a biography for each of these parts – longer than the twentieth-century ones because these new roles are not yet nearly so familiar. It is time to meet the twenty-first century's economic actors anew.

EARTH, which is life-giving – so respect its boundaries

Far from floating against a white background, the economy exists within the biosphere, that delicate living zone of Earth's land, waters and atmosphere. And it continually draws in energy and matter from Earth's materials and living systems, while expelling waste heat and matter back out into it. Everything that is produced – from clay bricks to Lego blocks, websites to construction sites, liver pâté to patio furniture, single cream to double glazing – depends upon this through-flow of energy and matter, from biomass and fossil fuels to metal ores and minerals. None of this is news. But if the economy is so evidently embedded in the biosphere, how has economics so blatantly ignored it?

Earth's importance for the economy was self-evident to the early economists. In the eighteenth century, François Quesnay and his fellow Physiocrats took their name from their belief that agrarian land was the key to understanding economic value. Yes, these early economists based their ecological thinking narrowly on agricultural land alone, but at least the living world got a mention. From there, however, things began to go awry, and there are many theories as to why.

Adam Smith, father of classical economic thinking, drew on the Physiocrats' work, believing that a nation's potential for wealth ultimately depended upon its climate and soil. But he also thought that the secret to productivity lay in the division of labour and so focused his attention on that. David Ricardo likewise believed that the 'original and indestructible powers of the soil' made scarce agricultural land a key determinant of economic value.[17] But as new lands were cultivated in Britain's colonies, he decided that land scarcity was no longer such a threat and so, like Smith, switched his attention to labour instead. John Stuart Mill also clearly saw the importance of Earth's materials and energy in all economic production, but he wanted to distinguish social science from natural science and so (rather unhelpfully) proposed that the field of political economy focus on the laws of the mind, not the laws of matter.[18] In the 1870s the radical American thinker Henry George pointed out that land gained value for its owners even if they did nothing to improve it, and so he advocated a land-value tax – prompting his influential (and land-owning) opponents to downplay the importance of land in economic theory from then on.[19]

The upshot of all this? The classical economists, led by Smith and Ricardo, had recognised labour, land and capital as three distinct factors of production. But by the late twentieth century, mainstream economics had reduced the focus to just two: labour and capital – and if ever land did get a mention, it was as just another form of capital, interchangeable with all the rest.[20] As a result, mainstream economics is still taught today with scant attention paid to the living planet that supports us and the blazing star whose energy we depend upon.[21] It relegates ecological stresses such as climate change, deforestation, and soil degradation to the periphery of economic thought, until they become so severe that their damaging economic impacts demand attention.

So let's restore sense from the outset and recognise that, far from being a closed, circular loop, the economy is an *open system* with constant inflows and outflows of matter and energy. The economy depends upon Earth as a *source* – extracting finite resources like oil, clay, cobalt and copper, and harvesting renewable ones like timber, crops, fish and fresh water. The economy likewise depends upon Earth as a *sink* for its wastes – such as greenhouse gas emissions, fertiliser run-off, and throwaway plastics. Earth itself, however, is a closed system because almost no matter leaves or arrives on this planet: energy from the sun may flow through it, but materials can only cycle within it.[22]

Redrawing the economy as an open subsystem of the closed Earth system is the major conceptual shift introduced by ecological economists such as Herman Daly in the 1970s. And it's a paradigm shift that has become increasingly important, given the economy's ever-growing scale. When Adam Smith published *The Wealth of Nations* in 1776, there were fewer than one billion people alive and, in dollar terms, the size of the global economy was 300 times smaller than it is today. When Paul Samuelson published *Economics* in 1948 there were not yet three billion people on Earth and the global economy was still ten times smaller than it is today. In the twenty-first century we have left behind the era of 'Empty World', when the flow of energy and matter through the global economy was small in relation to the capacity of nature's sources and sinks. We live now, says

Daly, in 'Full World', with an economy that exceeds Earth's regenerative and absorptive capacity by over-harvesting sources such as fish, and forests, and over-filling sinks such as the atmosphere and oceans.[23]

To this add a second shift in perspective: the economy's fundamental resource flow is not a roundabout of money but, rather, a one-way street of energy – and nothing can move, grow or work without using that energy. This is where Bill Phillips's MONIAC machine was fundamentally flawed. While brilliantly demonstrating the economy's circular flow of income, it completely overlooked its throughflow of energy. To make his hydraulic computer start up, Phillips had to flip a switch on the back of it to turn on its electric pump. Like any real economy it relied upon an external source of energy to make it run, but neither Phillips nor his contemporaries spotted that the machine's power source was a critical part of what made the model work. That lesson from the MONIAC applies to all of macroeconomics: the role of energy deserves a far more prominent place in economic theories that hope to explain what drives economic activity.

The vast majority of energy that powers today's global economy is from the sun. Some of that solar energy, such as sunshine and wind, arrives in real time each day. Some has been stored in recent times, like the energy bound up in crops, livestock and trees. And some has been stored up since ancient times, particularly the fossil fuels of oil, coal and gas. Which of these sources of solar energy the economy uses matters a great deal, and here's why. It was thanks to the balance between real-time solar energy entering Earth's atmosphere and heat escaping back out into space that Earth maintained a steady and benevolent average temperature during the Holocene. Over the past 200 years, however, and especially since 1950, humanity's use of ancient fossil-fuel energy has released carbon dioxide and other greenhouse gases into the atmosphere at an entirely unprecedented rate, with potentially dangerous consequences. Most of these gases occur naturally in the atmosphere and, together with water vapour, act like a blanket around the Earth, keeping its surface much warmer than it otherwise would be. Releasing more carbon dioxide, however, thickens that blanket and so further raises Earth's temperature, resulting in human-induced global warming.[24]

This wider perspective of the throughflow of energy and materials invites us to imagine the economy as a super-organism – think giant slug – that demands a continual intake of matter and energy from Earth's sources, and delivers a continual stream of waste matter and waste heat into its sinks. On a planet with intricately structured ecosystems and a delicately balanced climate, this begs a now obvious question: how big can the global economy's throughflow of matter and energy be in relation to the biosphere before it disrupts the very planetary life-support systems on which our well-being depends? The nine planetary boundaries give a compelling first answer to that question and in Chapter 6 we will explore just how the economy's use of matter and energy can be redesigned so that it works with, not against, the cycles of life that those boundaries seek to protect.

SOCIETY, which is foundational – so nurture its connections

When Thatcher declared that there is no such thing as society, it came as a surprise to many – not least to society. Political theorists such as Robert Putnam use the term 'social capital' to describe the wealth of trust and reciprocity that is created within social groups as a result of their networks of relationships.[25] Whether through local sports teams or international festivals, faith groups or social clubs, we build norms, rules and relations that enable us to cooperate with and depend upon one another. These connections build social cohesion and help to meet our fundamental human needs such as for participation, leisure, protection and belonging. 'Community connectedness is not just about warm fuzzy tales of civic triumph,' writes Putnam; 'In measurable and well-documented ways ... social capital makes us smarter, healthier, safer, richer, and better able to govern a just and stable democracy.'[26]

It's clear that an economy's vibrancy depends upon the trust, norms and sense of reciprocity nurtured within society – just as every sport depends upon its players abiding by a shared set of rules. But a society's vibrancy is, in turn, shaped by the structure of its economy: the relationships that it builds or weakens; the public spirit that it fosters or erodes; and the distribution of wealth that it generates, as Chapter 5 explores.

A thriving society, in addition, is more likely to build strong political engagement, starting with community meetings, grass-roots organising, voting in elections, and joining social and political movements that hold political representatives to account. 'Significant changes occur when social movements reach a critical point of power capable of moving cautious politicians beyond their tendency to keep things as they are,' writes the American historian Howard Zinn, pointing to his own country's nineteenth-century anti-slavery movement and twentieth-century civil rights movement.[27] Democratic governance of society and the economy rests on the right and capacity of citizens to engage in public debate – hence the importance of 'political voice' within the Doughnut's social foundation.

THE ECONOMY, which is diverse – so support all of its systems

Embedded within this rich web of society is the economy itself, the realm in which people produce, distribute and consume products and services that meet their wants and needs. One basic feature of the economy is rarely pointed out in Econ 101: that it is typically made up of four realms of provisioning: the household, the market, the commons and the state, as shown in the Embedded Economy diagram. All four are means of production and distribution, but they go about it in very different ways. Households produce 'core' goods for their own members; the market produces private goods for those willing and able to pay; the commons produce co-created goods for the communities involved; and the state produces public goods for all the populace. I wouldn't want to live in a society whose economy lacked any of these four realms of provisioning because each one has distinct qualities and much of their value arises through their interactions. In other words, they work best when they work together.

What's more, while the Circular Flow diagram identified people primarily as workers, consumers and capital owners, the Embedded Economy diagram invites us to acknowledge our many other social and economic identities. In the household we may be parents, carers and neighbours. In relation to the state we are members of the public, using public services and paying taxes in return. In the commons we are collaborative creators and stewards of shared wealth. In society we are citizens, voters, activists and volunteers. Every day we switch almost seamlessly between these different roles and relations: from customer to creator, from marketplace to meeting space, from bargaining to volunteering. So let's consider each realm in turn.

THE HOUSEHOLD, which is core – so value its contribution

The Circular Flow diagram depicted labour appearing – hey presto! – fresh and ready for work each day at the office or factory door. So who cooked, cleaned up, and cleared away to make that possible? When Adam Smith, extolling the power of the market, noted that, 'it is not from the benevolence of the butcher,

78

the brewer, or the baker that we expect our dinner', he forgot to mention the benevolence of his mother, Margaret Douglas, who had raised her boy alone from birth. Smith never married so had no wife to rely upon (nor children of his own to raise). At the age of 43, as he began to write his opus, *The Wealth of Nations*, he moved back in with his cherished old mum, from whom he could expect his dinner every day. But her role in it all never got a mention in his economic theory, and it subsequently remained invisible for centuries.[28]

As a result, mainstream economic theory is obsessed with the productivity of waged labour while skipping right over the unpaid work that makes it all possible, as feminist economists have made clear for decades.[29] That work is known by many names: unpaid caring work, the reproductive economy, the love economy, the second economy. However, as economist Neva Goodwin has pointed out, far from being secondary, it is actually the 'core economy' and it comes first every day, sustaining the essentials of family and social life with the universal human resources of time, knowledge, skill, care, empathy, teaching and reciprocity.[30] And if you have never really thought of it before, then it's time you met your inner housewife (because we all have one). She lives in the daily dealings of making breakfast, washing the dishes, tidying the house, shopping for groceries, teaching the children to walk and to share, washing clothes, caring for elderly parents, emptying the rubbish bins, collecting kids from school, helping the neighbours, making the dinner, sweeping the floor, and lending an ear. She carries out all those tasks – some with open arms, others through gritted teeth – that underpin personal and family well-being and sustain social life.

We all have a hand in this core economy, but some people (like Adam Smith's mum) spend far more time in it than others. Time may be a universal human resource but it varies hugely in terms of how we each get to experience and use it, how far we control it, and how it is valued.[31] In sub-Saharan Africa and South Asia, time spent in the core economy is particularly visible because, when the state fails to deliver and the market is out of reach, householders have to make provision for many more of their needs directly. Millions of women and girls spend hours walking miles each day, carrying their body weight in water, food or firewood on their heads, often with a baby strapped to their back – and all for no pay. But this gendered division of paid and unpaid work is prevalent in every society, albeit sometimes less visibly so. And since work in the core economy is unpaid, it is routinely undervalued and exploited, generating life-long inequalities in social standing, job opportunities, income, and power between women and men.

By largely ignoring the core economy, mainstream economics has also overlooked just how much the paid economy depends upon it. Without all that cooking, washing, nursing and sweeping, there would be no workers – today or in the future – who were healthy, well-fed, and ready for work each morning. As the futurist Alvin Toffler liked to ask at smart gatherings of business executives, 'How productive would your workforce be if it hadn't been toilet trained?'[32] The scale of the core economy's contribution is not to be dismissed lightly, either. In a 2002 study of Basle, a wealthy Swiss city, the estimated value of unpaid care being provided in the city's households exceeded the total cost of salaries paid in all of Basle's hospitals, daycare centres and schools, from the directors to the janitors.[33] Likewise, a 2014 survey of 15,000 mothers in the USA calculated that, if women were paid the going hourly rate for each of their roles – switching between housekeeper and daycare teacher to van driver and cleaner – then stay-at-home mums would earn around $120,000 each year. Even mothers who do head out to work each day would earn an extra $70,000 on top of their actual wages, given all the unpaid care they also provide at home.[34]

Why does it matter that this core economy should be visible in economics? Because the household provision of care is essential for human well-being, and productivity in the paid economy depends directly upon it. It matters because when – in the name of austerity and public-sector savings – governments cut budgets for children's daycare centres, community services, parental leave and youth clubs, the need for care-giving doesn't disappear: it just gets pushed back into the home. The pressure, particularly on women's time, can force them out of work and increase social stress and vulnerability. That undermines both well-being and women's empowerment, with multiple knock-on effects for society and the economy alike. In short, including the household economy in the new diagram of the macroeconomy is the first step in recognising its centrality, and in reducing and redistributing women's unpaid work.[35]

THE MARKET, which is powerful – so embed it wisely

Adam Smith's great insight was to show that the marketplace can mobilise diffuse information about people's wants and the cost of meeting them, thereby coordinating billions of buyers and sellers through a global system of prices – all without the need for a centralised grand plan. This distributed efficiency of the market is indeed extraordinary, and attempting to run an economy without it typically leads to short supplies and long queues. It was out of recognition of this power that the neoliberal scriptwriters put the market centre stage in their economic play. There is, however, a flip side to the market's power: it only values what is priced and only delivers to those who can pay. Like fire, it is extremely efficient at what it does, but dangerous if it gets out of control. When the market is unconstrained, it degrades the living world by over-stressing Earth's sources and sinks. It also fails to deliver essential public goods – from education and vaccines to roads and railways – on which its own success deeply depends. At the same time, as Chapter 4 will show, its inherent dynamics tend to widen social inequalities and generate economic instability. That is why the market's power must be wisely embedded within public regulations, and within the wider economy, in order to define and delimit its terrain.

It is also why, whenever I hear someone praising the 'free market', I beg them to take me there, because I've never seen it at work in any country that I have visited. Institutional economists – from Thorstein Veblen to Karl Polanyi – have long pointed out that markets (and hence their prices) are strongly shaped by a society's context of laws, institutions, regulations, policies and culture. As Ha-Joon Chang writes, 'A market looks free only because we so unconditionally accept its underlying restrictions that we fail to see them.'[36] From passports to medicines and AK-47s, many things cannot be legally bought or sold without official licence. Trade unions, immigration policies, and minimum wage laws all have an effect on a country's going wage rate. Company reporting requirements, the culture of shareholder primacy, and state-funded bailouts all influence the level of corporate profits. Forget the free market: think embedded market. And, strange though it sounds, that means there is no such thing as deregulation, only *reregulation* that embeds the market in a different set of political, legal and cultural rules, simply shifting who bears the risks and costs and who reaps the gains of change.[37]

THE COMMONS, which are creative – so unleash their potential

The commons are shareable resources of nature or society that people choose to use and govern through self-organising, instead of relying on the state or market for doing so. Think of how a village community might manage its only freshwater well and its nearby forest, or how Internet users worldwide collaboratively curate Wikipedia. Natural commons have traditionally emerged in communities seeking to steward Earth's 'common pool' resources, such as grazing land, fisheries, watersheds and forests. Cultural commons serve to keep alive a community's language, heritage and rituals, myths and music, traditional knowledge and practice. And the fast-growing digital commons are stewarded collaboratively online, co-creating open-source software, social networks, information and knowledge.

Garrett Hardin's description of the commons as 'tragic' – which fitted so neatly into the neoliberal script – arose from his belief that, if left as open access to all, then pastures, forests and fishing grounds would inevitably be overused and depleted. He was most probably right about that, but 'open access' is far from how successful commons are actually governed. In the 1970s, the little-known political scientist Elinor Ostrom started seeking out real-life examples of well-managed natural commons to find out what made them work – and she went on to win a Nobel-Memorial prize for what she discovered. Rather than being left 'open access', those successful commons were governed by clearly defined communities with collectively agreed rules and punitive sanctions for those who broke them.[38] Far from tragic, she realised, the commons can turn out to be a triumph, outperforming both state and market in sustainably stewarding and equitably harvesting Earth's resources, as Chapters 5 and 6 illustrate.

The triumph of the commons is certainly evident in the digital commons, which are fast turning into one of the most dynamic arenas of the global economy. It is a transformation made possible, argues the economic analyst Jeremy Rifkin, by the ongoing convergence of networks for digital communications, renewable energy and 3D printing, creating what he has called 'the collaborative commons'. What makes the convergence of these technologies so powerfully disruptive is their potential for distributed ownership, networked collaboration, and minimal running costs. Once the solar panels, computer networks and 3D printers are in place, the cost of producing one extra joule of energy, one extra download, one extra 3D printed component, is close to nothing, leading Rifkin to dub it 'the zero-marginal-cost revolution'.[39]

The result is that a growing range of products and services can be produced abundantly, nearly for free, unleashing potential such as open-source design, free online education, and distributed manufacturing. In some key sectors the twenty-first-century collaborative commons has started to complement, compete with, and even displace the market. What's more, the value generated is enjoyed directly by those who co-create in the commons, and it may never be monetised – with intriguing implications for the future of GDP growth, as Chapter 7 explores.

Despite their creative potential – and sometimes because of it – the commons have, for centuries, been encroached upon by the market and the state alike, through the enclosure of common land, the division of enterprise into workers and owners, and the rise of market-versus-state rivalry. All of this was aided by economic theory which purported to show that the commons were doomed to fail. But, thanks to Ostrom, widely documented evidence of success in the commons has generated growing interest in their resurgence – and that is why they must be drawn clearly into the Embedded Economy diagram.

THE STATE, *which is essential – so make it accountable*

As lead author of the neoliberal script, Milton Friedman was determined to limit the state's economic role to defending the nation, policing its streets, and enforcing its laws. Its legitimate purpose, he believed, was simply to secure private property and legal contracts, which he saw as the prerequisites for smoothly functioning markets.[40] In effect, he sought to relegate the state to a non-speaking part in the economic play: mentioned in the storyline, seen fleetingly on stage, but permitted little action. His rival, Paul Samuelson, strongly disagreed with that view. 'The creative role of government in economic life is vast and inescapable in an interdependent and crowded world,' he wrote in later editions of his textbook, but Friedman's stance still prevailed among those keen to 'roll back' the state.[41]

For the twenty-first-century economic story, the state's role must be rethought. Put it this way: in the film of the play, the state should be aiming all-out to win Best Supporting Actor at the Oscars – starring as the economic partner that supports the household, the commons and the market alike. First, by providing public goods – ranging from public education and healthcare to roads and street lighting – that deliver for all, not just for those who can pay, so enabling a society and its economy to thrive. Second, by supporting the core caring role of the household, such as with maternal and paternal leave policies that empower both parents, investment in early-years education, and care support for seniors. Third, by unleashing the dynamism of the commons, with laws and institutions that enable their collaborative potential and protect them from encroachment. Fourth, by harnessing the power of the market by embedding it in institutions and regulations that promote the common good – from banning toxic pollutants and insider trading to protecting biodiversity and workers' rights.

Like all best supporting actors, the state may also step centre stage, taking entrepreneurial risks where the market and commons can't or won't reach. The extraordinary success of tech companies like Apple is sometimes held up as evidence of the market's dynamism. But Mariana Mazzucato, an expert in the economics of government-led innovation, points out that the basic research behind every innovation that makes a smart phone 'smart' – GPS, microchips, touchscreens, and the Internet itself – was funded by the US government. The state, not the market, turns out to have been the innovating, risk-taking partner, not 'crowding out' but 'dynamising in' private enterprise – and this trend holds across other high-tech industries too, such as pharmaceuticals and biotech.[42] In the words of Ha-Joon Chang, 'If we remain blinded by the free market ideology that tells us only winner-picking by the private sector can succeed, we will end up ignoring a huge range of possibilities for economic development through public leadership or public-private joint efforts.'[43] Such state leadership is now needed worldwide to catalyse public, private, commons and household investments in a renewable energy future.

The state as empowering, enabling economic partner: it sounds so good – is it too good to be true? That crucially depends, argue the economist Daron Acemoglu and political scientist James Robinson, on whether, in each country, the state's economic and political institutions are inclusive or extractive. Put simply, inclusive institutions give many people a say in decision-making, unlike extractive ones that privilege the voice of the few and allow them to exploit and rule over others.[44] The threat of the authoritarian state is very real, but so too is the danger of market fundamentalism. To avoid the tyranny of the state and the tyranny of the market alike, democratic politics are key – thus reinforcing the foundational role played by society in generating the civic engagement needed for participation and accountability in public and political life.

FINANCE, which is in service – so make it serve society

Three long-held myths make up the traditional story of finance: that commercial banks work by turning people's savings into investments; that financial trading smoothes out the economy's fluctuations; and that, therefore, the financial sector provides a valuable service to the productive economy. All three of these myths were busted very publicly by the 2008 financial crisis. Far from simply lending out savings, banks magically create money as credit. Far from promoting stability, financial markets inherently generate flux. And far from providing a valuable service to the productive economy, finance has turned into the tail that wags the dog.

First, contrary to the textbook story and the Circular Flow diagram, banks do not merely lend out the money that has been deposited by their savers. They create money from nothing each time they issue loans – recording on their books both a liability (since the loan is withdrawn by the borrower) and a credit (since the loan will be repaid with interest over time). Such credit creation is hardly new – it started several thousand years ago – and it can play a valuable role, but it has grown hugely in scale since the 1980s. That expansion was triggered by financial deregulation (think *re*regulation) – including the 1986 Big Bang in the UK and the 1999 repeal of the Glass–Steagall Act in the US – which ended the requirement for banks to keep customers' savings and loans separate from their own speculative investments.

Second, financial markets do not tend to promote economic stability, despite the claims that they do. Thanks to financial deregulation, said US Federal Reserve Chair Alan Greenspan in 2004, 'not only have individual financial institutions become less vulnerable to shocks from underlying risk factors, but also the financial system as a whole has become more resilient.'[45] Four years later, the financial crash disproved that claim in a fairly decisive way. At the same time, Eugene Fama's efficient-market hypothesis – that financial markets are inherently efficient – lost credibility and has been countered by Hyman Minsky's financial-instability hypothesis – that financial markets are inherently volatile – as we will see in Chapter 4.

Lastly, far from playing a supporting role to the productive economy, finance has come to dominate it. In many countries, a small financial elite – based in just a handful of banking and financial firms – controls the public good of money creation and profits handsomely from it, while too often destabilising much of the wider economy in the process. It is time to turn this upside-down scenario the right way up and redesign finance so that it flows in service of the economy and society. Such a redesign also invites a rethink of how money could be created – not just by the market but by the state and the commons too – and Chapters 5, 6 and 7 explore some possibilities for that.

BUSINESS, which is innovative – so give it purpose

Operating within the realm of the market, business can be extraordinarily effective in combining people, technology, energy, materials and finance to create something new. The neoliberal narrative claimed that the market mechanism is what makes firms efficient, and so ignored what goes on inside them, just as it did with the household. But it is essential to lift the lid here too and look inside the black box of production.

Power is always at play between a firm's waged workers and its shareholding owners because of the vast inequalities between them, as Friedrich Engels and Karl Marx witnessed in the squalid factories of Victorian Britain. Such conditions can still be found in factories and farms across the world today where, in the name of profit, managers routinely flout the law, for example by locking workers in, banning toilet breaks, or sacking women if they become pregnant. But even when businesses operate within the law they can, in many countries, hire workers on insecure, zero-hour contracts, while paying a legal minimum wage that leaves them living below the poverty line.[46]

Ensuring workers' rights to organise and bargain collectively is one way of offsetting such deep power imbalances: another is to change the ownership structure of the firm itself, ending the centuries-old divide between workers and owners, as Chapter 5 explores. What's more, Friedman's narrow view on the business of business has lost credibility: in the face of twenty-first-century challenges, firms need a purpose far more inspiring than merely maximising shareholder value and, as Chapter 6 illustrates, a growing number of enterprises are finding ways to give themselves one.

TRADE, which is double-edged – so make it fair

The Embedded Economy diagram could be used to depict a single nation's economy, but it can likewise portray the global economy, and so includes international trade. Globalisation has led to the rapid expansion of cross-border flows in the last 20 years, thanks to shipping containers and the Internet slashing the costs of international transport and communications and, since 1995, thanks to the World Trade Organization's agenda of trade liberalisation.

Ricardo's influential theory of win–win trade was based on products like wine and cloth, and assumed that the factors of production – land, labour and capital – were immovable behind national borders. Today, everything but land moves, with cross-border flows including trade in products and services (from fresh fruit to legal advice); foreign direct investment (in businesses and properties); financial flows (from bank loans to corporate stocks), and the migration of people in search of a livelihood.

All of these cross-border flows have the potential to deliver benefits but they carry risks, too. When it is cheaper to import staple foods like rice and wheat than it is to grow them, trade can significantly reduce food prices for consumers. At the same time it may undermine domestic food production and leave the country highly vulnerable to international price hikes – as bread riots from Egypt to Burkina Faso revealed when the global price of wheat, corn and rice trebled during the food price crisis of 2007–8. When skilled workers migrate – such as doctors and nurses from sub-Saharan Africa working in Europe – they bring valuable skills and send much-needed remittances to their families back home, but this can also lead to a skill shortage in their own country's core services. When corporations offshore manufacturing, it often delivers cheaper products to consumers and creates new jobs overseas. But it can also result in domestic job losses that decimate whole communities – as experienced in America's 'rust belt', the nation's former industrial heartland. Likewise, financial inflows may boost an emerging economy's fledgling stock market but when international finance exits even faster than it entered, it can induce a near collapse of the currency, as Thailand, Indonesia and South Korea discovered the hard way during the Asian financial crisis of the late 1990s. Cross-border flows are always double-edged and so need to be managed.

Ricardo was right in thinking that very different nations may be able to trade to mutual gain, but comparative advantage is not only what you are blessed with: it is something you can build. As Ha-Joon Chang puts it, however, today's high-income countries are 'kicking away the ladder' that they once climbed, recommending that low- and middle-income countries open their borders to follow a trade strategy that they strategically avoided themselves. Despite their current rhetoric of 'free trade', when it comes to trade negotiations almost all of today's high-income countries – including the UK and the US – took the opposite route to ensure their own industrial success, opting for tariff protection, industrial subsidies and state-owned enterprises when it was nationally advantageous. And today they still keep tight control over their key traded assets such as intellectual property.[47]

Just as there is no such thing as the free market, it turns out that there is no such thing as free trade: all cross-border flows are set against the backdrop of national history, current institutions and international power relations. As the world's 2007–8 food price crisis followed by the 2008–10 financial crisis illustrated, it requires effective cooperation among governments to make sure that the benefits of cross-border flows are widely shared.

POWER, *which is pervasive – so check its abuse*

Search for the word 'power' in the index of a modern economics textbook and – if mentioned at all – it will probably refer you to an analysis of electricity sector reform. But power is at play in myriad places throughout the economy and society: in daily household decisions about who cares for the kids; in boss-versus-worker wage negotiations; in international trade and climate-change talks; and in humanity's domination over other species on the planet. Wherever people are present, so too are power relations: think of them as running throughout the Embedded Economy diagram, within each of its domains and at the interface between them too.

Out of all of these power relationships, when it comes to the workings of the economy, one in particular demands attention: the power of the wealthy to reshape the economy's rules in their favour. Samuelson's Circular Flow diagram inadvertently helped to gloss over this matter by depicting households as a homogeneous group, each one offering its labour and capital in return for wages and a share of profits – which are, in turn, paid out by a cluster of homogeneous firms. But, as the Occupy Movement made clear with its meme of the 1% and the 99%, that stylised picture doesn't quite do justice to the reality we have come to know. Inequality amongst households and firms alike has soared in many countries in recent decades. And the extreme concentration of income and wealth – in the hands both of billionaires and of corporate boards – rapidly turns into power over how and for whom the economy is run.

In politics, money talks – when it must in public, but preferably in private, with hidden handshakes, closed-door meetings, and under-the-table kickbacks. These relationships obey a powerful 'golden rule', says the political scientist Thomas Ferguson, based on his long analysis of US political funding. Business effectively invests in political candidates and expects a return on that investment in the form of favourable policies. 'To discover who rules, follow the gold,' he advises: trace the finance backing any major political campaign and you'll see what drives its policies.[48]

In the US, private and corporate funding for elections has increased more than twentyfold since 1976, and it topped $2.5 billion during the 2012 Obama–Romney presidential race.[49] Since 2005, the fossil-fuel industry alone has spent $1.7 billion in the USA on lobbying and campaign contributions, which explains their entrenched political support. In Europe, the EU–US Transatlantic Trade and Investment Partnership (TTIP) – a proposed trade treaty promising private court hearings for American and European corporations wishing to sue each other's governments – was drawn up under the heavy influence of big business. In 2012–13, as treaty discussions got under way, over 90% of meetings held by the European Union – 520 out of 560 – were with corporate lobbyists.[50] Such examples simply add to the reasons why, in the twenty-first-century story, the economy must be designed to be far more distributive not just of income but also of wealth, as Chapter 5 explores, in order to counter elite power with citizens' empowerment.

Raising the curtain on a twenty-first-century story

Stand back, survey the whole stage and the new cast of characters that this chapter has introduced: what difference does it all make? Simply putting aside the Circular Flow diagram and drawing the Embedded Economy instead transforms the starting point of economic analysis. It ends the myth of the self-contained, self-sustaining market, replacing it with provisioning by the household, market, commons and state – all embedded within and dependent upon society, which in turn is embedded within the living world. It shifts our attention from merely tracking the flow of income to understanding the many distinct sources of wealth – natural, social, human, physical and financial – on which our well-being depends.

This new vision prompts new questions. Instead of immediately focusing on making markets work more efficiently, we can start by considering: when is each of the four realms of provisioning – household, commons, market and state – best suited to delivering humanity's diverse wants and needs? What changes in technology, culture and social norms might alter that? How can these four realms most effectively work together – such as the market with the commons, the commons with the state, or the state with the household? Likewise, rather than focusing by default on how to increase economic activity, ask how the content and structure of that activity might be shaping society, politics and power. And just how big can the economy become, given Earth's ecological capacity?

At the end of Shakespeare's *Tempest* – when all wrongs have been righted – Prospero's daughter Miranda, who has lived a cloistered life on the island with her father, sees for the first time the scheming noblemen of Milan who were shipwrecked by the storm. 'Oh, wonder!' she exclaims, 'How many goodly creatures are there here! How beauteous mankind is! O brave new world / That has such people in't!' Twenty-first-century economists might share her wonder, but without her political naivety. Having been cloistered for seventy years within the confines of Samuelson's insular Circular Flow diagram and the Mont Pelerin Society's narrow neoliberal script, we can now start writing a new story simply by picking up a pencil and first drawing the Embedded Economy. And since this big-picture perspective puts the economy in context, it is far easier to see some of the big questions that the twenty-first-century economist must tackle. There's just one thing still missing and that is the play's protagonist: humanity.

3

NURTURE HUMAN NATURE

from rational economic man
to social adaptable humans

Think of the most famous portrait ever painted. It has to be the *Mona Lisa*, the enigmatic painting by Leonardo da Vinci that is reproduced on postcards and fridge magnets the world over. Leonardo was a master in oils but he was a pioneer of pen-and-ink sketches too. While people-watching in the streets of Milan he invented the art of caricature, those 'loaded' portraits that intentionally exaggerate a person's most distinctive features – be it a bulbous nose or protruding chin – to produce an image that, comic or grotesque, bears an unmistakable likeness to its model.

The *Mona Lisa* may top the list of famous portraits but it is far from the most influential one. That accolade belongs to an equally enigmatic yet utterly different character who more closely resembles one of Leonardo's caricatures. He is, of course, rational economic man, the self-centred depiction of humanity at the heart of economic theory, who is also known as *Homo economicus* (note how the Latin touch lends him an air of scientific credibility). His image has been drawn and redrawn over two centuries by successive generations of economists, and over time has become so exaggerated and embellished that what had started out as a portrait turned into a caricature and ended up as a cartoon.[1] Despite his absurdities, however, rational economic man's influence goes far beyond fridge magnets. He is the protagonist in every main-stream economics textbook; he informs policy decision-making world-wide; he shapes the way we talk about ourselves; and he wordlessly tells us how to behave. Which is precisely why he matters so much.

Homo economicus may be the smallest unit of analysis in economic theory – equivalent to the atom in Newton's physics – but, just like an atom, his composition has profound consequences. There are, most likely, going to be more than ten billion of us by 2100. If we head towards that future continuing to imagine, conduct and justify our-selves as *Homo economicus* – solitary, calculating, competing and insatiable – then we stand little chance of meeting the human rights of all within the means of our living planet. And so it is time to meet ourselves all over again by taking his cartoon depiction out of the economic gallery and painting, in its place, a new portrait of human-ity. It will turn out to be the most important portrait commissioned in the twenty-first century, mattering not just to economists but to us all. Its preparatory sketches are under way and, just as in Leonardo's workshop, many artists are collaborating in piecing them together, from psychologists, behavioural scientists and neurologists to soci-ologists, political scientists and, yes, economists.

This chapter traces the evolving portrayal of rational economic man that has come to define our economic selves, and reveals the pro-found impact that it has had upon us. But it also looks ahead to our emerging new portrait, exploring five broad shifts in the depiction of who we are. Each one of those shifts illuminates a critical aspect of human nature which, once better understood, can be nurtured in ways that help us move into the safe and just space for humanity.

The story of our self-portrait

Rational economic man stands at the heart of mainstream economic theory but the history of where he came from has been airbrushed

Rational Economic Man: the human character at the heart of mainstream economic theory.

from the textbooks. His portrait is painted in words and equations, not in pictures. If it were to be drawn, however, he would have to look something like this: standing alone, money in hand, calculator in head, and ego in heart.

Where did this infamous character come from? His most intimate early portrait was created by Adam Smith in two major works, his 1759 *Theory of Moral Sentiments* and his 1776 book known as *The Wealth of Nations*. Today Smith is best remembered for having noted the human propensity to 'truck, barter and exchange' and the role of self-interest in making markets work.[2] But although he believed self-interest was, 'of all virtues that which is most helpful to the individual', Smith also believed it was far from the most admirable of our traits, knocked off that top spot by our 'humanity, justice, generosity and public spirit . . . the qualities most useful to others'. Did he consider humankind to be motivated by self-interest alone? Not at all. 'How selfish soever man may be supposed,' he wrote, 'there are evidently some principles in his nature, which interest him in the fortune of others, and render their happiness necessary to him, though he derives nothing from it except the pleasure of seeing it.'[3] Furthermore, Smith believed that an individual's self-interest and concern for others combined with their diverse talents, motivations and preferences to produce a complex moral character whose behaviour could not easily be predicted.

Lacking a simplified, predictable character at its heart, political economy looked destined to remain mere art, not science. That frustration prompted John Stuart Mill to pare down the description and become – in the footsteps of Leonardo – the first economic caricaturist. Political economy 'does not treat the whole of man's nature . . . nor the whole conduct of man in society', he argued in 1844. 'It is concerned with him solely as a being who desires to possess wealth.' To this desire for wealth, Mill added two other exaggerated features: a deep dislike of work and a love of luxuries. He admitted that the resulting depiction was 'an arbitrary definition of man', based on 'premises which might be totally without foundation', making the conclusions of political economy 'only true . . . *in the abstract*'. But he justified his caricature, confident that no 'political economist was ever so absurd as to suppose that mankind are really thus constituted', while adding that 'this is the mode in which science must necessarily proceed'.[4]

Not everyone agreed: in the 1880s the political economist Charles Stanton Devas coined a now infamous nickname when he derided Mill for 'dressing up a ridiculous *homo oeconomicus*' and examining only the 'dollar-hunting animal'.[5] But by presenting a simplified and predictable character, Mill's caricature opened up the scope for economic theory and apparent scientific method, and so it stuck.

The economist most eager to further Mill's efforts at caricature was William Stanley Jevons. He was inspired by Newton's success in reducing the physical world to atoms and then constructing its laws of motion from a single atom up. So he attempted to model a nation's economy along the same lines, reducing economic activity to what he called the 'single average individual, the unit of which population is made up'.[6] To achieve this, he had to make the caricature even more exaggerated so that human behaviour could be described mathematically, which for Jevons was the ultimate in scientific credibility. He noted that the philosopher Jeremy Bentham had been busy expounding the idea of utility – a 'felicific calculus' based on an ambitious classification of 14 kinds of human pleasure and 12 kinds of pain – in order to provide the quantifiable basis for creating a universal moral and legal code. Seizing upon the mathematical potential of this concept, Jevons drew up 'calculating man', whose fixation on maximising his utility had him constantly weighing up the consumption satisfaction that he might derive from every possible combination of his options.[7]

With this move, Jevons placed utility at the heart of economic theory – a spot it occupies to this day – and from it he derived the law of diminishing returns: the more of a thing that you consume (be it bananas or shampoo), the less you will desire still more of it. But, despite each one of his desires following such a law of satiation, this economic man knew of no satiation overall. Alfred Marshall put it most vividly in his influential 1890 text *Principles of Economics*. 'Human wants and desires are countless in number and very various in kind,' he wrote. 'The uncivilized man indeed has not many more than the brute animal; but every step in his progress upwards increases the variety of his needs . . . he desires a greater choice of things, and things that will satisfy new wants growing up in him.'[8] Thus, by the end of the nineteenth century, the caricature clearly depicted a solitary man, ever calculating his utility, and insatiable in his wants.

It was a powerfully simple depiction which opened the way to new kinds of economic reasoning. But still it was not enough: the nineteenth-century model of economic man may have been ever-calculating but he was not all-knowing, and his inherent uncertainty (which forced him to act upon opinion rather than knowledge) barred the way to complete mathematical modelling. Hence in the 1920s, Chicago-school economist Frank Knight decided to endow economic man with two godlike traits – perfect knowledge and perfect foresight – enabling him to compare all goods and prices across all time. This was a decisive break with the old portrait: no longer merely exaggerating recognisably human features, Knight embellished his *Homo economicus* with superhuman powers. And with that, he had turned the caricature into a cartoon. He knew it, too: he admitted that his depiction of humanity was loaded with 'a formidable array' of artificial abstractions, resulting in a creature who 'treats other human beings as if they were slot machines'.[9] But economic science needed just such an idealised man to inhabit its idealised economic world, he reasoned, in order to unleash the potential of mathematical modelling, and so he became the world's first economic cartoonist.

Milton Friedman reinforced Knight's justifications in the 1960s, when he defended the cartoon character. He argued that since in real life people behaved 'as if' they were making the self-interested, all-knowing calculations ascribed to rational economic man, then the simplified assumptions – and the cartoon character they depicted – were legitimate.[10] Crucially, around the same time, that cartoon began to be seen by many leading economists of the day as an exemplar, a model for how real man *should* behave. Rational economic man came to define rationality, recounts the economic historian Mary Morgan, and turned into 'a normative model of behaviour for real economic actors to follow'.[11]

Life imitates art

Over the course of two centuries – from the 1770s to the 1970s, as economic man's depiction morphed from a nuanced portrait to a crude cartoon – what had started as a model *of* man had turned into a model *for* man. This matters, argues economist Robert Frank, because 'our beliefs about human nature help shape human nature itself'. Research by Frank and others has revealed, first, that the discipline of economics tends to attract self-interested people. Experimental research in Germany, for example, found that economics students were more likely than other students to be corruptible – willing to give a biased answer – if it led to a personal payout.[12] Research in the US likewise found that economics majors were more approving of their own and others' self-serving behaviour, while economics professors gave significantly less money to charity than their worse-paid colleagues in many other disciplines.[13]

Beyond attracting self-interested people, however, studying *Homo economicus* can alter us too, reshaping who we think we are and how we should behave. In Israel, third-year economics majors rated altruistic values – such as helpfulness, honesty and loyalty – as far less important in life than did their freshman equivalents. After taking a course in economic game theory (a study of strategy which assumes individual self-interest in its models), US college students behaved more selfishly, and expected others to do so as well.[14] 'The pernicious effects of the self-interest theory have been most disturbing,' concludes Frank. 'By encouraging us to expect the worst in others, it brings out the worst in us: dreading the role of the chump, we are often loath to heed our nobler instincts.'[15]

That's a clear caution to all students of economics. But rational economic man's influence on our behaviour goes far beyond the classroom. A striking example was uncovered at the Chicago Board Options Exchange (CBOE) which opened in 1973 and became one of the most important financial derivatives exchanges in the world. In the same year that the Exchange opened for trading, two influential economists, Fischer Black and Myron Scholes, published what came to be known as the Black–Scholes model, which used publicly available market data to calculate the expected price of options traded in the market. At first the formula's predictions deviated widely – by 30% to 40% – from actual market prices at the CBOE. But within a few years – and with no alter-ations to the model – its predicted prices differed by a mere 2% on average from actual market prices. The Black–Scholes model was soon heralded as 'the most successful theory not only in finance, but in all of economics' and its creators were awarded Nobel-Memorial prizes.

Two economic sociologists, Donald MacKenzie and Yuval Millo, decided to delve deeper into the matter, however, by interviewing some of the derivatives traders themselves. What did they discover? That the theory's increasing accuracy over time was because the traders had started to behave *as if* the theory were true, and so were using the model's predicted prices as a benchmark for setting their own bids. 'Financial economics,' they concluded, 'helped create in reality the kind of markets it posited in theory.'[16] And as financial markets later learned, when those theories turn out to be flawed, the consequences can be dire.

If rational economic man can reshape our behaviour in financial markets, he is very likely to be reshaping our behaviour in other parts of life too, especially when his priorities permeate our language. One experiment in the US found that after corporate executives were asked

The Chicago Board Options Exchange, where markets came to mimic market theory.

to solve simple riddles involving words like 'profits', 'costs' and 'growth', they tended to respond to their colleagues' needs with less empathy, and even worried that expressing concern for others at work would not seem professional.[17] Another experimental survey found that university students who were invited to take part in a 'Consumer Reaction Study' identified more strongly with notions of wealth, status and success than did their fellow students who were merely told instead that they were participating in a 'Citizen Reaction Study'.[18] Change one word and you can subtly but deeply change attitudes and behaviour. Throughout the twentieth century, widespread use of the word 'consumer' grew steadily in public life, policymaking and the media until it far outstripped the word 'citizen': in English-language books and newspapers, that happened in the mid 1970s.[19] Why does it matter? Because, explains the media and cultural analyst Justin Lewis, 'Unlike the citizen, the consumer's means of expression is limited: while citizens can address every aspect of cultural, social and economic life . . . consumers find expression only in the market place.'[20]

The twenty-first-century portrait

The portrait we paint of ourselves clearly shapes who we become. That is why it is essential for economics to portray humankind anew. By better understanding our own complexity, we can nurture human nature and give ourselves a far greater chance of creating economies that enable us to thrive within the Doughnut's safe and just space. The preliminary sketches for this updated self-portrait are under way, revealing five broad shifts in how we can best depict our economic selves. First, rather than narrowly self-interested we are social and reciprocating. Second, in place of fixed preferences, we have fluid values. Third, instead of isolated we are interdependent. Fourth, rather than calculate, we usually approximate. And fifth, far from having dominion over nature, we are deeply embedded in the web of life.

These five shifts in the emerging portrait are fascinating, but there's just one catch: the choice of the artist's model. Over the past forty years, behavioural psychology experiments have revealed a great deal about how people actually behave – but which people? Out of sheer convenience, the vast majority of experimental studies, which have been conducted by academic researchers in North America, Europe, Israel and Australia, have used their own universities' undergraduate students as their subjects. As a result, between 2003 and 2007, 96% of people studied in such behavioural experiments came from countries that were home to only 12% of the world's population. That would be no concern if those subjects' behaviour was representative of people everywhere. But it turns out that it is not. The few cases of research carried out in other countries and cultures reveal that those convenient-to-study university undergraduates actually behave quite differently from most people. That may well be because – unlike the vast majority of humanity – they live in WEIRD societies: ones that are Western, educated, industrialised, rich and democratic.[21]

What does that sampling bias mean for making sense of the emerging portrait? Understanding the range of behavioural differences between cultures and societies – and the reasons behind them – is clearly a subject for much-needed research, but for now we can count on two givens. First, although human behaviour may vary between societies, one important thing unites humanity: none of us resemble that narrow old model of rational economic man. Second, until a more nuanced and diverse image of humanity has been sketched out, the emerging portrait described in the five shifts below most closely resembles people in WEIRD societies.

From self-interested to socially reciprocating

Adam Smith spotted that self-interest is an effective human trait for making markets work, but he knew it was far from the only one required to make society and the wider economy work well too. Yet in *The Wealth of Nations* his sharp focus on the role of self-interest in markets overshadowed the rest of his rich observations about morals and motivation, and that trait alone was plucked out by his successors to provide the DNA for economic man. Over the following two centuries, economic theory came to be founded upon the fundamental assumption that competitive self-interest is not only man's natural state but also his optimal strategy for economic success.

Stand back and take a look at how people actually behave, however, and that assumption starts to look flimsy. Along with being self-regarding we are also other-regarding. We help strangers with heavy luggage, hold doors open for each other, share food and drink, give money to charity and donate blood – even body parts – to people we will never meet. Toddlers just 14 months old will help others by handing them out-of-reach objects, and children as young as three will share their treats with others. Of course children and adults alike often struggle to share – we certainly have the capacity to snatch and hoard too – but the striking fact is that we share at all.[22] *Homo sapiens*, it turns out, is the most cooperative species on the planet, outperforming ants, hyenas, and even the naked mole-rat when it comes to living alongside those who are beyond our next of kin.

In short, along with our propensity to trade, we are also drawn to give, share, and reciprocate. That may be because cooperation enhances our own group's chances of survival. In the simplest of terms, we send a clear message to each other: if you want to get by then learn to get along. And we have learned to get along in very particular ways. According to economists Sam Bowles and Herb Gintis, we WEIRD ones typically practise what is known as 'strong reciprocity': we are conditional cooperators (tending to cooperate so long as others do too) but also altruistic punishers (ready to punish defectors and free riders even if it costs us personally). And it is the combination of these two traits that leads to the success of large-scale cooperation in society.[23] No wonder rating and review systems are so popular in the otherwise anonymous online marketplace. From eBay to Etsy, they turn each participant's track record into their trading reputation, revealing who can be trusted, so allowing conditional cooperators to find each other and thrive even in the presence of free riders.[24]

Our readiness to cooperate and to punish defectors has been most famously demonstrated in the Ultimatum Game, which has been played in many societies beyond Western, educated, industrial, rich and democratic ones. Two players – a proposer and responder who are anonymous to each other – are offered a sum of money to share, typically equivalent to two days' earnings. The proposer suggests how to divide it and, if the responder accepts that division, they each receive their respective shares; if the responder rejects the proposal, however, they both go empty-handed. And they only get to play the game once. If, as mainstream theory assumes, people were purely self-interested then responders would accept any amount offered: to turn it down would be to reject free money. But what happens in practice? Responders typically reject proposals that they think are unfair, even if it means they walk away with no money at all.[25] We humans are ready to punish others for their selfishness, even if it costs us.

The most interesting results, however, emerge from the contrasting ways that different societies play the game. Among North American university students – the archetypal WEIRD community – proposers tend to offer the other player a 45% share, and offers below 20% tend to be rejected. Meanwhile, among the Machiguenga living in the Peruvian Amazon, proposers tend to offer far less – around just 25% – and responders almost always accept their share, no matter how small it is. By contrast, among the villagers of Lamelara, Indonesia, proposers offer to give away almost 60% of the money, and rejections are rare.

What explains these wide variations in cultural norms of

reciprocity? In large part, the diverse societies and economies in which we live. North Americans live in a highly interdependent market-based economy that relies upon a culture of reciprocity to make it work. In contrast the hunter-gatherer Machiguenga live in small family groups and meet most of their needs within their own households, with little trade between: as a result their dependence on community reciprocity is relatively low. The Lamelara, in turn, depend upon communal whale hunting for their livelihoods, heading out to sea in large canoes carrying a dozen or more men who must then share each day's catch: strong norms of sharing are essential to their collective success, and are reflected in their high offers in the game.

Across diverse cultures, social norms of reciprocity clearly vary according to the structure of the economy, particularly the relative importance of the household, market, commons or state in provisioning for society's needs.[26] People's sense of reciprocity appears to co-evolve with their economy's structure: a fascinating finding with important implications for those aiming to rebalance the roles of the household, market, commons and state in any society.

From fixed preferences to fluid values

Economic theory curiously begins with the over-18s: it is rational economic man, not rational economic boy, that we first meet – but why? Because the theory hinges on being able to assume that people have pre-set tastes, formed independently of the economy. Few would attempt to deny that corporate advertising grooms children, making the most of their pester power today while seeding the tastes and desires that will draw their purchasing power tomorrow. But adults can perhaps be portrayed as sovereign consumers, with firms merely aiming to deliver the products and services that match their existing preferences. Under this set-up, any changes in people's shopping habits must largely be due to new product information, a shift in relative prices, or a change in their incomes.

This story is, of course, far from credible. Adults, like children, are by no means immune to the marketeer's message, as Sigmund Freud's nephew, Edward Bernays, realised in the 1920s. 'We are governed, our minds are molded, our tastes formed, our ideas suggested, largely by men we have never heard of,' he wrote in his book *Propaganda*, '. . . It is they who pull the wires which control the public mind.'[27] Bernays invented the 'public relations' industry and rapidly became America's master wire-puller, convincing women (on behalf of the American Tobacco Corporation) that cigarettes were their 'torches of freedom', while persuading the nation (on behalf of the Beech-Nut Packing Company's pork department) that bacon and eggs were the 'hearty' all-American breakfast.[28] Drawing on his uncle's insights into the workings of the human mind, Bernays knew that the secret to influencing preferences lay not in advertising a product's attributes (it's bigger, faster, shinier!) but in associating that product with deeply held values, such as freedom and power.

Those deep values that Bernays masterfully tapped into have since been systematically researched, with profound results. Since the 1980s the social psychologist Shalom Schwartz and colleagues have surveyed people of all ages and backgrounds in over 80 countries, identifying ten clusters of basic personal values that are recognised across cultures: self-direction, stimulation, hedonism, achievement, power, security, conformity, tradition, benevolence and universalism. When it comes to nurturing human nature, three things stand out in their findings.

First, all ten basic values are present in us all, and each one of us is motivated by their full array, but to widely differing degrees that vary between cultures and individuals. Power and hedonism, for example, may predominate for some people, while in others benevolence and tradition prevail. Second, each of the values can be 'engaged' in us if it is triggered: when reminded of security, for example, we are likely to take fewer risks; when power and achievement are brought to mind, we are less likely to take care of others' needs. Third, and most interestingly, the relative strength of these different values changes in us not just over the course of a lifetime, but in fact many times in a day, as we switch between social roles and contexts, whether moving from the workplace to the social space, the kitchen table to the conference table, from the commons to the market to the home. And – just like muscles – the more often any one value is engaged, the stronger it becomes.

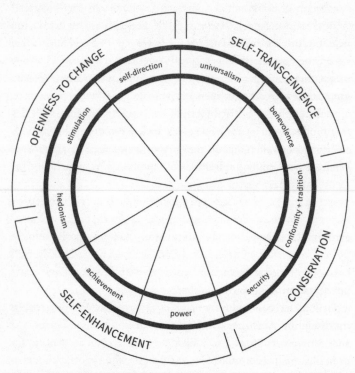

Schwartz's value circumplex, which shows the ten basic personal values that are common across cultures.

Schwartz further found that the ten basic values can be grouped around two key axes, as illustrated in his circumplex. The first axis juxtaposes *openness to change* (which concerns independence and novelty) with *conservation* (concerning self-restriction and resistance to change). The second axis juxtaposes *self-enhancement* (focused on status and personal success) with *self-transcendence* (having concern for the wellness of all). That divide between self-enhancement and self-transcendence is echoed in the contrast between *extrinsic* motivation – which moves us to act in order to achieve a further outcome, such as gaining status, money, or some other benefit – and *intrinsic* motivation, which moves us to do something because it is inherently engaging or satisfying.[29] What's more, the ten values tend to influence one another in push–pull ways across these axes. Engaging one value, such as stimulation, tends to activate its neighbours, hedonism and self-direction, while simultaneously suppressing its opposites, security, conformity and tradition.[30]

Such insights into the responsiveness and fluidity of the values that motivate our actions bring far greater nuance to humanity's emerging portrait than did the pre-set preferences of *Homo economicus*, with many implications for how we can nurture human nature, as will emerge below.

From isolated to interdependent

Depicting rational economic man as an isolated individual – unaffected by the choices of others – proved highly convenient for modelling the economy, but it was long questioned even from within the discipline. At the end of the nineteenth century, the sociologist and economist Thorstein Veblen berated economic theory for depicting man as a 'self-contained globule of desire', while the French polymath Henri Poincaré pointed out that it overlooked 'people's tendency to act like sheep'.[31] He was right: we are not so different from herds as we might like to imagine. We follow social norms, typically preferring to do what we expect others will do and, especially if filled with fear or doubt, we tend to go with the crowd.

One telling experiment with the musical tastes of WEIRD teenagers demonstrated just how influential social norms can be. Participants were recruited – 14,000 of them – through a teen website and were invited to listen to a set of 48 songs (all unknown tunes by unknown bands) to give them a rating and then, if they wished, to download their favourites. In a control group, participants were given only the name of each band, the title of the song, and a recording of the music before they gave their ratings. In eight other separate groups, however, participants could also see how many times each tune had already been downloaded by others within their group.

The outcome? Across all eight experimental groups, each song's popularity was partly determined by its quality (as rated independently by those in the control group): the 'best' songs rarely did poorly and the 'worst' rarely did well. But a good deal of each song's popularity was also due to social influence: the participants preferred songs that they knew others liked. And the more prominently that other participants' ratings were displayed on the website, the more likely it was for a 'smash hit' to emerge within each group – but, fascinatingly, the harder it became to predict which song the hit would turn out to be.[32] This kind of herd behaviour can be highly contagious and highly uncertain. And it explains the unpredictability not only of the next chart-topping song, but also of next summer's fashion craze – not to mention the 'animal spirits' driving boom and bust in stock markets – revealing the strength of social networks in shaping our preferences, purchases and actions.

Social influence of this kind is set to grow as people's lives come to be more tightly networked than ever before, albeit in new ways. As network theorist Paul Ormerod points out, we are more aware than ever before of the opinions, decisions, choices and behaviours of other people. In 1900, around 10% of people worldwide lived in cities; by 2050 around 70% of us will. Couple this proximity of city dwellers with worldwide communications transmitting news and views, data and ads, and what emerges is a dynamic global network-of-networks of human beings.[33]

For Veblen, one of the most pernicious effects of such social influence was the rise of what he called 'conspicuous consumption': the appeal of buying luxury products and services to signal our status to others in the hope of 'keeping up with the Joneses'. Joseph Stiglitz points out that this effect is particularly concerning today in the context of high inequality, both within and between countries. There is a 'well-documented lifestyle effect', he notes, in which 'people outside the top 1 percent increasingly live beyond their means. Trickle-down economics may be a chimera, but trickle-down behaviourism is very real.'[34]

What is the implication for economic policy aiming to influence how we behave? Economists have traditionally sought to change people's behaviour by changing the relative price of things, be it through a tax on sugar or a discount on solar panels. But such price signals often fail to achieve their expected results, Ormerod points out, because they can be drowned out by far stronger network effects, thanks to social norms and expectations of what others in the network are doing.[35] At the same time, it may be possible to harness such interdependence for behavioural change, as we will see.

From calculating to approximating

Homo sapiens clearly can't match the infallibility of rational economic man. That much has been agreed upon since the 1950s when Herbert Simon broke rank with his fellow economists and started to study how people actually behaved, finding their rationality to be severely 'bounded'. His findings, augmented by those of psychologists Daniel Kahneman and Amos Tversky in the 1970s, gave birth to the field now known as behavioural economics, which studies the many kinds of 'cognitive bias' that systematically cause humans to deviate from the ideal model of rationality.

Examples abound. We (the WEIRD ones, at least) typically exhibit: availability bias – making decisions on the basis of more recent and more accessible information; loss aversion – the strong preference to avoid a loss rather than to make an equivalent gain; selective cognition – taking on board facts and arguments that fit with our existing frames; and risk bias – underestimating the likelihood of extreme events, while overestimating our ability to cope with them. There are many more. Indeed one Wikipedia page lists over 160 cognitive biases, like a jumbo-size game of spot-the-difference between rational economic man and his fallible human equivalent.[36]

What to do in the face of such irrational shortcomings? Introduce nudge policies, say Richard Thaler and Cass Sunstein, which they define as 'any aspect of the choice architecture that alters people's behaviour in a predictable way without forbidding any options or significantly changing their economic incentives'.[37] Thanks to Edward Bernays, brands and retailers have been nudging us for almost a century in the implicit messaging of advertisements, in the placements of products in shops and TV shows, and in the psychology of sales. But public policy can be designed to nudge us too. Displaying fruit at eye level in a school canteen is a healthy eating nudge. Structuring company pension schemes to be opt-out rather than opt-in is a nudge towards long-term income security. Nudge policies, in essence, can be used to encourage us to mimic the way that we would behave if we were as rational as economic man.

Policy nudges can clearly work but the ever-growing catalogue of cognitive biases makes humans start to look rather incompetent: indeed it starts to seem a miracle that we have survived at all. Just the opposite is the case, argues the evolutionary psychologist Gerd Gigerenzer: we have survived and thrived not despite our cognitive biases but because of them. These so-called biases are the underpinnings of our heuristics, the unconscious mental short cuts we take every time we use a 'rule of thumb' to make decisions. Over millennia, the human brain has evolved to rely on quick decision-making tools in a fast-moving and uncertain world and in many contexts those heuristics lead us to make better decisions than exact calculations would do.

The take-the-best heuristic, for example, provides a 'fast and frugal' way of making decisions under uncertainty. Working with hospital medics, Gigerenzer helped to create a simple three-question decision tree allowing doctors to use the best, or most pertinent, information in rapidly assessing whether patients are at risk of a heart attack and should be admitted for coronary care. First ask Question 1: are there irregularities in the electrocardiogram? If yes, admit for coronary care. If no, ask Question 2: are chest pains the primary symptom? If yes, admit for coronary care. If no: ask Question 3: is any one of five other specific symptoms present? If yes, admit for coronary care; if no, provide a bed in the general ward. Fascinatingly, this method has been found to make more accurate predictions than a medical computer program that gathers and weighs up around 50 pieces of information about each patient.[38] Given the value of fast and frugal heuristics like this one, perhaps we should think of ourselves not as rational man but as heuristic man and be proud of it too: what first appears to be a failure of rationality might be better thought of as a triumph of evolution.

The power of such heuristics led Gigerenzer to disagree with the prescriptions of behavioural economists who, he says, 'think that people are basically hopeless when it comes to understanding risk, and we need to nudge them into behaviour from birth to death'. Rather than overriding our rules of thumb with a nudge, he argues, we should nurture those heuristic abilities while bolstering them with basic skills in assessing risk. 'We live in the 21st century, surrounded by complex technology, and there are things that we will not be able to anticipate,' argues Gigerenzer. 'What we need is not just better technology, bigger bureaucracy and stricter laws . . . but risk-savvy citizens.' And he has demonstrated that we can indeed learn to become more risk-savvy, by successfully teaching everyday statistical-reasoning skills to German doctors, American judges and Chinese schoolchildren alike. Rather than be passively nudged into acting wisely, he believes, we can be learn to be risk-savvy with the rule of thumb and so choose to act wisely ourselves.[39]

It's an appealing and empowering approach, but one problem with relying upon heuristics won't go away: they work best in the context for which they evolved. Humanity's context, however, has changed over the past 10,000 years and particularly dramatically in the last 200 years. Take the devastating effects of climate change, for example: at first they tend to be invisible, delayed, gradual and distant: four characteristics that our heuristic decision tools are infamously bad at handling well. The smart way forward, then, for policymakers seeking to promote behaviour change may lie in encouraging a judicious mix of risk-savvy heuristics and behavioural nudges, based on a much-needed understanding of when each approach might work best.

From dominant to dependent

A new economic self-portrait must reflect the way that we see humanity's place in the world. The traditional Western depiction of man has nature lying at his feet and at his disposal. 'Let the human race recover that right over nature which belongs to it by divine bequest,' wrote the seventeenth-century philosopher Francis Bacon.[40] That perspective was echoed by W. Arthur Lewis, founder of development economics, in his 1949 book *Economics: Man and His Material Means*, which set out to study 'the ways in which mankind tries to wrest a living from the Earth' by making 'the most efficient use of scarce resources'. This presumption of man's dominion over nature runs far back in Western culture, at least to the Bible's opening verses. It also underpins the language of environmental economics, which frames the living world as a storehouse of 'natural resources', as if it were waiting – like a pile of Lego blocks – to be transformed by man into something useful to man.

Rather than presiding at the pinnacle of nature's pyramid, however, humanity is woven deep into nature's web. We are embedded in the living world, not separate from or above it: we live within the biosphere, not on the planet. As the American ecologist Aldo Leopold deftly put it, we need to transform the way we see ourselves, 'from conqueror of the land-community to plain member and citizen of it'.[41] Thanks to forty years of Earth-system research, we have a rapidly improving scientific understanding of how the Holocene epoch – with its stable climate, ample fresh water, protective ozone layer, and abundant biodiversity – has enabled humanity to thrive, and hence how we depend upon Earth's continual flourishing in turn.

This shift in perspective – from pyramid to web, from pinnacle to participant – also invites us to move beyond anthropocentric values and to recognise and respect the intrinsic value of the living world. 'What's really needed,' suggests the thinker Otto Scharmer, 'is a deeper shift in consciousness so that we begin to care and act, not just for ourselves and other stakeholders but in the interests of the entire ecosystem in which economic activities take place.'[42] The need for such a shift in consciousness is particularly strong in WEIRD societies: in the US, for example, children growing up in urban centres today have a far more simplistic and anthropomorphic understanding of the living world than do children raised in rural Native American communities.[43] One practical way to address this would be to teach and embody eco-literacy in every school so that coming generations develop a worldview based upon understanding the living world's interdependent systems that make life on Earth possible.

Changing our sense of how we belong in the world also depends upon finding better words to describe it. The political theorist Hannah Arendt once noted that a stray dog has a greater chance of surviving if it is given a name.[44] Perhaps in that spirit, mainstream environmental economists now describe the living world in terms of the 'ecosystem services' that it provides and the wealth of 'natural capital' it contains. But the names we choose matter: calling a stray dog Champ rather than Scamp switches just a couple of letters but utterly transforms how he is seen in the world. And that is precisely why talking of 'natural capital' and 'ecosystem services' is so double-edged: it may give the stray dog a name but the chosen name simply shifts the living world from being man's material means to being an asset on his balance sheet. When Chief Oren Lyons of the Iroquois Onondaga Nation was invited to address students at the University of Berkeley's College of Natural Resources, he highlighted this risk. 'What you call resources we call our relatives,' he explained. 'If you can think in terms of relationships, you are going to treat them better, aren't you? ... Get back to the relationship because that is your foundation for survival.'[45]

No wonder new economic thinkers are searching for words that better describe how we belong in the world. The biomimicry expert Janine Benyus – whose ideas we will explore in Chapter 6 – eloquently speaks of Earth as 'this home that is ours but not ours alone'. For the ecological writer Charles Eisenstein, it is time to recognise ourselves as 'the connected living self in co-creative partnership with the Earth'.[46] This kind of language makes some people squirm, but perhaps that is because it confronts us with the awkwardness of acknowledging our most profound yet most neglected relationships. It also indicates just how unused we are to talking about ourselves this way, a little like fish searching for a word for water. How do we belong in this world, and what is our role? Finding the words to say it may turn out to be more important than we can imagine in determining whether or not we as a species can learn to thrive with others.

These five shifts provide preparatory sketches for humanity's twenty-first-century portrait, but the work is still far from finished.

First, we need to understand more about our economic selves beyond how we behave around money. Just as WEIRD students turn out to behave unlike most other people, so too money may turn out to affect our behaviour quite differently to the way that most other things that matter to us do. How might the Ultimatum Game be played if those involved were asked to share not money but food, water, healthcare, time or political voice? It is deeply unlikely that money invokes the very same sense of fairness as do these other things that we value deeply. In addition, we need to understand a good deal more about who all of us are, not just the WEIRD ones. A greater diversity in experimental research will no doubt reveal some more fascinating differences between peoples and cultures, but we may ultimately discover that – in the words of the late British MP Jo Cox – we have 'far more in common with each other than things that divide us'.[47]

How, then, can the insights from these five shifts in our self-portrait be harnessed in ways that can help to bring all of humanity into the Doughnut? This question will keep returning throughout the following chapters but one issue deserves particular attention here: the growing use of monetary incentives in policies aimed at ending human deprivation and ecological degradation. Initial evidence suggests that monetary payments often crowd out existing motivations by activating extrinsic rather than intrinsic values. As the case studies described below reveal, there may be far wiser ways – drawing on what we now know about values, nudges, networks and reciprocity – to nurture human nature towards the Doughnut's safe and just space.

Markets and matches: handle with care

Traditional economic policy presumes that a reliable way to change people's behaviour is to change relative prices, whether through creating markets, assigning property rights or enforcing regulations. 'Just get the prices right,' a typical economist will tell you: sort that and the rest will follow.

Prices certainly do matter. When Malawi, Uganda, Lesotho and Kenya stopped charging fees for children to attend state primary schools from the late 1990s, school enrolments – especially for girls and for children from the poorest families – increased dramatically, taking those countries far closer to the goal of providing education for all. In 2004 the German government introduced a feed-in tariff for households and institutions generating renewable energy, offering to pay above the retail price of electricity. It helped to trigger transformative national investments in wind, solar, hydro and biomass energy technologies, which were powering the country with 30% renewable energy just ten years later.[48]

But while prices matter, getting them 'right' is not such a simple solution as it first promises to be: twentieth-century theory has led economists to overestimate the effectiveness of price as a lever, and to underestimate the role of values, sense of reciprocity, networks, and heuristics. Crucially, the theory overlooks the fact that some things may be put in jeopardy when they are given a price. That is especially true when it comes to relationships that we have traditionally managed with our morals. Here's why. Setting a price is like striking a match: it sparks intense interest but that spark ignites both power and danger. As Chapter 2 suggested, the market – like fire – can be extremely efficient at doing what it does, but it can also be a challenge to contain. And if it becomes all-consuming, it may transform the very ground across which it burns.

Richard Titmuss first raised this concern in his 1970 book, *The Gift Relationship*, which contrasted the blood donor service in the US, where people were paid for their contributions, with the far more successful service in the UK, where volunteers gave more and healthier blood for free.[49] That contrast prompted a fascinating question: do monetary incentives serve to reinforce and 'crowd in'

118

people's intrinsic motivation to act, or instead crowd it out by replacing it with the extrinsic motivation of money? This question has only become more pertinent since Titmuss's study, given the growing international use of cash incentives and payment schemes for addressing both social and ecological challenges.

Take, for example, Colombia's experiments with educational schemes that offer conditional cash transfers to families of secondary school students. In 2005 teenage children from low-income families in Bogotá were randomly chosen to take part in a pilot scheme, which transferred 30,000 pesos (around $15) per month to their parents if they attended school at least 80% of the time and passed their end-of-year exams. The World Bank economists who designed and monitored the scheme found that students selected for the scheme were 3% more likely to attend school regularly than students who were not, and 1% more likely to re-enrol the following year. It was the positive response they had expected, albeit a small one.

But the economists also uncovered a troubling flip side to the experiment that they had not been expecting. Students who were not selected by the scheme, but had siblings who were, became less likely to attend school regularly – and more likely to drop out – than students from similar families in which no one took part in the scheme. Most strikingly, this was particularly true amongst girls: those with siblings in the scheme were 10% more likely to drop out of school than girls from similar families in which no one was participating.[50] What's more, this unintended negative drop-out effect turned out to be far stronger than the positive effect on attendance and re-enrolment that the scheme was set up to achieve in the first place. The World Bank economists conducting the study described these findings – which were incidental to their research – as 'worrisome' and 'intriguing' because they inexplicably defied their theory and expectations.

Perhaps what they had accidentally uncovered was the role that money can play in eroding social norms, such as student pride and parental responsibility, by replacing them with market norms, such as payment for effort and reward for compliance. The philosopher Michael Sandel has raised concerns about these very effects, arguing that cash payments can crowd out intrinsic motivations and the values that underpin them. He points, as an example, to the *Earning by Learning* programme, set up in low-achieving primary schools in Dallas, Texas, which paid six-year-old children $2 for every book that they read. Researchers found that the children's literacy skills improved over the year, but what effect might such payments have on their longer-term motivation to learn? 'The market is an instrument, but not an innocent one,' Sandel remarks. 'The obvious worry is that the payment may habituate children to think of reading books as a way of making money, and so erode, or crowd out, or corrupt the love of reading for its own sake.'[51]

Despite such concerns, financial incentives are increasingly being introduced in social realms, bringing our market identities – as consumers, customers, service providers and workers – to the forefront of our attention. And when market norms displace social norms, the effects can be hard to reverse, as demonstrated in an experimental study in Haifa, Israel in the 1990s. Ten children's day-nurseries all introduced a small fine for parents who were more than 10 minutes late collecting their children at the end of the day. The parental response? Rather than arriving more promptly, twice as many parents started arriving late. Introducing a monetary fine effectively wiped out any feelings of guilt, and was interpreted as a market price for overtime care. Three months later when the experiment ended and the fine was removed, the number of late pick-ups rose higher still: the price had gone, but the guilt hadn't come back. The temporary marketplace had, in essence, erased the social contract.[52] 'As markets reach into spheres of life traditionally governed by nonmarket norms, the notion that markets don't touch or taint the goods they exchange becomes increasingly implausible,' warns Sandel. 'Markets are not mere mechanisms; they embody certain values. And sometimes, market values crowd out nonmarket norms worth caring about.'[53]

Merely mentioning market roles can crowd out our intrinsic motivation. One online survey asked participants to imagine themselves as one among four households facing a water shortage due to a drought affecting their shared well. Crucially, the survey described the whole scenario in terms of 'consumers' to one half of the participants, and in terms of 'individuals' to the other half. What difference did that single word change make? Those labelled 'consumers' reported feeling less personal responsibility to take action and less trust in others to do the same than did those referred to as 'individuals'.[54] Simply thinking like a consumer, it seems, triggers self-regarding behaviour, and divides rather than unites groups who are facing a common scarcity. In the context of twenty-first-century pressures on Earth's sources and sinks – from fresh water and fish to the oceans and atmosphere – that insight could turn out to have pivotally important implications for how we describe ourselves in the challenges that we collectively face. Suddenly the words 'neighbours', 'community members', 'community of nations' and 'global citizens' seem incredibly precious for securing a safe and just economic future.

Research into the use of valuations, prices, payments and markets to shape people's ecological behaviour has turned up similar findings. In villages around Morogoro, Tanzania, community members were asked to spend half a day cutting grass and planting trees together in their local schoolyard. In villages where they were offered a small payment to take part, 20% fewer people were willing to participate than in villages where no mention was made of money at all. Furthermore, among those who were paid for the work – with a typical day's wage – most said on completion that they were dissatisfied with the task and its pay, while those with whom money was not discussed at all overwhelmingly expressed satisfaction at having done something useful for their village.[55]

Likewise, as part of a forest conservation scheme in Chiapas, Mexico, many farmers are compensated in cash for refraining from cutting trees, hunting, poaching, or expanding their herd of cattle. The more years that they participate in the scheme, however, the more their stated motivation to conserve the forest becomes financial rather than intrinsic, and their readiness for future conservation efforts depends increasingly upon the promise of future payments. In other parts of Chiapas, however, where the forest is managed through community planning and projects, it initially takes longer to generate the farmers' engagement but the social capital that they build is far greater and their motivation remains centred on the inherent benefits of long-term forest conservation.[56] Bringing money into the mix, it seems, can significantly alter our regard for the living world.

These examples are not mere exceptions to the rule. The most comprehensive survey yet of research into the impacts of payments to promote ecological conservation – whether to collect more litter and plant more trees or harvest less timber and catch fewer fish – finds that most of the schemes studied were unintentionally crowding out, rather than crowding in, people's intrinsic motivation to act.[57] Instead of engaging existing intrinsic commitments, such as pride in cultural heritage, respect for the living world, and trust in the community, some schemes inadvertently serve to erode those very values and replace them with financial motivation. 'Using money to motivate people can throw up surprising results,' says Erik Gómez-Baggethun, one of the study's authors, 'we often don't understand the complex interplay of human values and motivations well enough to anticipate what will happen, and so that calls for caution.' Given that markets do indeed seem to be like fire, here's one way to sum up the moral of the story:

> Beware before you strike a match or start a market:
> you never know what riches it may reduce to ashes.

Evidence from a wide range of policy initiatives – from school enrolments to forest conservation – raises a warning signal around introducing cash incentives in social spaces: their deeper effects are still so little understood and the evidence to date shows that they can so often go wrong. Furthermore, there are other means of motivating behaviour change – drawing on reciprocity, values, nudging and networks – that may cost far less, in both cash and consequences.

Tapping into nudge, networks and norms

As our emerging self-portrait makes clear, we are motivated by far more than cost and price. So instead of turning first to markets to mediate our social and ecological relationships, the twenty-first-century economist would be wise to start by asking what social dynamics are already in play. What are the values, heuristics, norms and networks that currently shape human behaviour – and how could they be nurtured or nudged, rather than ignored and eroded? With this question as a starting point, economists will become far savvier in blending the blunt power of markets with the subtle force of morals. And empirical evidence hints at the possibility that this strategy could help to bring us into the Doughnut.

Nudges can have a big effect for a small cost, and digital technology makes smart nudging easier and cheaper than ever before. Take prescription medicines, for example: people often forget to take them regularly, undermining both their own health and possibly the drug's long-term efficacy too. In the UK, where an estimated £300 million is spent annually on unused prescription medicines, researchers found that a simple text message reminder significantly increased the proportion of patients who were taking their medicines on time.[58] A similar experiment among people living with HIV/AIDS in Kenya found that a weekly text message likewise led to 25% more of them strongly adhering to their course of antiretrovirals.[59] No money sent, just a simple text.

Environmental nudges can be effective too. 'We have long

showers, leave appliances turned on and throw away rubbish as part of daily routines that involve little thought,' says Pelle Hansen, chair of the Danish Nudging Network. Basic nudges can easily be designed into buildings to offset these habits – using automated taps, shower timers, and motion-activated lighting – delivering substantial cuts in water and energy use. They work in public spaces too. In the streets of Copenhagen, Hansen and his students handed out sweets to passers-by and documented how many of the wrappers ended up on the pavement, in bins, or in other people's bike baskets. They then painted green footprints leading up to the rubbish bins and found that littering fell by 46%. No need for fines or rewards to encourage compliance: the little green footprints artfully amplified an existing social norm.[60]

Network effects also influence social behaviour, as illustrated by the power of a prominent example. In October 2011, Brazil's former president Lula da Silva went public with news of his throat cancer, saying he believed it was due to smoking cigarettes. Over the following four weeks, there was a national surge in Google searches for information about quitting smoking – far greater than similar searches made on World No Tobacco Day or even on New Year's Day, when resolutions to quit are common. Likewise, when the UK reality TV star Jade Goody went public with her diagnosis of cervical cancer in 2009, there was a 43% increase in women making appointments to be tested.[61] Those cases acted as warnings, but network effects can inspire too. Thanks to the courageous stance of the Pakistani educational activist Malala Yousafzai, millions of girls worldwide have been inspired by 'the Malala effect' to demand and cherish their right to an education. Such effects work on a local scale too. Researchers in West Bengal, India found that when women started being appointed to lead village councils for the first time, local teenage girls began to have higher aspirations for their education and themselves, as did their parents. No prices, no payments, just pride.[62]

Nudges and network effects often work because they tap into underlying norms and values – such as duty, respect and care – and those values can be activated directly. That's what researchers in the US discovered when they set out to explore how to prompt pro-environmental behaviour. They set up signs at a petrol station inviting passing motorists to have a free tyre check, offering either financial, safety or environmental reasons for doing so. The forecourt sign saying 'Care about your finances? Get a free tire check!' triggered no interest at all from passing motorists, whereas the sign saying 'Care about the environment? Check your car's tire pressure!' prompted the most. Activating the right values clearly makes quite a difference to action.[63]

In communities that are low on income but high on social capital, activating social norms can have far-reaching effects, as researchers in Uganda discovered when they set out to improve rural healthcare simply by creating a renewed sense of social contract. In 50 districts with poorly performing clinics, they brought local community members together with health centre staff to assess current practices and to draw up their own agreement setting out the standards that the community expected. Each community established a system for monitoring its own local clinic, such as staff duty rosters, suggestion boxes, and numbered waiting room tickets, then posted the monthly results on a public notice board. One year on, the quality and quantity of primary healthcare provided had dramatically improved: 20% more patients were being seen and with shorter waiting times; absenteeism among doctors and nurses had plummeted; and – most strikingly – 33% fewer children under the age of five were dying in those communities. All of this was achieved without fees, fines or a bigger budget, but thanks to the expectations of a social contract backed up with public accountability.[64]

These small-scale examples of tapping into people's values are compelling, but some might dismiss their successes as inherently incremental, merely tweaking at the margins of humanity's grand challenges. Tom Crompton and Tim Kasser, experts in environmental values, attitudes and behaviour, would disagree. They argue that when it comes to creating deep and lasting social and ecological behaviour change, the most effective approach is precisely to connect with people's values and identity, not with their pocket and budget. Their research finds that people in whom self-enhancing values and extrinsic motivations have come to predominate tend to seek wealth, possessions and status. They are also less likely to care about the living world, to make an effort to cut their ecological footprint, to use public transport, or to recycle household waste. Moreover, when faced with environmental threats – such as the prospects of climate change – they are more likely to seek diverting distractions which might further raise the pressure on the planet. In contrast, people in whom self-transcending values and intrinsic motivations have come to dominate express greater concern about ecological issues and are more motivated to get involved in local action or global movements that proactively engage with the issues at hand.[65] The challenge now is to discover how lessons from street-level success with sweet wrappers and text messages could be scaled up to nudge and network whole cities, nations, and international negotiations, into the Doughnut.

Meeting ourselves all over again

If a picture speaks a thousand words, how then should we literally draw our new self-portrait? I have playfully but seriously posed this question in Doughnut discussions in many countries, to students, corporate executives, policymakers and activists – each time inviting the group to visualise and literally sketch out figures that would best replace the cartoon of rational economic man. Three images keep cropping up time and again: humanity as a community, as sowers and reapers, and as acrobats.

The image of community reminds us that we are the most social of species, dependent upon each other throughout the cycles of our

A new portrait of humanity: preparatory sketches.

lives. The sower-reaper embeds us within the web of life, making clear that our societies co-evolve with the living world on which we depend. And the acrobats exemplify our skill of trusting, reciprocating and cooperating with each other to achieve things that none of us could alone. There are, no doubt, many other ways we can sketch ourselves: this portrait is far from complete. But it already takes us far. We wasted two hundred years staring at the wrong portrait of ourselves: *Homo economicus*, that solitary figure poised with money in his hand, calculator in his head, nature at his feet, and an insatiable appetite in his heart. It is time to redraw ourselves as people who thrive by connecting with each other and with this living home of ours that is not ours alone.

It was Henri Poincaré who first remarked that we were more like sheep than we care to imagine. If today we could bring him up to speed on the insights of behavioural psychology and hand him a snorkel and flippers, I think he would beg to expand on his animal analogies. Thanks to our multiple values and motivations we also bear an uncanny resemblance to the octopus. Like its many tentacles – each of which has something akin to its own personality – we have many different roles in relation to the economy, as employees, citizens, entrepreneurs, neighbours, consumers, voters, parents, collaborators, competitors and volunteers. What's more, octopuses have the dazzling ability to keep changing colour, shape and texture to reflect their mood and their ever-shifting surroundings. We humans can be just as fluid, engaging a wide range of our values many times a day as we switch from bargaining to giving to competing to sharing in our constantly changing economic landscape.[66]

If we are to bid farewell to the name *Homo economicus* too, what should take its place? Many new names have been proposed, from *Homo heuristicus* and *Homo reciprocans* to *Homo altruisticus* and *Homo socialis*. But it makes no sense to pin ourselves down to just one of these identities: we inhabit them all simultaneously. Adam Smith was right when he said that we love to truck, barter and exchange, but he was also right that we and our societies flourish best when we display our 'humanity, justice, generosity and public spirit'. Rather than pick and choose just one of these many names for our new self-portrait, we should convey all of them within it. Having taken the cartoon of rational economic man down from the gallery wall, perhaps the most apt thing to do is replace it with a hologram of humanity, ever changing in the light.

The economic stage is now set, the cast drawn up, and the play's protagonist – humanity – amply introduced. It is time then, to explore the ways in which our collective behaviour plays out on that stage, as reflected in the economy's dynamics. And for insight into that, we need look no further than an apple tree.

4

GET SAVVY WITH SYSTEMS

from mechanical equilibrium
to dynamic complexity

Newton's apple has a lot to answer for. In 1666 as the brilliant young scientist sat in his mother's Lincolnshire garden, he marvelled – it is said – at how an apple fell: why never sideways or up, but always *down*? The answer prompted his famous insight into gravity and the laws of motion, which went on to revolutionise science. But, two centuries later, those same laws also gave rise to physics envy, misplaced metaphors, and painfully narrow thinking in economics. If only – just before that apple fell – young Isaac had also marvelled at how it grew: in a fascinating, ever-evolving interplay of trees and bees, sun and leaves, roots and rain, blossom and seeds. It might have led him to equally revolutionary insights into the nature of complex systems, thus transforming the history of science. It would have changed the course of economics, too, inspiring his economic admirers with a far more fruitful metaphor. Today we would be talking not of the market mechanism but of the market organism – and we'd be so much the wiser for it.

So much for that fantasy. It was the apple as it fell that grabbed Isaac's attention and led to his groundbreaking discoveries. Craving the authority of science, economists then mimicked Newton's laws of motion in their theories, describing the economy as if it were a stable, mechanical system. But we now know it is far better understood as a complex adaptive system, made up of interdependent humans in a dynamic living world. So if we are to have half a chance of bringing ourselves into the Doughnut, then it is essential to shift the economist's attention from the apple as it falls to the apple as it grows, from linear mechanics to complex dynamics. Bid farewell to the market as mechanism and discard the engineer's hard hat: it's time to don a pair of gardening gloves instead.

Overcoming our inheritance

Thanks to the last 100,000 years of evolution that fine-tuned *Homo sapiens*, we humans don't find it so easy to think in terms of complex systems. For millennia, people lived relatively short lives in small groups, learned from quick feedback (put your hand in the fire: it gets burned) and had little impact on their wider surroundings. Hence our brains evolved to cope with the near, the short term and the responsive, while expecting incremental, linear change. Add to that our evident desire for equilibrium and resolution: we promise it in our stories, with their happily-ever-after endings, and seek it in our music with harmonic melodies that resolve. But these traits leave us ill equipped when the world turns out to be dynamic, unstable and unpredictable.

Of course we know that counter-intuitive things do happen, so we warn ourselves with folk sayings. It was the straw that broke the camel's back (incremental change can lead to sudden collapse). Don't put all your eggs in one basket (a lack of diversity makes you vulnerable). A stitch in time saves nine (beware of escalating effects). What goes around comes around (everything is connected). Wise advice, but it still doesn't make it easy for us to anticipate and interpret the complex world as it comes at us.

If our understanding of complexity has been hampered by 100,000 years of evolution, then it has been topped off by 150 years of economic theory that has reinforced our biases with mechanistic models and metaphors. In the late nineteenth century a handful of mathematically minded economists set out to make economics a science as reputable as physics. And they turned to differential calculus – which could so elegantly describe the trajectory of falling apples and orbiting moons – to describe the economy with a set of axioms and equations. Just as Newton had uncovered the physical laws of motion that explained the world from the scale of a single atom to the movement of the planets, they sought to uncover the economic laws of motion that explained the market, starting with a single consumer and scaling up to national output.

The British economist William Stanley Jevons set the metaphorical ball rolling in the 1870s when he claimed that 'the Theory of Economy . . . presents a close analogy to the Science of Statical Mechanics, and the Laws of Exchange are found to resemble the Laws of Equilibrium of a lever'.[1] Over in Switzerland, the engineer-turned-economist Léon Walras had a similar vision, declaring that 'the pure theory of economics . . . is a science which resembles the physio-mathematical sciences in every respect' and – as if to prove it – he started referring to market exchange as 'the mechanism of competition'.[2] They and others likened the role played by gravity in pulling a pendulum to rest to the role played by prices in pulling markets into equilibrium. As Jevons put it:

> Just as we measure gravity by its effects in the motion of a pendulum, so we may estimate the equality or inequality of feelings by the decisions of the human mind. The will is our pendulum, and its oscillations are minutely registered in the price lists of the markets. I know not when we shall have a perfect system of statistics, but the want of it is the only insuperable obstacle in the way of making Economics an exact science.[3]

Such mechanical metaphors – from the lever to the pendulum – must have seemed cutting edge in their day. No wonder these economists put them at the heart of their theories of how individuals and firms behave, thus founding a field that came to be known as microeconomics. But in order to make this new theory echo Newton's laws and conform to the rigours of differential calculus, Jevons, Walras and their fellow mathematical pioneers had to make some heroically simplifying assumptions about how markets and people work. Crucially, the nascent theory hinged on assuming that, for any given mix of preferences that consumers might have, there was just one price at which everyone who wanted to buy and everyone who wanted to sell would be satisfied, having bought or sold all that they wanted for that price. In other words, each market had to have one single, stable point of equilibrium, just as a pendulum has only one point of rest. And for that condition to hold, the market's buyers and sellers all had to be 'price-takers' – no single actor being big enough to have sway over prices – and they had to be following the law of diminishing returns. Together these assumptions underpin the most widely recognised diagram in all of microeconomic theory, and the first one that must be mastered by every novice student: the diagram of supply and demand.

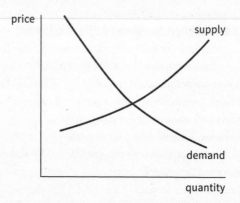

Supply and demand: the point at which price matches supply with demand is the point of market equilibrium.

What lies behind this iconic pair of crossing lines? Think of a good, any good (let's say pineapples) and here's how it works. The demand curve shows how many pineapples customers will want to buy at each price, given their aim of maximising their utility, or satisfaction. The curve slopes downwards because the more pineapples a customer buys, the less utility they are likely to gain from buying yet one more – an assumption known as the diminishing marginal utility of consumption – and so they will be willing to pay a little less for each successive one. The supply curve, in contrast, shows how many pineapples the sellers will be prepared to supply for any given price, given their aim of maximising their profits. Why does the curve slope upwards? Because – the theory goes – if each pineapple farmer has a fixed plot of land, then the cost of growing yet more pineapples on it will start to rise – that's the law of diminishing marginal returns – and so they will require a higher price for supplying each successive piece of fruit.

Alfred Marshall, who drew the definitive version of this diagram in the 1870s, likened the criss-crossing of its lines to a pair of scissors – yet another mechanical analogy – to explain the mystery of how market prices are set. Just as a pair of scissors does not cut paper with its upper blade or lower blade alone but precisely where the two blades cross, so, he argued, market price is set not by suppliers' costs nor consumers' utility alone, but precisely where costs and utility meet – and there lies the point of market equilibrium.

Walras had an ambitious agenda for these scissors: he was convinced it was possible to scale the analysis up from a single commodity to all commodities, so creating a model of the whole market economy. And, he reasoned, if those markets were comprised of fully informed, small-scale competitive sellers and buyers, then the economy would reach a point of equilibrium that maximised total utility. In other words – in a neat echo of Smith's invisible hand – it would, for any given income distribution, produce the best possible outcome for society as a whole. The mathematical techniques did not yet exist for Walras to prove his hunch but his agenda was later picked up by Kenneth Arrow and Gerard Debreu, who set out its equations in their 1954 model of general equilibrium. It appeared to be a landmark proof, giving microeconomic under-pinning to macroeconomic analysis, launching a seemingly unified economic theory and laying the foundations of what has been known ever since as 'modern macro'.[4]

The theory looks complete, sounds impressively like physics, and is set out in authoritative equations. But it is deeply flawed. Thanks to the interdependence of markets within an economy, it is just not possible to add up all individuals' demand curves to get a reliable downward-sloping demand curve for the economy as a whole. And without that, there is no promise of equilibrium. This is not news to economists, or at least it shouldn't be: in the 1970s several smart theorists realised (to their own horror) that the foundations of equi-librium theory didn't hold up. But the implications of their insight (catchily known as the Sonnenschein–Mantel–Debreu conditions) were so devastating for the rest of the theory that the disproof seems to have been hidden, ignored or brushed aside in the textbooks and the teaching, leaving students ever since unaware that anything was fundamentally out of whack with the equilibrating pulleys and pen-dulum of the market mechanism.[5]

As a result, general equilibrium theories dominated macroeco-nomic analysis through the second half of the twentieth century, and all the way up to the 2008 financial crash. The 'New Classical' variants of equilibrium theory – which assume that markets adjust instantly to shocks – jostled for attention with so-called 'New Keynesian' variants that assume there will be adjustment delays due to 'sticky' wages and prices. Both variants failed to see the crash coming because – being built on the presumption of equilibrium, while simultaneously overlooking the role of the financial sector – they had little capacity to predict, let alone respond to, boom, bust and depression.

With such ill-fitting models dominating macroeconomic analysis, some big-name insiders began to critique the very theories that they had helped to legitimise. Robert Solow, known as the father of neoclassical economic growth theory and long-time collaborator of Paul Samuelson, became an outspoken critic, first in his 2003 speech bluntly entitled 'Dumb and Dumber in Macroeconomics', then in analyses that mocked the theory's stringent assumptions.[6] The general equilibrium model, he pointed out, in fact depends upon there being just one single, immortal consumer-worker-owner maximising their utility into an infinite future, with perfect foresight and rational expectations, all the while served by perfectly competitive firms. How on earth did such absurd models come to be so dominant? In 2008, Solow gave his view:

> I am left with a puzzle, or even a challenge. What accounts for the ability of 'modern macro' to win hearts and minds among bright and enterprising academic economists? . . . There has always been a purist streak in economics that wants everything to follow neatly from greed, rationality, and equilibrium, with no ifs, ands, or buts . . . The theory is neat, learnable, not terribly difficult, but just technical enough to feel like 'science.' Moreover it is practically guaranteed to give laissez-faire-type advice, which happens to fit nicely with the general turn to the political right that began in the 1970s and may or may not be coming to an end.[7]

One thing that is clearly coming to an end is the credibility of general equilibrium economics. Its metaphors and models were devised to mimic Newtonian mechanics, but the pendulum of prices, the market mechanism, and the reliable return to rest are simply not suited to understanding the economy's behaviour. Why not? It's just the wrong kind of science.

No one made this point more powerfully than Warren Weaver, the director of natural sciences at the Rockefeller Foundation, in his

1948 article, 'Science and Complexity'. Looking back over the last three hundred years of scientific progress, while simultaneously looking forward at the challenges facing the world, Weaver clustered together three kinds of problems that science can help us to understand. At one extreme lie *problems of simplicity*, involving just one or two variables in linear causality – a rolling billiard ball, a falling apple, an orbiting planet – and Newton's laws of classical mechanics do a great job of explaining these. At the other extreme, he wrote, are *problems of disordered complexity* involving the random movement of billions of variables – such as the motion of molecules in a gas – and these are best analysed using statistics and probability theory.

In between these two branches of science, however, lies a vast and fascinating realm: *problems of organised complexity*, which involve a sizeable number of variables that are 'interrelated in an organic whole' to create a complex but organised system. Weaver's examples came close to asking the very questions that Newton's apple failed to prompt. 'What makes an evening primrose open when it does? Why does salt water fail to satisfy thirst? . . . Is a virus a living organism?' He noted that economic questions came into this realm, too. 'On what does the price of wheat depend? . . . To what extent is it safe to depend on the free interplay of such economic forces as supply and demand? . . . To what extent must systems of economic control be employed to prevent the wide swings from prosperity to depression?' Indeed, Weaver recognised that most of humanity's biological, ecological, economic, social and political challenges were questions of organised complexity, the realm that was least understood. 'These new problems, and the future of the world depends on many of them, require science to make a third great advance,' he concluded.[8]

That third great advance got under way in the 1970s when complexity science – which studies how relationships between the many parts of a system shape the behaviour of the whole – began to take off. It has since transformed many fields of research, from the study of ecosystems and computer networks to weather patterns and the spread of disease. And although it is all about complexity, its core concepts are actually quite simple to grasp – meaning that, despite our instincts, we can all learn, through training and experience, to be better 'systems thinkers'.

A growing number of economists are thinking in systems too, making complexity economics, network theory, and evolutionary economics among the most dynamic fields of economic research. But, thanks to the lasting influence of Jevons and Walras, most economics teaching and textbooks still introduce the essence of the economic world as linear, mechanical and predictable, summed up by the market's equilibrating mechanism. It's a mindset that will leave future economists deeply ill-equipped to handle the complexity of the contemporary world.

In a playful 'look back from 2050' the economist David Colander recounts that, by 2020, the majority of scientists – from physicists to biologists – had already realised that complexity thinking was essential for understanding much of the world. Economists, however, were a little slower on the uptake and it was not until 2030 that 'most economic researchers believed that the economy was a complex system that belonged within complexity science'.[9] If his history of the future should turn out to be right, it may well be too late. Why wait until 2030 when we can ditch the ill-chosen metaphors of Newtonian physics and get savvy with systems now?

The dance of complexity

At the heart of systems thinking lie three deceptively simple concepts: stocks and flows, feedback loops, and delay. They sound straightforward enough but the mind-boggling business begins when they start to interact. Out of their interplay emerge many of the surprising, extraordinary and unpredictable events in the world.

If you have ever been mesmerised by the sight of thousands of starlings flocking at sunset – in a spectacle poetically known as a murmuration – then you'll know just how extraordinary such 'emergent properties' can be. Each bird twists and turns in flight, using phenomenal agility to stay a mere wingspan apart from its neighbours, while tilting as they tilt. But as tens of thousands of birds gather together, all following these same simple rules, the flock as a whole becomes an astonishing swooping, pulsing mass against the evening sky.

So what is a system? Simply a set of things that are interconnected in ways that produce distinct patterns of behaviour – be they cells in an organism, protestors in a crowd, birds in a flock, members of a family, or banks in a financial network. And it is the relationships between the individual parts – shaped by their stocks and flows, feedbacks, and delay – that give rise to their emergent behaviour.

Stocks and flows are the basic elements of any system: things that can get built up or run down – just like water in a bath, fish in the sea, people on the planet, trust in a community, or money in the bank. A stock's levels change over time due to the balance between its inflows and outflows. A bathtub fills or empties depending on how fast water pours in from the tap versus how fast it drains out of the plughole. A flock of chickens grows or shrinks depending on the rate of chicks born versus chickens dying. A piggy bank fills up if more coins are added than are taken away.

If stocks and flows are a system's core elements, then feedback loops are their interconnections, and in every system there are two kinds: reinforcing (or 'positive') feedback loops and balancing (or 'negative') ones. With reinforcing feedback loops, the more you have, the more you get. They amplify what is happening, creating vicious or virtuous circles that will, if unchecked, lead either to explosive growth or to collapse. Chickens lay eggs, which hatch into chickens, and so the poultry population grows and grows. Likewise, in the vengeful tit-for-tat of playground fights, a single rough shove can soon escalate into a full-blown bust-up. Interest earned on savings adds to those savings, increasing future interest payments, and so wealth accumulates. But reinforcing feedback can lead to collapse too: the less you have, the less you get. If people lose confidence in their bank and withdraw their savings, for example, it will start to run out of cash, deepening the loss of confidence and leading to a run on the bank.

If reinforcing feedbacks are what make a system move, then balancing feedbacks are what stop it from exploding or imploding. They counter and offset what is happening, and so tend to regulate systems. Our bodies use balancing feedbacks to maintain a healthy temperature: get too hot and your skin will start sweating in order to cool you down; get too cold and your body will start shivering in an attempt to warm itself up. A household's thermostat works in a similar way to stabilise room temperature. And in a playground scuffle, someone is likely to step in and try to break it up. In effect, balancing feedbacks bring stability to a system.

Complexity emerges from the way that reinforcing and balancing feedback loops interact with one another: out of their dance emerges the system's behaviour as a whole, and it can often be unpredictable. The simplest depiction of the ideas at the heart of systems thinking is a pair of feedback loops, and the one shown here tells a simple story of chickens, eggs, and crossing the road.[10]

Each arrow shows the direction of causation and comes with a plus or minus sign. A plus sign indicates that the effect is positively related to the cause (more chickens result in more attempted road crossings, for example) while a minus sign stands for the reverse (more attempted road crossings result in fewer chickens). Each pair of arrows creates a loop, labelled R if it is reinforcing and B if it is balancing. On the left, more chickens lay more eggs that hatch into more chickens: a reinforcing loop. On the right, more chickens make more attempted road crossings, which results in fewer chickens: a balancing loop. When both feedback loops are in play in a highly

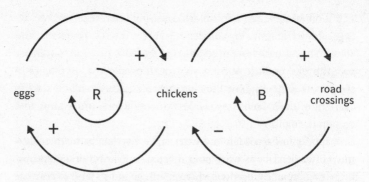

Feedback loops: the fundamentals of complex systems. Reinforcing feedback (R) amplifies what is happening, while balancing feedback (B) counters it. Their interaction creates complexity.

simplified system like this one (assuming there is at least one rooster in the flock and no shortage of grain), what might happen to the size of the poultry population over time? Depending on the relative strength of the two loops – the rate at which chickens produce chicks versus the rate at which chickens get hit – the flock might grow exponentially, collapse, or even come to oscillate continuously around a stable size if there is a significant delay between chicks hatching and their attempting to cross the road.

Delays such as this – between inflows and outflows – are common in systems and can have big effects. Sometimes they bring useful stability to a system, allowing stocks to build up and act as buffers or shock absorbers: think energy stored in a battery, food in the cupboard, or savings in the bank. But stock–flow delays can produce system stubbornness too: no matter how much effort gets put in, it takes time to, say, reforest a hillside, build trust in a community, or improve a school's exam grades. And delay can generate big oscillations when systems are slow to respond – as anyone knows who has been scalded then frozen then scalded again while trying to master the taps on an unfamiliar shower.

It is out of these interactions of stocks, flows, feedbacks and delays that complex adaptive systems arise: complex due to their unpredictable emergent behaviour, and adaptive because they keep evolving over time. Beyond the realm of starlings and chickens, bathtubs and showers, it soon becomes clear just how powerful systems thinking can be for understanding our ever-evolving world, from the rise of corporate empires to the collapse of ecosystems. Many events that first appear to be sudden and external – what mainstream economists often describe as 'exogenous shocks' – are far better understood as arising from endogenous change. In the words of the political economist Orit Gal, 'complexity theory teaches us that major events are the manifestation of maturing and converging underlying trends: they reflect change that has already occurred within the system'.[11]

From this perspective, the 1989 fall of the Berlin Wall, the 2008 collapse of Lehman Brothers and the imminent collapse of the Greenland ice sheet have much in common. All three are reported in the news as sudden events but are actually visible tipping points that result from slowly accumulated pressure in the system – be it the gradual build-up of political protest in Eastern Europe, the build-up of sub-prime mortgages in a bank's asset portfolio, or the build-up of greenhouse gases in the atmosphere. As Donella Meadows, one of the early champions of systems thinking, put it, 'Let's face it, the universe is messy. It is nonlinear, turbulent, and chaotic. It is dynamic. It spends its time in transient behaviour on its way to somewhere else, not in mathematically neat equilibria. It self-organises and evolves. It creates diversity, not uniformity. That's what makes the world interesting, that's what makes it beautiful, and that's what makes it work.'[12]

Complexity in economics

The realisation that economics needs to embrace dynamic analysis is by no means a recent one. Over the past 150 years, economists of all stripes tried to break away from imitating Newtonian physics, but their efforts were all too often steam-rolled by the dominance of equilibrium theory and its satisfyingly neat equations. Jevons himself had a hunch that economic analysis should be dynamic but, lacking the mathematics to do it, he settled for comparative statics, which compares snapshots of two points in time: it was an unfortunate compromise because it led him away from, rather than towards, the insight he ultimately sought.[13] In the 1860s, Karl Marx described how the relative income shares of workers and capitalists would continually rise and fall, due to self-perpetuating cycles of output and employment.[14] By the end of the nineteenth century, Thorstein Veblen was criticising economics for being 'helplessly behind the times in not being evolutionary' and therefore unable to explain change or development,[15] while Alfred Marshall argued against mechanical metaphors and, instead, for seeing economics as 'a branch of biology, broadly interpreted'.[16]

Twentieth-century attempts to recognise the economy's inherent dynamism were likewise made by deeply opposing schools of thought but even they couldn't dislodge equilibrium thinking. In the 1920s John Maynard Keynes critiqued the use of comparative statics, pointing out that it is precisely what happens in between those snapshots of economic events that is of greatest interest. 'Economists set themselves too easy, too useless a task,' he wrote, 'if in tempestuous seasons they can only tell us that when the storm is long past the ocean is flat again.'[17] In the 1940s, Joseph Schumpeter drew on Marx's insights into dynamism to describe how capitalism's inherent process of 'creative destruction', through continual waves of innovation and decline, gave rise to business cycles.[18] In the 1950s, Bill Phillips created his MONIAC precisely with the aim of replacing comparative statics with system dynamics, complete with the time lags and fluctuations that can be observed as water flows into and out of tanks. In the 1960s Joan Robinson lambasted equilibrium economic thinking, insisting that, 'a model applicable to actual history has to be capable of getting out of equilibrium; indeed it must normally not be in it'.[19] And in the 1970s, the father of neo-liberalism, Friedrich Hayek, decried the economist's 'propensity to imitate as closely as possible the procedures of the brilliantly successful physical sciences – an attempt which in our field may lead to outright error'.[20]

So let's finally heed their collective advice, push equilibrium thinking to one side, and start to think in systems instead. Imagine pulling the iconic supply and demand curves out of their rigid criss-cross and twisting them into a pair of feedback loops. At the same time, drop the economist's beloved notion of 'externalities', those incidental effects felt by people who were not involved in the transactions that produced them – like toxic effluent that affects communities living downstream of a river-polluting factory, or the exhaust fumes inhaled by cyclists biking through city traffic. Such negative externalities, remarks the ecological economist Herman Daly, are those things that 'we classify as "external" costs for no better reason than because we have made no provision for them in our economic theories'.[21] The systems dynamics expert John Sterman concurs. 'There are no side effects – just *effects*,' he says, pointing out that the very notion of side effects is just 'a sign that the boundaries of our mental models are too narrow, our time horizons too short'.[22] Due to the scale and interconnectedness of the global economy, many economic effects that were treated as 'externalities' in twentieth-century theory have turned into defining social and ecological crises in the twenty-first century. Far from remaining a peripheral concern 'outside' of economic activity, addressing these effects is of critical concern for creating an economy that enables us all to thrive.

From this vantage point – counter-intuitive though it may sound – equilibrium economics actually turns out to be a form of systems analysis, just an extremely limited one. It get the results it seeks by imposing severely restrictive assumptions about how market systems behave – assumptions including perfect competition, diminishing returns, full information, and rational actors – so that no errant effects get in the way of the price mechanism's ability to act as the balancing feedback loop that restores market equilibrium. Think of it in terms of starlings: what restrictions would you have to impose on a large flock of these birds if you wanted to make sure that they all stayed still? You could place each bird in its own narrow little coop and shut them all away in a dark, quiet room: that should encourage them to stay put. But don't expect the flock to behave like that once you remove these unnatural confines and release them into the air. They will twist and turn, putting on an extraordinary aerial display of a complex system in action. So it is with economic actors trapped in the narrow confines of an equilibrium model: when all the restrictive assumptions are in place, they will indeed behave as required. But remove those assumptions – enter the real world – and all havoc could break loose. It often does, of course, in the boom-to-bust of financial crash, in the rise of the 1%, and in the tipping points of climate change.

Bubble, boom, and bust: the dynamics of finance

If financial traders were birds, their antics would indeed resemble those of a flock of starlings cavorting in the sky (the obvious difference being that starlings never crash). Those financial antics are due to what the speculator George Soros has called 'the reflexivity of markets': the pattern of feedbacks that kick in when market participants' views influence the course of events, and the course of events, in turn, influences participants' views.[23] Whether we are financial traders or teenagers (or indeed both), our emerging self-portrait reveals that we are not isolated individuals driven by fixed preferences: we are deeply influenced by what goes on around us – and we often have fun being part of it. Trends are launched when a product's popularity boosts its desirability to others, further raising its popularity, generating this season's must-have toy, the hottest me-too gadget, and the latest viral dance craze (who can forget 'Gangnam Style'?).

Less fun but almost as frequent are asset bubbles in which the price of a stock builds higher and higher before it ultimately bursts. The name of that phenomenon originated with the South Sea Bubble of 1720, an event that the great Sir Isaac Newton forbade to be mentioned in his presence ever after. In March of that year, the price of shares in the South Sea Company – which had been granted a British monopoly on trading with South American colonies – began to rise fast as false rumours of its successes abroad started to spread. Newton had already bought a few shares in the company and so in April he cashed them in for a large profit. But the South Sea stock price kept on rising fast and so, swept along by the nation's enthusiasm, Isaac couldn't resist the market's lure. He jumped back in at a much higher price in June – just two months before the bubble finally peaked and burst. Newton lost his life savings as a result. 'I can calculate the movement of stars, but not the madness of men,' he famously said in the bubble's aftermath.[24] The master of mechanics had been confounded by complexity.

Like Newton, we all pay a high price when we don't understand the dynamic systems on which our lives and livelihoods depend. That certainly became clear in the wake of the 2008 financial crash, which famously prompted the Queen to ask, 'Why did no one see it coming?' Before it happened, the equilibrium-thinking underpinning mainstream economic theory had lulled the vast majority of economic analysts into paying scant attention to the banking sector – both its structure and its behaviour. Incredible though it now seems, many major financial institutions – from the Bank of England and the European Central Bank to the US Federal Reserve – were using macroeconomic models in which private banks played no role at all: an omission that turned out to be a fatal error. As economist Steve Keen – one of the few who did see a crash coming – pithily put it, 'Trying to analyse capitalism while leaving out banks, debt, and money is like trying to analyse birds while ignoring that they have wings. Good luck.'[25]

Thanks to the dominance of equilibrium thinking, most economic policymakers eschewed the idea that instability could arise from the dynamics at play within the economy itself. In the decade running up to the crash, and oblivious to the build-up of systemic risk, the UK's chancellor, Gordon Brown, hailed the end of boom and bust,[26] while Ben Bernanke, Governor of the Federal Reserve Board welcomed what he called 'the Great Moderation'.[27] After 2008, when the boom went very bust, many started to search for insights in the long-ignored work of the economist Hyman Minsky, especially his 1975 financial-instability hypothesis, which put dynamic analysis at the heart of macroeconomics.

Minsky had realised that – counter-intuitive though it sounds – when it comes to finance, stability breeds instability. Why? Because of reinforcing feedback loops, of course. During good economic times, banks, firms and borrowers all gain in confidence and start to take on greater risks, which pushes up the price of housing and other assets. This asset price rise, in turn, reinforces borrowers' and lenders' confidence along with their expectations that asset values will keep on rising. In Minsky's own words, 'The tendency to transform doing well into a speculative investment boom is the basic instability in a capitalist economy.'[28] When prices eventually don't keep pace with expectations, as will inevitably happen, mortgage defaults kick in, assets fall further in value, and – in what has been dubbed a 'Minsky moment' – finance goes off the cliff of insolvency, bringing on a crash. Guess what happens post-crash? Confidence gradually rebuilds and the process begins all over again in a rolling cycle of dynamic disequilibrium. There's still a lot to learn from the chicken that crossed the road.

In 2008 the fallout from this inherent market instability was compounded by the financial regulators' failure to understand the inherent dynamics of banking networks. Before the crash, those regulators worked on the assumption that networks always serve to disperse risk, and so the regulations that they devised only monitored the nodes in the network – individual banks – rather than overseeing the nature of their interconnections. But the crash made clear that a network's structure can be robust-yet-fragile: usually behaving as a robust shock-absorber, but then – as the character of the network evolves – switching to becoming a fragile shock-amplifier. That switch is more likely to be triggered, discovered the Bank of England's Andy Haldane, when networks have a few super-nodes acting as key hubs, too many connections between the nodes, and the small-world trait of creating short-cut connections between otherwise distant nodes. Between 1985 and 2005, the global financial network evolved to feature all three of these trigger traits but, lacking a systems perspective, regulators did not pick up on them.[29] As Gordon Brown later admitted, 'we created a monitoring system that was looking at individual institutions. That was the big mistake. We didn't understand how risk was spread across the system, we didn't understand the entanglements of different institutions with each other, and we didn't understand – even though we talked about it – just how global things were.'[30]

Prompted by the 2008 crash, new dynamic models of financial markets are being built. Steve Keen has teamed up with computer programmer Russell Standish to develop the first systems-dynamics computer program – aptly named Minsky – which is a disequilibrium model of the economy that takes the feedbacks of banks, debt and money seriously. As Keen told me in his characteristic style, 'Minsky finally gives wings to the economic bird, so at last we'll have a chance of understanding how it flies.'[31] Theirs is one among several promising complexity approaches to understanding the effects of financial markets on the macroeconomy.

Success to the successful: the dynamics of inequality

Inequality features only as a peripheral concern in the world of equilibrium economics. Given that markets are efficient at rewarding people, goes the theory, then those with broadly similar talents, preferences, and initial endowments will end up equally rewarded: any remaining differences must be due to differences in effort, and that provides a spur for innovation and hard work. But in the disequilibrium world that we inhabit – where powerful reinforcing feedbacks are in play – virtuous cycles of wealth and vicious cycles of poverty can send otherwise similar people spiralling to opposite ends of the income-distribution spectrum. It's due to what systems experts have come to call the 'Success to the Successful' trap, which kicks off when the winners in one round of a game reap rewards that raise their chances of winning again in the next.

Equilibrium theory acknowledges that reinforcing feedbacks might sometimes prevail in business, resulting in oligopoly – the rule of the few – but it presents these cases as exceptions to the rule. As early as the 1920s, however, the Italian economist Piero Sraffa argued the opposite: when it comes to firms' supply curves, increasing returns – not the so-called law of diminishing returns – are often likely to be the norm. As Sraffa pointed out, everyday experience shows that firms in many industries face falling unit costs as they expand their production, and so those industries tend towards oligopoly or even monopoly, rather than perfect competition.[32] That perspective certainly resonates with the corporate landscape we know today. In the food sector alone, four agribusiness giants known as the ABCD group (ADM, Bunge, Cargill, and Louis Dreyfus) control over 75% of the global grain trade. Another four account for over 50% of global seed sales, and just six agrochemical firms control 75% of the world's fertiliser and pesticide market.[33] In 2011, just four Wall Street banks – JPMorgan Chase, Citigroup, Bank of America, and Goldman Sachs – accounted for 95% of the financial industry's derivatives trading in the US.[34] It is a pattern of concentration that prevails in many other industries too, from media and computing to telecoms and supermarkets.

Anyone who has played the board game Monopoly is well versed in the dynamics of Success to the Successful: players who are lucky enough to land on expensive properties early in the game can buy them up, build hotels, and reap vast rents from their fellow players, thus accumulating a winning fortune as they bankrupt the rest. Fascinatingly, however, the game was originally called 'The Landlord's Game' and was designed precisely to reveal the injustice arising out of such concentrated property ownership, not to celebrate it.

The game's inventor Elizabeth Magie was an outspoken supporter of Henry George's ideas and when she first created her game in 1903 she gave it two very different sets of rules to be played in turn. Under the 'Prosperity' set of rules, every player gained each time someone acquired a new property (echoing George's call for a land value tax), and the game was won (by all) when the player who had started out with the least money had doubled it. Under the second, 'Monopolist' set of rules, players gained by charging rent to those who were unfortunate enough to land on their properties – and whoever managed to bankrupt the rest was the sole winner. The purpose of the dual sets of rules, said Magie, was for players to experience a 'practical demonstration of the present system of land grabbing with all its usual outcomes and consequences' and so understand how different approaches to property ownership can lead to vastly different social outcomes. 'It might well have been called "The Game of Life",' remarked Magie, 'as it contains all the elements of success and failure in the real world.' But when the games manufacturer Parker Brothers bought the patent for The Landlord's Game from Magie in the 1930s, they relaunched it simply as Monopoly, and provided the eager public with just one set of rules: those that celebrate the triumph of one over all.[35]

Distributional dynamics that play out in board games show up in computer simulations of the economy too. It was Robert Solow, the outspoken critic of modern macro, who ridiculed equilibrium economic models by demonstrating that, far from modelling markets of many players, they were actually made up of a single 'representative agent' – reducing the economy to just one typical consumer-worker-owner who responds predictably to 'external' shocks. Since the 1980s, complexity economists have been developing alternative approaches including 'agent-based' modelling which starts out with a diverse array of agents all following a simple set of rules as they continually respond and adapt to their surroundings. Once the computer model is set up, the programmers essentially press 'go', launching those agents into action, then sit back to watch and learn from the dynamic patterns that emerge from their interplay. And there is a lot to learn.

In a 1992 landmark computer simulation known as Sugarscape, modellers Joshua Epstein and Robert Axtell created a miniature virtual society to see how wealth would be distributed over time. Sugarscape consists of a 50-by-50 grid-based landscape – like a giant chessboard – featuring two large sugar mountains that are separated by sugar-sparse plains.[36] Scattered across that landscape are many sugar-hungry agents, some able to move faster than others, some seeing further, and some burning sugar faster, as they all scan the grid, competing to move on to the squares piled high with the sugary fuel that will sustain them. At the outset, sugar stocks are randomly distributed between the agents: a few have more, a few less, but most have a middling share. As the simulation gets under way, however, it doesn't take long for these sweet-toothed agents to find themselves deeply divided into a small elite of sugar super-rich and the vast mass of sugar-poor. Yes, their varying attributes of speed, eyesight, metabolism and starting point can explain some of this divergence, but – importantly – these attributes alone cannot account for the striking extremes of inequality that arise.

That inequality emerges, in fact, largely from the dynamics inherent in Sugarscape society: sugar is wealth, and having more helps in getting more, a classic case of Success to the Successful at work. Most striking, however, is that even small chance differences between the agents – like having an early lucky break or making a first false move in the search for sugar – can rapidly amplify into big differences, propelling them to vastly different fates in their starkly split saccharine society.[37] The computer world of Sugarscape is of course not reality but its familiar dynamics further debunk the claim that income inequalities mostly reflect talent and merit in society.

The Success to the Successful dynamic was spotted long before Monopoly and Sugarscape came along. Two thousand years ago, the notion that 'the rich get richer and the poor get poorer' was noted in the Bible and hence came to be known as 'the Matthew Effect'. Its tell-tale pattern of accumulative advantage, coupled with spiralling disadvantage, can be seen in children's educational outcomes, in adults' employment opportunities, and of course in terms of income and wealth. And that financial dynamic is certainly alive today. Between 1988 and 2008, the majority of countries worldwide saw rising inequality within their borders, resulting in a hollowing out of their middle classes. Over those same 20 years, global inequality fell slightly overall (mostly thanks to falling poverty rates in China) but it increased significantly at the extremes. More than 50% of the total increase in global income over that period was captured by just the richest 5% of the world's population, while the poorest 50% of people gained only 11% of it.[38] Getting into the Doughnut requires reversing these widening gaps of income and wealth, so finding ways to offset and weaken the Success to the Successful feedback loop will be key, and we will explore some of them in Chapter 5.

Water in the tub: the dynamics of climate change

Economic externalities are framed – thanks to their very name – as a peripheral concern in mainstream theory. But when we recast them as effects and recognise that the economy is embedded within the biosphere – as we did in Chapter 2 – it quickly becomes clear that those effects could build up as feedback and disrupt the economic system that first generated them. That is certainly the case with so-called environmental externalities, like the build-up of greenhouse gases in the atmosphere, which risk triggering catastrophic effects of climate change. No wonder systems thinkers like John Sterman, director of MIT's systems dynamics group, are intent on finding ways to overcome policymakers' blind spots when it comes to tackling climate change because, unlike in banking crises, there is no chance of a last-minute bail-out.

Understanding the build-up of pressure in the climate system depends upon understanding a basic relationship between the flow of carbon dioxide emissions and their stock, or concentration, in the atmosphere. To his alarm, Sterman discovered that even his top students at MIT had a surprisingly poor intuitive grasp of how such stock–flow dynamics work: most thought that simply stopping global CO_2 emissions from rising would be enough to halt the increase of CO_2 in the atmosphere. So he turned to a classic analogy and drew the atmosphere as a giant bathtub with an open tap and open plughole: the tub fills as new emissions pour in and empties as carbon dioxide is both taken up by plant photosynthesis and dissolved in the oceans. The metaphor's message? Just as a bathtub will only start to empty if water pours in from the tap more slowly than it drains out of the plughole, so carbon dioxide concentration in the atmosphere will only fall if new emissions flow in more slowly than CO_2 is drawn out. When Sterman first drew the carbon bathtub in 2009, global annual inflows of CO_2 were 9 billion tons, compared to outflows of just 5 billion tons: it meant that annual emissions had to fall by half merely to start reducing atmospheric concentrations. If MIT students found that hard to grasp, he realised, then no doubt policymakers did as well and, 'that means they think it's easier to stabilize greenhouse gases and stop warming than it is', he warned.[39]

Following in the footsteps of Elizabeth Magie, Sterman and his colleagues set out to create a game that would teach climate dynamics to its players through experience. They came up with a user-friendly computer simulation, known as C-ROADS (short for Climate Rapid Overview and Decision Support) to help governments see the impacts of their policy plans. C-ROADS instantly adds up all nations' greenhouse gas reduction pledges to show their combined long-term implications for global emissions, atmospheric concentrations, temperature change, and sea-level rise. It has been used by negotiating teams in the US, China, the EU and beyond, transforming their understanding of the speed and scale of cuts needed worldwide. 'Without tools like these,' explains Sterman, 'there is no hope for developing the systems-thinking capabilities or understanding of the climate among any of the constituent stakeholder groups.'[40]

C-ROADS has been highly valuable for running role-plays of international climate negotiations over the past decade, often with real policymakers. Seeking to recreate the power dynamics at play, the C-ROADS team offer those representing powerful countries a literal seat at the table which is loaded with plentiful snacks, whilst leaving least developed country representatives to sit on the floor. So when the President of Micronesia took part in a role-play in 2009, he duly insisted on taking his place on the floor. As the mock negotiations got under way and the major powers made their usual inadequate pledges, the simulated sea level rose by one metre. So the C-ROADS team duly covered up all those on the floor – including the Micronesian President – with a big blue sheet. 'He was thrilled,' recounted Sterman, 'because for the first time people saw what the implications of sea level rise would be.'[41] Without understanding or experiencing the effects of stock and flow dynamics, we have little chance of recognising the speed and scale of energy transformation required to bring ourselves back within the planetary boundary for climate change.

Avoiding collapse

A systems perspective makes clear that the prevailing direction of global economic development is caught in the twin dynamics of growing social inequality and deepening ecological degradation. To put it bluntly, these trends echo the conditions under which earlier civilisations – from the Easter Islanders to the Greenland Norse – have collapsed. When a society starts to destroy the resource base on which it depends, argues the environmental historian Jared Diamond, it is going to be far less adept at changing its ways if it is also stratified, with a small elite that is quite separate from the masses. And when the short-term interests of that decision-making elite diverge from the long-term interests of society as a whole it is, he warns, 'a blueprint for trouble'.[42] Instances of collapse are sometimes assumed to be rare aberrations along the path of human progress, but they have been surprisingly common. Indeed, the breakdown of civilisations ranging from the Roman Empire and China's Han Dynasty to the Mayan civilisation of Mesoamerica makes clear that even complex and inventive civilisations are vulnerable to downfall.[43] So can systems thinking help us to discover whether it might happen again?

That question was most famously explored in the 1972 study *Limits to Growth*, whose team of authors based at MIT created one of the first dynamic computer models of the global economy, known as World 3. The team's aim was to explore a range of economic scenarios up to 2100, taking account of five factors that they saw as determining – and ultimately limiting – output growth: population, agricultural production, natural resources, industrial production, and pollution. According to their projections for the business-as-usual scenario, as global population and output expanded, non-renewable resources like oil, minerals and metals would be depleted, leading to a drop in industrial output and food production, ultimately resulting in famine, a large fall in the human population, and greatly reduced living standards for all. When launched, their analysis simultaneously raised the alarm about the state of the world, introduced systems thinking widely into policy debates, and caused an uproar amongst those committed to the goal of growth.[44]

Mainstream economists were quick to deride the model's design on the basis that it underplayed the balancing feedback of the price mechanism in markets. If non-renewable resources became scarce, they argued, their prices would rise, triggering greater efficiency in their use, the wider use of substitutes, and exploration for new sources. But in dismissing World 3 and its implied limits to growth, they too quickly dismissed the role and effects of what the 1970s model simply called 'pollution', which – unlike metals, minerals and fossil fuels – typically carries no price and so generates no direct market feedback. World 3's modelling of pollution turned out to be prescient: today we can name it in far more specific terms as the many forms of ecological degradation that put pressure on planetary boundaries, from climate change and chemical pollution to ocean acidification and biodiversity loss. What's more, recent data comparisons with the 1972 model find that the global economy appears to be closely tracking its business-as-usual scenario – and that doesn't end well.[45]

This should set the alarm bells ringing: in the early twenty-first century, we have transgressed at least four planetary boundaries, billions of people still face extreme deprivation, and the richest 1% own half of the world's financial wealth. These are ideal conditions for driving ourselves towards collapse. If we are to avoid such a fate for our global civilisation, we clearly need a transformation and it can be summed up like this:

Today's economy is divisive and degenerative by default.
Tomorrow's economy must be distributive and regenerative by design.

An economy that is distributive by design is one whose dynamics tend to disperse and circulate value as it is created, rather than concentrating it in ever-fewer hands. An economy that is regenerative by design is one in which people become full participants in regenerating Earth's life-giving cycles so that we thrive within planetary boundaries. This is our generational design challenge, and its possibilities are explored in Chapters 5 and 6. But what kind of systems-thinking economist can help to make it happen?

Goodbye spanner, hello secateurs

Thinking in systems transforms the way we view the economy and invites economists to drop off their old metaphorical baggage. Say farewell to economy-as-machine and embrace economy-as-organism. Let go of the imaginary controls that promised to pull markets into equilibrium and, instead, get a feel for the pulse of the feedback loops that keep them continually evolving. It is time for economists to make a metaphorical career change, too: discard the engineer's hard hat and spanner, and pick up some gardening gloves and secateurs instead.

It's a vocational shift that has been a long time coming: back in the 1970s, Friedrich Hayek himself suggested that economists should aim to be less like craftsmen shaping their handiwork and more like gardeners tending their plants. Yes, the metaphor may have come from a thinker with extreme laissez-faire leanings but, if anything, it

Economists need a metaphorical career change: from engineer to gardener (as demonstrated by Charlie Chaplin and Josephine Baker).

suggests that Hayek never did a hard day's work in the garden: as any true plantsman knows, gardening is far from laissez-faire. In their book *The Gardens of Democracy*, Eric Liu and Nick Hanauer argue that moving from 'machinebrain' to 'gardenbrain' thinking calls for a simultaneous shift away from believing that things will self-regulate to realising that things need stewarding. 'To be a gardener is not to let nature take its course; it is to *tend*,' they write, 'Gardeners don't make plants grow but they do create conditions where plants can thrive and they do make judgments about what should and shouldn't be in the garden.'[46] That is why economic gardeners must get stuck in, nurturing, selecting, repotting, grafting, pruning and weeding the plants as they grow and mature.

One approach to economic gardening is to embrace evolution. Rather than aiming to predict and control the economy's behaviour, says Eric Beinhocker, a leading thinker in this field, economists should 'think of policy as an adapting portfolio of experiments that helps to shape the evolution of the economy and society over time'. It's an approach that aims to mimic the process of natural selection, often summed up as 'diversify–select–amplify'. Set up small-scale policy experiments to test out a variety of interventions, put a stop to the ones that don't work well, and scale up those that do.[47] This kind of adaptive policymaking is crucial in the face of today's ecological and social challenges because, as Elinor Ostrom put it, 'We have never had to deal with problems of the scale facing today's globally interconnected society. No one knows for sure what will work, so it is important to build a system that can evolve and adapt rapidly.'[48]

This has empowering implications: if complex systems evolve through their innovations and deviations then that gives added importance to novel initiatives, from new business models to complementary currencies and open-source design. Far from being mere fringe activities, these experiments are at the cutting edge – or rather, the evolving edge – of economic transformation towards the distributive and regenerative dynamics that we need.

If the economy is constantly evolving, how best can we steward its process? Learn to find the 'leverage points', said Donella Meadows – those places in a complex system where making a small change in one thing can lead to a big change in everything. She believed that most economists spend too much time tweaking low leverage points such as adjusting prices (which merely alters the rate of flow), when they could have far greater leverage through rebalancing the economy's feedback loops, or even by changing its goal (she had little time, remember, for that cuckoo goal of GDP growth). In addition, instead of jumping straight in with plans for change, she advised, be humble and try to get the beat of the system, even if it is an ailing economy, a dying forest, or a broken community. Watch and understand how it currently works and learn its history. It's obvious to ask what's wrong, so also ask: how did we get here, where are we headed, and what is still working well? 'Don't be an unthinking intervenor and destroy the system's own self-maintenance capacities,' she warned. 'Before you charge in to make things better, pay attention to the value of what's already there.'[49]

Meadows was a skilled economic gardener in this sense, having spent much of her life watching the dance of social-ecological systems in action, and observing the value of what was already there. In fact, she noted, effective systems tend to have three properties – healthy hierarchy, self-organisation and resilience – and so should be stewarded to enable these characteristics to emerge.

First, healthy hierarchy is achieved when nested systems serve the greater whole of which they are a part. Liver cells serve the liver, which in turn serves the human body; if those cells start to multiply rapidly, they become a cancer, no longer serving but destroying the body on which they depend. In economic terms, healthy hierarchy means, for example, ensuring that the financial sector is in service to the productive economy, which in turn is in service to life.[50]

Second, self-organisation is born out of a system's capacity to make its own structures more complex, like a dividing cell, a growing social movement, or an expanding city. In the economy much self-organising goes on in the marketplace through the price mechanism – that was Adam Smith's insight – but it also takes place in the commons and in the household too – the insight of Elinor Ostrom and generations of feminist economists. All three of these realms of provisioning can self-organise effectively to meet people's wants and needs, and the state should support all three in doing so.

Lastly, resilience emerges out of a system's ability to endure and bounce back from stress, like a jelly that wobbles on a plate without losing its form, or a spider's web that survives a storm. Equilibrium economics became fixated on maximising efficiency and so overlooked the vulnerability that it can bring, as we will see in the next chapter. Building diversity and redundancy into economic structures enhances the economy's resilience, making it far more effective in adapting to future shocks and pressures.

Getting ethical

There is one further important consequence of recognising the economy's inherent complexity and it concerns the ethics of economic policymaking. Ethics are at the core of other professions, such as medicine, that combine the uncertainty inherent in intervening in a complex system (like the human body) with having responsibility for significant impacts upon other people's lives. Hippocrates, the father of medicine, inspired a set of ethical principles, summed up in the modern Hippocratic Oath, that still guide doctors today, including: first do no harm; prioritise the patient; treat the whole person, not just the symptom; obtain prior informed consent; and call on the expertise of others when needed.

Xenophon, the father of economics, conceived of household management as a domestic affair and so suggested no ethics to guide it (since he believed he already knew how to manage women and slaves). But economics now guides the management of nations and of our planetary household, profoundly influencing the lives of us all. Is it, then, time for economists to get serious about ethics? George DeMartino, economist and ethicist at the University of Denver, certainly thinks so. 'When a profession seeks influence over others, it necessarily takes on ethical obligations – whether it recognizes them or not,' he argues, bluntly adding, 'I'm aware of no other profession that has been so cavalier regarding its responsibilities.'[51]

DeMartino believes that economic policy advisers too often follow what he calls the 'maxi-max' rule: when considering all possible policy options, recommend the one that would work best *if* it worked – without fully assessing whether it is *likely* to work. 'Maxi-max has been the primary decision rule in the most important economic interventions over the past 30 years,' he argues, pointing to the damage wrought by the shock policies of privatisation and market liberalisation implemented in Latin America, sub-Saharan Africa, and the former Soviet Union during the 1980s and 1990s.[52]

Economics is more than two thousand years behind medicine in honing the ethics of its own profession. That's quite some catching up to do, so to get the ball rolling – and with inspiration from DeMartino – here are four ethical principles for the twenty-first-century economist to consider. First, *act in service* to human prosperity in a flourishing web of life, recognising all that it depends upon. Second, *respect autonomy* in the communities that you serve by ensuring their engagement and consent, while remaining ever aware of the inequalities and differences that may lie within them. Third, *be prudential* in policymaking, seeking to minimise the risk of harm – especially to the most vulnerable – in the face of uncertainty. Lastly, *work with humility*, by making transparent the assumptions and shortcomings of your models, and by recognising alternative economic perspectives and tools. Principles such as these may one day be included in an Economist's Oath, to be recited by aspiring professionals upon graduation. But with or without the ceremony, what matters most is to bring such ethical principles to life in every economics student's training and every policymaker's practice.

'The future can't be predicted,' wrote Donella Meadows, 'but it can be envisioned and brought lovingly into being. Systems can't be controlled, but they can be designed and redesigned . . . We can listen to what the system tells us, and discover how its properties and our values can work together to bring forth something much better than can ever be produced by our will alone.'[53]

If the global economy's current dynamics continue – with their divisive and degenerative effects – then we face the very real risk of heading towards collapse. This overriding generational challenge calls on the twenty-first-century economist to embrace complexity and draw on its insights in order to transform economies – local to global – to make them distributive and regenerative by design, as the following chapters explore. If he were alive today I bet that Newton, apple in hand, would be up for the task.

5

DESIGN TO DISTRIBUTE

from 'growth will even it up again'
to distributive by design

'No pain no gain': it's the best-known saying of the world's greatest ever bodybuilder and it has motivated millions of people to grit their teeth and pump iron. In the 1980s Arnold Schwarzenegger's punishing workout routines took the fitness world by storm, and his favourite catchphrase became a celebrated gym motto that lives on today. Its message is simple: you have to push through intense physical pain if you want to build an incredible physique. That motto also happens to sum up an economic philosophy that came to dominate the late twentieth century: nations have to push through the social pain of high inequality if they want to create a richer, more equitable society for all.

The motto of no pain no gain clearly still inspires plenty of policymakers today, especially when justifying belt-tightening austerity measures that widen inequalities and hit the poorest hardest. But, as this chapter reveals, as far as the economy is concerned it's a false belief based not on evidence, but on an erroneous yet deeply influential diagram. Far from being a necessary phase in every nation's progress, rising inequality is a policy choice. It is a widely damaging one at that, with multiple repercussions that push humanity further out of the Doughnut.

Rather than accept growing inequality as a law of economic

development, an inevitability that must be endured, twenty-first-century economists will regard it as a failure of economic design, and will seek to make economies far more distributive of the value that they generate. Instead of focusing primarily on redistributing income earned, they will aim to redistribute wealth too – especially the wealth that comes from controlling land, money creation, enterprise, technology and knowledge. And instead of focusing on market and state solutions alone, they will also harness the power of the commons. It's a fundamental shift in perspective, and it is well under way.

The economic rollercoaster ride

If humanity is to thrive within the Doughnut, every human being must have the capabilities needed to lead a life of dignity, opportunity and community. Yet as we know from Chapter 1, many millions of people still lack the most basic means to do so. Where, then, do these people live?

Twenty years ago, the answer was easy to guess: almost all of them lived in the world's poorest countries, classified by the World Bank as low-income, with GDP per person of less than $1,000 per year. As a result, tackling global poverty was seen to be a matter of channelling global aid transfers to provide basic public services and stimulate economic growth in those low-income countries. But today, the answer has changed and at first it seems counter-intuitive: three quarters of the world's poorest people now live in middle-income countries. Not because they have moved but because their nations have become better off overall and so have been reclassified by the World Bank as middle-income. Many of those countries, however – including the largest such as China, India, Indonesia and Nigeria – are becoming more unequal, which explains how they can simultaneously be home to most of the world's poorest people.

Wide inequalities lead to poverty in high-income countries too, where the gap between the rich and the poor is now at its highest level for 30 years, leaving a striking number of people short of their essential needs.[1] In the US, for example, one child in five lives below the federal poverty line, while in the UK food banks have given out over one million packages of emergency food supplies each year since 2014.[2]

For the first time, ending human deprivation is becoming as much a question of tackling national distribution as of international redistribution, argues Andy Sumner, the expert who crunched the data on where the world's poorest people now live. 'A fundamental reframing of global poverty is approaching,' he writes, 'and the core variable to explain global poverty is increasingly national distribution and thus national political economy.'[3] Of course international redistribution from rich to poor countries continues to be essential for the 300 million people who live in poverty in countries still classified as low-income, which are mainly in sub-Saharan Africa. But the new geography of deprivation puts tackling national inequalities high on the agenda of ending poverty for all.

If tackling national inequality is essential for getting into the Doughnut, what does economic theory have to say about it? Inequality was a topic of great interest to many of the founding fathers of economics, but their views differed widely over how income would be distributed between labour, landlords and capitalists as market economies grew. While Karl Marx argued that incomes would tend to diverge, with the rich getting richer while workers were kept poor, Alfred Marshall claimed the opposite: that incomes across society would tend to converge as the economy expanded. In the 1890s, however, the Italian engineer-turned-economist Vilfredo Pareto stepped back from theoretical debate and searched for a pattern in the data. Having gathered income and tax records from England and from German states, from Paris and Italian towns, he plotted them on a graph and saw a curiously striking pattern emerge. In each case, he found, around 80% of national income was in the hands of just 20% of people, while the remaining 20% of income was spread among 80% of people. Pareto was delighted: he appeared to have discovered an economic law, which is still known today as Pareto's 80–20 rule. What's more, he argued, the steep 'social pyramid' that his data had repeatedly revealed must be a fixed fact of human nature, making attempts at redistribution counterproductive. The way to help the worst off was to expand the economy, he concluded, and the wealthy were best placed to make that happen.[4]

Converging, diverging, or ever-fixed? Debates over the likely path of income inequality raged on, but in 1955 the story took a crucial turn, quite literally. When Simon Kuznets – the brilliant inventor of national income accounting – gathered together long-run trend data on incomes in the US, UK and Germany, he was taken aback by what he found. In all three countries, income inequality measured before tax had been falling at least since the 1920s, and even possibly before the First World War. Contrary to Pareto's static social pyramid, Kuznets believed he had uncovered a different law: a social rollercoaster ride on which income inequality first rose, then levelled out, and eventually fell again, all while the economy grew.

It was an intriguing finding, but it jarred with his intuitive understanding of the Success to the Successful trap. Since the wealthy have higher savings and since savings generate more wealth, he reasoned, inequality should tend to rise over time, not fall – so what was going on? He offered up a possible explanation: the process of rural to urban migration. In the early stages of economic development, Kuznets suggested, as workers are drawn into cities, they leave behind low-paid but fairly egalitarian rural life to earn higher but more unequal urban wages, and so inequality increases as industrialisation gets under way. At a certain point, however, once enough workers are earning those higher urban wages, and they start demanding better pay for the low-waged among them, inequality begins to fall again, resulting in both a more prosperous and more equal society.[5]

It was a clever theory but it was wrong, not least because rural incomes were in fact far from egalitarian – a false assumption, for which Kuznets privately admitted he had 'no evidence whatsoever'.[6] But to his credit, he was cautious when publishing his conjectures, noting that the 'scant' data he drew on were specific to a particular historical context and should not be used for making 'unwarranted dogmatic generalisations'. He openly admitted that his explanations came 'perilously close to pure guesswork', thus making his conclusion, '5 per cent empirical information and 95 per cent speculation, some of it possibly tainted by wishful thinking'.[7]

So much for the caveats and warnings. His underlying message – that rising inequality is an inevitable stage on the journey towards economic success for all – was too good a story to doubt. The image that Kuznets had already sketched in every economist's mind was soon drawn on to the economist's page and named 'the Kuznets Curve'. With income per person on the x axis and a measure of national income inequality on the y axis, the curve – shaped like an upside-down U – appeared to present an economic law of motion. And it whispered a powerful message: if you want progress, inequality is inevitable. It's got to get worse before it can get better, and growth will make it better. Or, as Arnold would say, 'No pain, no gain'.

The inverted-U rapidly became an iconic economic diagram, especially in the nascent field of development economics, where it bolstered the theory that poor countries should concentrate income in the hands of the wealthy since only they would save and invest enough of it to kick-start GDP growth. In the blunt words of the field's founding theorist, W. Arthur Lewis, 'development must be inegalitarian'.[8] In the 1970s, both Kuznets and Lewis won the Nobel-Memorial prize in economics for their respective theories on

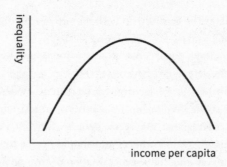

The Kuznets Curve, which suggests that as countries get richer, inequality must rise before it will eventually fall.

growth and inequality, while the World Bank treated the curve as an economic law and used it to publish projections of how long it would take for poverty levels to start falling in low- and middle-income countries.[9]

Economists, meanwhile, kept searching for real-world examples of the rollercoaster's rise and fall. Lacking good time-series data for any individual country, they relied instead on momentary snapshots of inequality across a wide array of countries. The results roughly, albeit rather loosely, seemed to fit the curve: middle-income countries tended to be more unequal than low-income and high-income ones alike. But it was still no proof that any single country had ever travelled up the painful hump and down the happy other side. It was only in the 1990s, when sufficient time-series data were available, that the Kuznets Curve could be thoroughly tested. The result? As a leading economist of the day put it, 'the pattern is that there is no pattern'.[10] As countries moved from low- to middle- to high-income, some saw inequality rise then fall then rise again; others saw it fall then rise; in others still it only rose, or only fell. As far as inequality and growth are concerned – as it turns out – everything is possible.

Striking regional events even more deeply debunked the curve's erroneous law. The East Asian 'miracle' – from the mid 1960s to 1990 – saw countries such as Japan, South Korea, Indonesia and Malaysia combine rapid economic growth with low inequality and falling poverty rates. It was achieved largely thanks to rural land reform that boosted the incomes of smallholder farmers, coupled with strong public investments in health and education, and industrial policies that raised workers' wages while restraining food prices. Far from being inevitable, the Kuznets process had turned out to be avoidable: it was indeed possible to achieve growth with equity. What's more, starting in the early 1980s, many high-income countries that believed they had successfully made it over the curve's hump saw their income distribution begin to widen again, resulting in the infamous rise of the one percent accompanied by flat or falling wages for the majority.

It was, however, the economist Thomas Piketty's 2014 long view of the dynamics of distribution under capitalism that made the underlying story plain to see. By asking not just who *earns* what but also who *owns* what, he distinguished between two kinds of households: those that own capital – such as land, housing, and financial assets which generate rent, dividends and interest – and those households that own only their labour, which generates only wages. He then scoured old tax records from Europe and the US to compare the growth trend of these different sources of income and concluded that Western economies – and others like them – are on track for dangerous levels of inequality. Why? Because the returns to capital have tended to grow faster than the economy as a whole, leading wealth to become ever more concentrated. That dynamic is then reinforced through political influence – from corporate lobbying to campaign financing – that further promotes the interests of the already wealthy. In Piketty's words, 'Capitalism automatically generates arbitrary and unsustainable inequalities that radically undermine the meritocratic values on which democratic societies are based.'[11]

Kuznets, it turns out, had been partially right: income inequality – and even wealth inequality – did fall in the US and Europe in the first half of the twentieth century. But what Piketty's analysis revealed was that Kuznets had conducted his study in the midst of an exceptional economic era. The equalising trend that he had ascribed to the inherent logic of capitalist development was actually due to the capital-depleting impacts of two world wars and the Great Depression, combined with unprecedented post-war public investment in education, healthcare and social security, all funded through progressive taxation. Kuznets's first intuition had in fact been right: when wealth is concentrated in few hands – and when the returns to capital are growing faster than the economy itself – inequality does indeed tend to rise. Success to the Successful rules after all, unless governments take action to offset it.

The Kuznets Curve may have been debunked, along with the claim that inequality is necessary for progress. But, like all powerful pictures, its memory lingers on, lending credence to the myth of trickle-down economics. In 2014 even economists at the International Monetary Fund (IMF) noted with frustration that, despite evidence to the contrary, 'the notion of tradeoff between redistribution and growth seems deeply embedded in policymakers' consciousness'.[12] Perhaps that is why, in the midst of severe recession following the 2008 financial crash, the vice-chairman of Goldman Sachs, Lord Griffiths, felt he could justify a return to lavish bonuses for his city traders with the claim that, 'We have to tolerate the inequality as a way to achieve greater prosperity and opportunity for all.'[13]

Why inequality matters

Inequality may not be inevitable but, in line with the neoliberal script, it was until recently seen as no cause for alarm, and certainly not as an appropriate target for policy. 'Of all the tendencies that are harmful to sound economics, the most seductive, and in my opinion the most poisonous, is to focus on questions of distribution,' wrote the influential economist Robert Lucas in 2004.[14] For most of the last 20 years at the World Bank, according to one of its lead economists, Branko Milanovic, 'even the word *inequality* was not politically acceptable, because it seemed like something wild or socialist'.[15] For others, the acceptable degree of social inequality came to be a matter of personal or political preference – as Britain's former prime minister Tony Blair quipped of the UK's top foot-baller, 'It's not a burning ambition for me to make sure that David Beckham earns less money.'[16] Over the past decade, however, per-spectives on inequality have shifted dramatically as its systemically damaging effects – social, political, ecological and economic – have become all too clear.

Societies can be deeply undermined by income inequality. When epidemiologists Richard Wilkinson and Kate Pickett studied a range of high-income countries in their 2009 book, *The Spirit Level,* they discovered that it is national inequality, not national wealth, that most influences nations' social welfare. More unequal countries, they found, tend to have more teenage pregnancy, mental illness, drug use, obesity, prisoners, school dropouts, and community breakdown, along with lower life expectancy, lower status for women, and lower levels of trust.[17] 'The effects of inequality are not confined to the poor,' they concluded; 'inequality damages the social fabric of the whole society.'[18] More equal societies, be they rich or poor, turn out to be healthier and happier.

Democracy, too, is jeopardised by inequality when it concentrates power in the hands of the few and unleashes a market in political influence. That is probably nowhere more evident than in the United States, which by 2015 was home to more than 500 billionaires. 'We are now seeing billionaires becoming much more active in trying to influence the election process,' observes political analyst Darrell

West, who has studied the antics of his nation's richest citizens, 'They're spending tens or hundreds of millions of dollars pursuing their own partisan interests, often in secret from the American public.'[19] The US former vice-president Al Gore concurs. 'American democracy has been hacked,' he says, 'and the hack is campaign finance.'[20]

Higher levels of national inequality, it turns out, also tend to go hand in hand with increased ecological degradation. Why so? In part because social inequality fuels status competition and conspicuous consumption, summed up in the only-half-joking US bumper sticker, 'He who dies with the most toys wins'. But also because inequality erodes social capital – built on community connections, trust and norms – that underpins the collective action needed to demand, enact and enforce environmental legislation.[21] Research into households' use of water in Costa Rica and use of energy in the US found that social pressure to reduce consumption to the community norm was far stronger within communities that considered themselves to be a group of peers.[22] Little surprise, then, that a study of all 50 US states found that those states marked out by larger inequalities of power – in terms of income and ethnicity – had weaker environmental policies and suffered greater ecological degradation.[23] Furthermore, one study covering 50 countries found that the more unequal a country is, the more likely is the biodiversity of its landscape to be under threat.[24]

Economic stability, too, is jeopardised when resources become concentrated in too few hands. That certainly became clear in the 2008 financial crisis. When the high-paid took on high-risk assets that turned out to be the bundled debts of the low-paid taking on mortgages that they could not afford, the result was system fragility and financial crash. Michael Kumhof and Romain Rancière, two economists at the IMF, analysed the 25-year run-up to that crash and found it bore uncanny similarities to the decade-long run-up to the Great Depression of 1929: both eras saw a large increase in the income share of the rich, a fast-growing financial sector, and a large increase in the indebtedness of the rest of the population – culminating in financial and social crisis.[25]

It is clear, then, that high income inequality entails many damaging effects. For low-income economies, these might once have seemed an unfortunate but necessary trade-off for the role that inequality was believed to play in generating faster economic growth – but that myth, too, has been debunked. Contrary to the founding theories of development economics, inequality does not make economies grow faster: if anything, it slows them down. And it does so by wasting the potential of much of the population: people who could be schoolteachers or market traders, nurses or micro-entrepreneurs – actively contributing to the wealth and well-being of their community – instead have to spend their time desperately trying to meet their families' most basic daily needs. When the poorest families in society have no money to pay for their essential needs, the poorest workers in society can get no work in supplying them, and so the market stagnates among those who need its dynamism most.

Such intuitive reasoning is backed by analysis: economists at the IMF have found strong evidence that, across a wide range of countries, inequality undercuts GDP growth.[26] 'More unequal societies have slower and more fragile economic growth,' writes Jonathan Ostry, the lead economist behind the IMF study. 'It would thus be a mistake to imagine that we can focus on economic growth and let inequality take care of itself.'[27] That is a powerfully important message, especially for policymakers in today's low- and middle-income countries, and one that clearly contradicts the 'no pain, no gain' myth of the Kuznets Curve.

Get with the network

With the Kuznets Curve debunked, and the damaging effects of inequality now starkly clear, a new mindset is emerging. Its message is simple:

Don't wait for economic growth to reduce inequality – because it won't.
Instead, create an economy that is distributive by design.

Such an economy must help to bring everyone above the Doughnut's social foundation. To do so, however, it must alter the distribution not only of income but also of wealth, time and power. A tall order? For sure. But many possibilities emerge if we set out with a

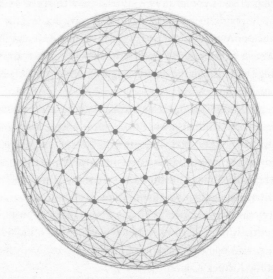

A network of flows: structuring an economy as a distributed network can more equitably distribute the income and wealth that it generates.

systems-thinker's mindset. A compelling starting place is to draw a new image, so what picture best encapsulates the principle of distributive design? In contrast to Pareto's pyramid and Kuznets's rollercoaster ride, its essence is a distributed network whose many nodes, larger and smaller, are interconnected in a web of flows.

As their recurring success in nature's designs shows, networks are excellent structures for reliably distributing resources throughout a whole system. In order to better understand the kind of networks that can make us thrive, network theorists Sally Goerner, Bernard Lietaer and Robert Ulanowicz studied the branching patterns and resource flows that are found in nature's ecosystems. From the cold-water springs of Iowa to the alligator-filled wetlands of South Florida, they found that the answer lies – as it so often does – in structure and in balance.

Nature's networks are structured by branching fractals, ranging from a few larger ones to many medium-sized ones and then myriad smaller ones, just like tributaries in a river delta, branches in a tree, blood vessels in a body, or veins in a leaf.[28] Resources such as energy, matter and information can flow through these networks in ways that achieve a fine balance between the system's *efficiency* and its *resilience*. Efficiency occurs when a system streamlines and simplifies its resource flow to achieve its aims, say by channelling resources directly between the larger nodes. Resilience, however, depends upon diversity and redundancy in the network, which means that there are ample alternative connections and options in times of shock or change. Too much efficiency makes a system vulnerable (as global financial regulators realised too late in 2008) while too much resilience makes it stagnant: vitality and robustness lie in a balance between the two.

What design principles can nature's thriving networks teach us for creating thriving economies? In two words: diversity and distribution. If large-scale actors dominate an economic network by squeezing out the number and diversity of small and medium players, the result will be a highly unequal and brittle economy. This certainly sounds familiar, given the current scale of corporate concentration across many industrial sectors, from agribusiness, pharmaceuticals and the media to the banks that are deemed too big to fail.

As Goerner and colleagues point out, the fragility generated by such concentration is reviving appreciation for the small, diverse enterprises that make up the bulk of an economy's network. 'Because we have over-emphasized large-scale organisations, the best way to restore robustness today would be to revitalize our small-scale fair-enterprise root system,' they conclude. 'Economic development must become more focused on developing human, community, and small-business capital because long-term, cross-scale vitality depends on these.'[29] The question, then, is how to design economic networks so that they distribute value – from materials and energy to knowledge and income – in a far more equitable way.

Redistributing income – and redistributing wealth

In the latter half of the twentieth century, policies aimed at national redistribution fell into three broad categories: progressive income taxes and transfers; labour market protections such as a minimum wage; and providing public services such as health, education and social housing. Beginning in the 1980s, the authors of the neoliberal script pushed back on each one. Fierce debate rose up over whether higher income taxes discouraged the high-paid from working more, and whether higher welfare payments trapped the low-paid into not working at all. Minimum wages and labour unions were portrayed not as protection for the poorest of workers but as a barrier to their employment. And the state's role in providing quality education, universal healthcare and affordable housing was depicted as an increasingly prohibitive public expense that simultaneously encouraged dependency.

Thanks to international public outrage over widening inequalities, ambition for greater redistribution has returned in the early twenty-first century. Many mainstream economists in high-income countries now advocate raising top marginal income tax rates along with higher taxes on interest, rent and dividends. Social activists worldwide have put companies and governments under pressure to pay living wages; the Asia Wage Floor Alliance, for example, is demanding a living wage for garment workers across Asia.[30] Others call for a maximum wage too, set within each company at around 20 to 50 times its lowest earner's wage, in order to curb excessive executive pay and ensure that corporate profits are more equitably shared amongst the workforce.[31] Some governments now offer guaranteed access to work, such as India's nationwide scheme that promises 100 days of minimum-wage employment each year to every rural household that needs it.[32] And citizens – from Australia and the USA to South Africa and Slovenia – are campaigning for a national basic income paid unconditionally to all, in order to ensure that, job or no job, every person has sufficient income to meet life's essentials.[33]

Such redistributive policies can be life-changing for those who benefit from them. But they still may not get to the root of economic inequalities, because they focus on redistributing income, not the wealth that generates it. Tackling inequality at root calls for democratising the ownership of wealth, argues the historian and economist Gar Alperovitz, because 'political-economic systems are largely defined by the way property is owned and controlled'.[34] So in addition to redistributing income, the economist's focus shifts towards redistributing sources of wealth too. If that sounds entirely unfeasible, a foolish pipe dream, then read on. Distributive design has an unprecedented opportunity this century to transform the dynamics of wealth ownership. Five opportunities stand out, concerning who controls land, money creation, enterprise, technology and knowledge – and all five are explored below.

Some of these opportunities depend upon state-led reforms, and so have to be seen as part of a long-term process of change. But others, crucially, can be initiated by grass-roots movements and emerge bottom-up, so can start now. Of course, many have already started. And by transforming the underlying dynamics of wealth, these innovations are helping to turn today's divisive economies into distributive ones, reducing both poverty and inequality in the process.

Who owns the land?

Redistributing land ownership has historically been one of the most direct ways to reduce national inequalities, as post-Second World War experience in countries like Japan and South Korea demonstrated. For people whose livelihoods and culture depend upon the land, secure land rights are essential. They enable farmers to take out loans, increase their crop yields, and build a secure future for their families and communities. That's especially true for women farmers: with strong land-inheritance rights, they can earn almost four times more income than those left land-insecure. In the village of Santinagar, West Bengal, 36 landless families became a community of landowners in 2010 thanks to a low-cost land purchase scheme devised by the land rights organisation, Landesa, and the state government. Among them were Suchitra Dey, her husband, and nine-year-old daughter. 'People used to call us rootless creatures,' she said, 'but now we feel proud as we have our own address.' On their micro-plot – roughly the size of a tennis court – they have built a house and grow vegetables. Selling the surplus has doubled the family's income, enabling Suchitra to put aside savings for her daughter's education.[35] It is clearly the start of a better life.

The trouble is, as populations and economies grow, the price of land rises, but no more of it can be supplied and so that shortage generates ever-higher rents for landowners. Mark Twain had his eye on this trend in nineteenth-century America: 'Buy land,' he quipped. 'They're not making it anymore.' His contemporary Henry George was struck by the inequity inherent in this set-up, which he witnessed first hand on his travels around America in the 1870s. But instead of encouraging his fellow citizens to buy land, he called on the state to tax it. On what grounds? Because much of land's value comes not from what is built on the plot but from nature's gift of water or minerals that may lie beneath its surface, or from the communally created value of its surroundings: nearby roads and railways; a thriving economy, a friendly neighbourhood; good local schools and hospitals. That certainly explains the real estate agent's timeless mantra: What determines house value? Location, location, location.

In 1914, one of George's supporters, Fay Lewis, decided to make this point with what today would be called political performance art. He bought up an empty lot on a street in his home town of

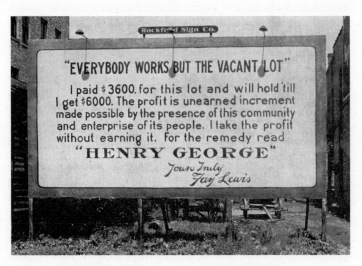

Political performance art by Fay Lewis, Rockford, Illinois, 1914.

179

Rockford, Illinois and left it derelict, erecting only a giant billboard to explain why. He even turned it into a postcard to spread the message far and wide.[36]

George's proposal for a land-value tax – an annual levy on underlying land values as a fair means of generating public revenue – echoed John Stuart Mill's earlier call to tax 'rentier landlords' who 'grow richer, as it were in their sleep, without working, risking, or economising'.[37] Inspired by such reasoning, land-value taxes are now in use – albeit in diluted form – from Denmark and Kenya to the US, Hong Kong and Australia. But taxation to George was essentially a substitute for a more systemic fix: land, he believed, should be owned in common by a community, rather than by landowners. 'The equal right of all men to the use of land,' he wrote, 'is as clear as their equal right to breathe the air.'[38] This view was a reaction against the long history of land enclosure, dating back to Henry VIII's strategy of disbanding England's monasteries in the sixteenth century and selling off their land. Over the following two centuries, the new land-owning aristocracy fenced off the collectively grazed village commons to establish vast private estates, simultaneously creating a large class of landless workers who had to choose between ploughing their landlords' fields or heading to industrial centres to find waged work. In the blunt words of the 1960s historian E. P. Thompson, 'Enclosure (when all the sophistications are allowed for) was a plain enough case of class robbery.'[39]

That historic takeover of rural England is emblematic of the centuries-long global trend of both the state and the market encroaching on common land, at first through colonisation, then through corporate expansion. It is on the rise again today, with renewed international investor interest triggered by the 2007–8 global food price crisis. Since 2000, foreign investors have made over 1,200 large-scale land deals in low- and middle-income countries, acquiring more than 43 million hectares of land – an area bigger than Japan.[40] In the majority of cases, those deals were land grabs:

signed without the free prior and informed consent of the indigenous and local communities that had inhabited and collectively stewarded that land for generations. In case after case, investors' promises to create new jobs, enrich community infrastructure and skill-up local farmers have come to nothing: instead many communities have found themselves dispossessed, dispersed and impoverished.[41]

Adam Smith's celebration of the self-organising market underpinned the justification given for turning land into private property, a justification that was later reinforced by Garrett Hardin's claim that the commons are inherently tragic. But, as we saw in Chapter 2, Elinor Ostrom challenged that belief when she started drawing attention to the equally powerful alternative of self-organising in the commons, and proved Hardin wrong. Gathering a rich array of case studies of 'common-pool' resource users, from Southern India to Southern California, she and her colleagues analysed how diverse communities had, sometimes for generations, successfully collaborated in harvesting, stewarding, and sustaining forests, fishing grounds and waterways.[42]

Many of those communities, in fact, managed their land and its common-pool resources better than markets did, and better than comparable state-run schemes. In Nepal, where rice farmers face the challenge of ensuring that every farmer gets sufficient water for irrigation, Ostrom and her colleagues compared irrigation schemes constructed and operated by the state with ones that were built and run by the farmers themselves. And they found that although the farmer-run irrigation schemes were more basic in build, they were kept in better repair, produced more rice, and distributed the available water more fairly among all their members. This self-organising system worked because the farmers developed their own rules for water use, met regularly in meetings and in the fields, set up a monitoring system, and sanctioned those who broke the rules.[43]

There are clearly many ways to share more equitably the wealth that lies beneath our feet. Ostrom was quick to point out, however, that there is no panacea for managing land and its resources well: neither the market, the commons, nor the state alone can provide an infallible blueprint. Approaches to distributive land design must fit the people and the place, and may well work best when they combine all three of these approaches to provisioning.[44]

Who makes your money?

We live in a monoculture of money, one so familiar and established that – like fish that have never noticed the water – we are barely aware of it. The money we know, be it dollars, euros, rupees or yen, is based on just one among many possible currency designs. This matters because money is not merely a metal disc, piece of paper, or electronic digit. It is, in essence, a social relationship: a promise to repay that is based on trust.[45] And the design of money – how it is created, the character it is given, and how it is to be used – has widespread distributive consequences. So what is this monetary water in which we swim?

In the majority of countries, the privilege of creating money has been handed to commercial banks, which create money every time they offer loans or credit. As a result, more money is made available only by their issuing more interest-bearing debt, and that debt is increasingly being channelled into activities like buying houses, land, or stocks and shares. Investments such as these do not create new wealth that generates additional income with which to pay the interest, but instead earn a return simply by pushing up the price of existing assets.[46] In the UK, for example, 97% of money is created by commercial banks and its character takes the form of debt-based interest-bearing loans. As for its intended use? In the ten years running up to the 2008 financial crash, over 75% of those loans were granted for buying stocks or houses – so fuelling the house-price bubble – while a mere 13% went to small businesses engaged in productive enterprise.[47] When such debt increases, a growing share of a nation's income is siphoned off as payments to those with interest-earning investments and as profit for the banking sector, leaving less income available for spending on products and services made by people working in the productive economy. 'Just as landlords were the archetypal rentiers of their agricultural societies,' writes economist Michael Hudson, 'so investors, financiers and bankers are in the largest rentier sector of today's financialized economies.'[48]

Once the current design of money is spelled out this way – its creation, its character, and its use – it becomes clear that there are many options for redesigning it, involving the state and the commons along with the market. What's more, many different kinds of money can coexist, with the potential to turn a monetary monoculture into a financial ecosystem.

Imagine, for starters, if central banks were to take back the power to create money and then issue it to commercial banks, while simultaneously requiring them to hold 100% reserves for the loans that they make – meaning that every loan would be backed by someone else's savings, or the bank's own capital. It would certainly separate the role of providing money from the role of providing credit, so helping to prevent the build-up of debt-fuelled credit bubbles that burst with such deep social costs. That idea may sound outlandish, but it is neither a new nor a fringe suggestion. First proposed during the 1930s Great Depression by influential economists of the day such as Irving Fisher and Milton Friedman, it obtained renewed support after the 2008 crash, gaining the backing of mainstream financial experts at the International Monetary Fund and Martin Wolf of the UK's *Financial Times*.[49]

State-owned banks could, furthermore, use money from the central bank to channel substantial low- or zero-interest loans into investments for long-term transformation, such as affordable and carbon-neutral housing and public transport. It would give a crucial boost to building the transformative assets that every economy now needs, and would shift power away from what Keynes called 'the rentier . . . the functionless investor'. Indeed, if the state intentionally kept interest rates very low, he argued:

> it would mean the euthanasia of the rentier, and, consequently, the euthanasia of the cumulative oppressive power of the capitalist to exploit the scarcity-value of capital. Interest today rewards no genuine sacrifice, any more than does the rent of land. The owner of capital can obtain interest because capital is scarce, just as the owner of land can obtain rent because land is scarce.[50]

States could also transform the distributive impact of monetary policy measures used during recessions. In mild recessions, central banks normally seek to boost the money supply by cutting interest rates in order to stimulate commercial bank lending and hence money creation. In deep recessions, however, once interest rates have already been cut very low, central banks attempt to further boost the money supply by buying back government bonds from commercial banks – a practice known as quantitative easing, or QE – in the hope that the banks will then seek to invest the extra money in expanding productive businesses. But as post-financial-crash experience demonstrated, commercial banks used that extra money to rebuild their own balance sheets instead, buying speculative financial assets like commodities and shares. As a result, the price of commodities such as grain and metals rose, along with the price of fixed assets like land and housing, but new investments in productive businesses didn't.[51]

What if, instead, central banks tackled such deep recessions by issuing new money directly to every household as windfall cash to be used specifically for paying down debts – an idea that has come to be known as 'People's QE'.[52] Rather than inflating the price of bonds, which tends to benefit wealthy asset owners, this approach – which resembles a one-off tax rebate for all – would benefit indebted households. Additionally, suggests the tax expert Richard Murphy, central banks could channel new money into national investment banks for 'green' and social infrastructural projects, such as community-based renewable energy systems, as part of the long-term infrastructural transformation that is urgently needed – an idea now known as 'Green QE'.[53]

Such ideas for state-led monetary redesign at first seem radical, but they are increasingly looking feasible. And at the same time as promoting greater economic stability, they would promote greater equality, tending to favour the low-income and indebted rather than favouring banks and asset owners.

Monetary redesign is under way in the commons too, with diverse communities creating their own complementary currencies to be used alongside a nation's official currency. 'Wherever there are unmet needs and spare resources,' explains financial economist Tony Greenham, 'we can find new ways of creating money.'[54] Issued from within their community of users, these currencies are sometimes paper, sometimes electronic, and are usually interest-free. Whether their use is intended to boost the local economy, empower marginalised communities, or reward work that is traditionally unpaid, such currency schemes are thriving, creating more resilient and more equitable local monetary ecosystems.

Take Bangladesh – not the country, but the sprawling slum district on the outskirts of Mombasa, Kenya, where money is tight and business is highly volatile, leaving many families frequently short of cash for life's essentials. In 2013, Bangla Pesa was launched as a complementary currency for use by small businesses within that community. The government's first response? To arrest the scheme's founder, Will Ruddick, an American community development worker, along with five of the currency's first users, for fear that its paper vouchers were aiming to oust the official Kenyan Shilling. But once government officials understood that Bangla Pesa actually served to complement, not compete with, Kenyan shillings, they released the group and instead began supporting them in spreading the scheme.

Over 200 traders, the majority of them women – from bakers and fruit sellers to carpenters and tailors – are now members of the network. Every new member must be endorsed by four others before being issued with Bangla vouchers, which they must commit to back with their own goods and services – thus ensuring that the scheme is underwritten by its own members.[55] Within two years of the scheme's launch, traders' total revenues had increased substantially, in good part thanks to the economic stability and liquidity provided by the scheme. Using Bangla vouchers to buy and sell within the network allows members to keep their Kenyan shillings to pay for essentials like electricity that demand hard cash. Furthermore, the complementary currency provides a buffer against the frequent slumps in cash spending in the community. When a three-day power cut hit the district in 2014, small businesses like John Wacharia's barber shop lost customers and cash revenue. But as a member of the network, he had an alternative means of exchange at hand. 'Bangla Pesa allowed me to provide for my family, eat, and survive when I could no longer work,' he said.[56]

Complementary currencies are not only for the cash-poor. Take St Gallen, a wealthy Swiss city that introduced time banking in 2012 in order to provide more care for elderly people. Its scheme, Zeitvorsorge, literally meaning 'time-provision', invites every citizen over the age of 60 to earn care-time credits by helping a local elderly resident with everyday tasks such as shopping and cooking, while also keeping them company. This makes it an ideal way for senior citizens to build up a 'time pension' to cover their own future needs for care and companionship. Zeitvorsorge distributes an initial stock of care-time credits – which are essentially its currency – among the city's more needy elderly residents, making the scheme socially redistributive from the outset. Each carer can earn up to 750 hours of time credits and the city council acts as guarantor, promising to redeem those credits for cash should the initiative fail.[57]

So far the scheme is only growing in popularity. Once a week Elspeth Messerli, aged 73, spends a day helping 70-year-old Jacob Brasselberg, whose multiple sclerosis confines him to a wheelchair. Why does Elspeth do it? 'The first two years after retirement I enjoyed life – and then I needed a goal again,' she explains, 'so I give today and I will take tomorrow, if I should need it.'[58] Of course schemes such as this one – in which care-currency is earned by giving care – are open to the concern that, like paying kids to read books, they risk replacing morals with money, albeit money of a very different kind. As such schemes spread, research is needed to investigate the full ripple of their social effects, and to explore how they can be designed in ways that serve to reinforce rather than replace the human instinct to care for others.

Complementary currencies can clearly enrich and empower communities but game-changing ones are now emerging, thanks to the invention of Blockchain. Combining database and network technologies, Blockchain is a digital peer-to-peer decentralised platform for tracking all kinds of value exchanged between people. Its name derives from the blocks of data – each one a snapshot of all transactions that have just been made in the network – which are linked together to create a chain of data blocks, adding up to a minute-by-minute record of the network's activity. And since that record is stored on every computer in the network, it acts as a public ledger that cannot be altered, corrupted or deleted, making it a highly secure digital backbone for the future of e-commerce and transparent governance.

One fast-rising digital currency that uses blockchain technology is Ethereum, which, among its many possible applications, is enabling electricity microgrids to set up peer-to-peer trading in renewable energy. These microgrids allow every nearby home, office or institution with a smart meter, Internet connection, and solar panel on its roof to hook in and sell or buy surplus electrons as they are generated, all automatically recorded in units of the digital currency. Such decentralised networks – ranging from a neighbourhood block to a whole city – build community resilience against blackouts and cut long-distance energy transmission losses at the same time. What's more, the information embedded in every Ethereum transaction allows network members to put their values into action in the microgrid market, for example by opting to buy electricity from the nearest or greenest suppliers, or only from those that are community-owned or not-for-profit.[59] And this is just one example of its potential. 'Ethereum is a currency for the modern age,' says the cryptocurrency expert David Seaman. 'It's a platform that could be really important to society down the road in ways that we can't even predict yet.'[60]

These very different examples illustrate a few of the myriad possibilities of monetary redesign, involving the market, the state and the commons. But each one makes clear that the way that money is designed – its creation, its character, and its intended use – has far-reaching distributional implications. Recognising this invites us to escape the monoculture of money and put the potential of distributive design at the heart of a new financial ecosystem.

Who owns your labour?

Stagnant wages have become a familiar story. Over the past three decades, the majority of workers across high-income countries have seen their wages barely increase, flatline, or even fall while executive pay has ballooned. In the UK, GDP has grown far faster than the average worker's wages since 1980, and the wage gap has widened too, resulting in the average worker earning 25% less than they otherwise would have done by 2010.[61] In the US, the years 2002–12 have been dubbed 'the lost decade for wages': while the economy's productivity grew by 30%, wages for the bottom 70% of workers were stagnant or in decline.[62] Even in Germany – where trade unions have far greater influence over industrial policy – the share of wages in national output fell from 61% of GDP in 2001 to just 55% by 2007, its lowest level in five decades.[63] Indeed, across all high-income countries, while workers' productivity grew by over 5% from 2009 to 2013, their wages rose just 0.4%.[64]

At the heart of this inequity lies a simple design question: who owns the enterprise, and so captures the value that workers generate? When the founding fathers of economics disagreed over how income would be distributed between labour, landlords and capitalists, they could all agree on one thing: that these were obviously three distinct groups of people. In the midst of the industrial revolution – when industrialists issued shares to wealthy investors while hiring penniless workers at the factory gate – that was a fair assumption. But what determined each group's respective share of earnings? Economic theory says it is their relative productivity, but in practice it has largely turned out to be their relative power. The rise of shareholder capitalism entrenched the culture of shareholder primacy, with the belief that a company's primary obligation is to maximise returns for those who own its shares.

There's a deep irony to this model. Employees who turn up for work day-in, day-out are essentially cast as outsiders: a production cost to be minimised, an input to be hired and fired as profitability requires. Shareholders, meanwhile, who probably never set foot on the company premises, are treated as the ultimate insiders: their narrow interest of maximising profits comes before all. No wonder that, under this set-up, the average worker has been losing out, especially since trade unions in many countries were stripped of their bargaining power from the 1980s onwards.

But this set-up is, of course, just one among many possible enterprise designs. It happens to have dominated the nineteenth and twentieth centuries but that doesn't mean it has to dominate the twenty-first. The analyst Marjorie Kelly has dedicated her career to understanding the effects of alternative enterprise designs, ranging from Fortune 500 corporations to local not-for-profits. For enterprise to be inherently distributive of the value it creates, she argues, two design principles are particularly key: *rooted membership* and *stakeholder finance*, and together they flip the dominant ownership model on its head.[65] Imagine if labour ceased to be the expendable outsider and became, instead, the ultimate insider, rooted in employee-owned firms. Imagine, too, if those enterprises raised finance not by issuing shares to outside investors but by issuing bonds, promising their stakeholder-investors not a slice of ownership but a fair fixed return. No need only to imagine, of course: such enterprises are growing fast.

Employee-owned companies and member-owned cooperatives have long been a cornerstone of distributive enterprise design, born out of the cooperative movement that took off in mid nineteenth-century England, offering its members better pay, greater job security, and a say in managing the business. It is a model that thrives today, from the Evergreen Cooperatives running greenhouses, laundries and solar installation services in Cleveland, Ohio to the Mamsera Rural Cooperative in Rombo, Tanzania, whose members grow high-quality coffee and manage tree nurseries. They are both part of a growing force: in 2012 the 300 largest cooperatives worldwide, covering agriculture, retail, insurance, and healthcare, generated $2.2 trillion in revenue – equivalent to the world's seventh largest economy.[66] In the UK, the John Lewis Partnership, a leading retailer for almost a century, has over 90,000 permanent staff named as Partners in the business. In 2011 the company raised £50 million in capital by inviting employees and customers to purchase five-year bonds in return for an annual 4.5% dividend plus 2% in shop vouchers.[67]

Other new business designs are now joining this long-established model to create a veritable ecosystem of enterprises. It is happening, in good part, thanks to innovative entrepreneurs and lawyers teaming up to write new kinds of corporate charters and company articles of association, which are effectively a company's user manual, setting out its objectives, structure, and employee or members' rights and duties. Redesign that and you've redesigned the DNA of business. From not-for-profits to community interest companies, the bottom-up experiment in business redesign is giving rise to a network of enterprise alternatives operating alongside the old-style corporate mainstream. 'What's underway is an ownership revolution,' says Todd Johnson, one of the innovative US lawyers rewriting corporate charters. 'It's about broadening economic power from the few to the many and about changing the mindset from social indifference to social benefit.'[68] These are the foundations of a dynamic and inspiring movement, but critics point out that mainstream corporate practice, driven by shareholder primacy, still dominates. 'Ultimately we will need to change the operating system at the heart of major corporations,' Kelly acknowledges. 'But if we begin there, we will fail. The place to begin is with what's doable, what's enlivening – and what points toward bigger wins in the future.'[69]

Who will own the robots?

'The digital revolution is far more significant than the invention of writing or even of printing,' said Douglas Engelbart, the acclaimed American innovator in human–computer interaction. He may well turn out to be right. But the significance of this revolution for work, wages and wealth hinges on how digital technologies are owned and used. So far, they have generated two opposing trends whose implications are only just beginning to unfold.

First, the digital revolution has given rise to the network era of near zero-marginal-cost collaboration, as we saw in the dynamic rise of the collaborative commons in Chapter 2. It is essentially unleashing a revolution in distributed capital ownership. Anyone with an Internet connection can entertain, inform, learn, and teach worldwide. Every household, school or business rooftop can generate renewable energy and, if enabled by a blockchain currency, can sell the surplus in a microgrid. With access to a 3D printer, anyone can download designs or create their own and print-to-order the very tool or gadget they need. Such lateral technologies are the essence of distributive design, and they blur the divide between producers and consumers, allowing everyone to become a prosumer, both a maker and user in the peer-to-peer economy.

So far, so empowering. But a parallel process of winner-takes-all dynamics is also in play. Instead of promoting a diversity of web-based enterprises and information providers, the Internet's strong network effects (with everyone wanting to be on the networks that everyone else is on) have transformed individual providers – like Google, YouTube, Apple, Facebook, eBay, Paypal, and Amazon – into digital monopolies that sit at the heart of the network society. They are now effectively running the global social commons in the interest of their own commercial ventures, while aggressively arming themselves with patents to guard that privilege.[70] The global governance to regulate these divisive dynamics is still sorely lacking yet is clearly going to be essential in order to reverse this rapid enclosure of the twenty-first century's most creative commons.

Alongside this, the digital revolution has brought a second trend of concentration. Just as it is empowering people with near zero-marginal-cost production, it is displacing people with near zero-humans-required production. Thanks to the rise of robots – machines that can mimic and outperform humans – many millions of jobs are at risk. Whose jobs exactly? Anyone with a role involving tasks, skilled or not, that a programmer could write software to perform, from warehouse stackers, car welders and travel agents to taxi drivers, paralegal clerks and heart surgeons. This wave of digital automation is still in its infancy, but it has already led to what the digital economy expert Erik Brynjolfsson has called the 'great decoupling' of production from jobs, seen most clearly in the United States. From the end of the Second World War until 2000, US productivity and employment were closely intertwined, but they have strongly diverged ever since: while productivity has kept on rising, employment levels have fallen flat.[71]

Technology has of course replaced workers before, and it can be to society's broad benefit when it frees people up to engage in other productive enterprise. In 1900, half of the US labour force worked in agriculture, assisted by over 20 million horses. Just over a century later, thanks to mechanisation only 2% of US workers are employed in agriculture, and the horses have all but gone.[72] But economic analysts worry that today's robot replacements are cutting across so many industrial and service sectors so fast that job creation in other fields simply cannot keep up. Millions of mid-skill jobs lost in the recession of 2007–09 have not come back because they have been replaced by software. Meanwhile, the jobs that have returned post-recession are typically menial, creating an hourglass economy that offers a few high-skill and many low-skill jobs with little in between. Analysts predict that five million jobs across 15 major economies could well be lost to automation by 2020.[73] And it is a worldwide trend, with the fastest-growing market for robots in China. There, the electronics manufacturing giant Foxconn, which employs around a million workers, plans to create a 'million robot army' and has already replaced 60,000 workers with robots in one factory alone.[74]

So how could distributive design help to prevent the economic segregation that technology appears to be driving? An obvious starting point is to switch from taxing labour to taxing the use of non-renewable resources: it would help to erode the unfair tax advantage currently given to firms investing in machines (a tax-deductible expense) rather than in human beings (a payroll tax expense). At the same time, invest far more in skilling people up where they beat robots hands-down: in creativity, empathy, insight and human contact – skills that are essential for many kinds of work, from primary school teachers and artistic directors to psychotherapists, social workers and political commentators. As Erik Brynjolfsson and his co-author Andrew McAfee put it, 'Humans have economic wants that can be satisfied only by other humans, and that makes us less likely to go the way of the horse.'[75]

That's reassuring, but only partly, because if most workers continue to earn income just from selling their labour alone, they will simply not earn enough. Wages, analysts anticipate, will fail to capture a big enough slice of the economic pie to ensure that everyone gets some of it, let alone a fair share of it. The future returns to paid employment are on track to create a deeply split labour market with vast inequalities – a prospect that strongly reinforces the rationale behind the many national campaigns demanding a basic income for all.

Human-niche work for some and a guaranteed income for all would make a smart start to handling the rise of the robots but it would leave low-wage workers and the workless forever lobbying to maintain such high levels of redistribution year on year. Far more secure is for every person to have a stake in owning the robot technology itself. What might that look like? Some advocate a 'robot dividend', an idea inspired by the Alaska Permanent Fund, which grants every Alaskan citizen, through a state constitutional amendment, an annual slice of the state's income arising from the oil and gas industry, a dividend that exceeded $2,000 per resident in 2015.[76]

That model could work for robots too but, thanks to current tax loopholes and a culture of privatised returns, many nation states – the US included – currently earn surprisingly little direct revenue from the multibillion-dollar digital economy, despite having invested substantial public money in the research, development and infrastructure underpinning it. That needs to change, argues the economist Mariana Mazzucato: when the state takes a risk, it deserves a return, which could be collected through royalties from co-owned public–private patents, or through state banks owning significant equity in businesses that use robot technologies based on publicly funded research.[77] Given the extreme disruption to work and hence incomes that is anticipated by the rise of the robots, more such innovative proposals are needed to ensure that the wealth generated by their productivity is widely distributed. That said, it is also time to look beyond the traditional binary choice of market versus state when it comes to controlling technology. Turn instead to the innovation taking place in the collaborative commons, which have the potential to transform the control of knowledge.

Who owns the ideas?

The international regime of intellectual property rights has significantly shaped the control and distribution of knowledge for hundreds of years. It's a story that began innocently enough in the fifteenth century, when Venice started awarding its famed glass-blowers 10-year patents to protect their novel creations from imitators. Show us how you made it, promised the law, and no one is permitted to copy you for a decade. It was a clever way for the city state to reward ingenuity, but as Venetian artisans emigrated, they took their demands for patents with them, so spreading the practice across Europe and across industries.[78]

The rise of patents, followed by copyright and trademarks, created intellectual property regimes that initially spurred on the industrial revolution but then began colonising the commons of traditional knowledge, with a growing number of patents seeking to monopolise know-how that had been collectively developed. With great irony, the intensive overuse and abuse of intellectual property law today is widely acknowledged to be stifling the very innovation that it was originally created to promote. Patents now last 20 years and are granted for a wide array of spurious inventions – ranging from Amazon's US patent on 'one-click' purchasing to the medical firm Myriad Genetics' patents on cancer-related genes.[79] And in many high-tech industries patents are frequently acquired tactically with the specific aim of blocking or suing competitors. 'We have designed an expensive and unfair intellectual property regime,' writes economist Joseph Stiglitz, 'that works more to the advantage of patent lawyers and large corporations than to the advancement of science and small innovators.'[80]

Mainstream economic theory claims that without intellectual property protection, innovators lack the incentive to bring new products to market because they cannot recoup their costs. But in the collaborative commons, millions of innovators are defying this received wisdom, co-creating and using free open-source software, known as FOSS, as well as free open-source hardware, or FOSH. It's a spirit embodied by Marcin Jakubowski, physicist and Missourian farmer, who – frustrated by the extortionate cost of farm machinery that kept breaking down – decided to build his own, while sharing his ever-improving designs online for free. His idea soon grew into the Global Village Construction Set, which aims to demonstrate step-by-step how to build from scratch 50 universally useful machines, from tractors, brick makers and 3D printers to sawmills, bread ovens and wind turbines. The designs have so far been recreated by innovators in India, China, the US, Canada, Guatemala, Nicaragua, Italy and France. Based on these successes, Jakubowski and his collaborators have since launched the Open Building Institute, which aims to make open-source designs for ecological, off-grid, affordable housing available to all.[81] 'Our goal is decentralized production,' he explains. 'I'm talking about a business case for efficient enterprise where the traditional concept of scale becomes irrelevant. Our new concept of scale is about distributing economic power far and wide.'[82]

Open-source design also promises large social benefits and vast cost savings for state-funded institutions in every country, says Joshua Pearce, a leading academic and engineer in free open-source hardware. His research into the economics of FOSH manufacturing finds that using open-source 3D printers and designs to produce essential scientific equipment – like the precision syringes used widely in labs and hospitals – slashes costs, making such equipment far more affordable and accessible worldwide. 'The inescapable conclusion,' says Pearce, 'is that FOSH development should be funded by organizations interested in maximizing return on public investments particularly in technologies associated with science, medicine and education.'[83]

The digital revolution has clearly unleashed an era of collaborative knowledge creation that could radically decentralise the ownership of wealth. But, argues the commons theorist Michel Bauwens, it is unlikely to reach its potential without state support. Just as corporate capitalism has long depended on the backing of government policies, public funding, and pro-business legislation, so now the commons need the backing of a Partner State whose aim is to enable the creation of common value.[84] How can the state start helping the knowledge commons to realise its potential? In five key ways.

First, invest in human ingenuity by teaching social entrepreneurship, problem-solving and collaboration in schools and universities worldwide: such skills will equip the next generation to innovate in open-source networks like no generation before them. Second, ensure that all publicly funded research becomes public knowledge, by contractually requiring it to be licensed in the knowledge commons, rather than permitting it to be locked away under patents and copyright for private commercial gain. Third, roll back the excessive reach of corporate intellectual property claims in order to prevent spurious patent and copyright applications from encroaching on the knowledge commons. Fourth, publicly fund the set-up of community makerspaces – places where innovators can meet and experiment with shared use of 3D printers and essential tools for hardware construction. And lastly, encourage the spread of civic organisations – from cooperative societies and student groups to innovation clubs and neighbourhood associations – because their interconnections turn into the very nodes that bring such peer-to-peer networks alive.

Going global

Due to the legacies of colonialism, unjust debt, forced privatisation and skewed trade rules imposed on the Global South, international inequalities are still extreme. Since 2000, global income inequality has narrowed slightly – largely thanks to poverty reduction in China – but the world as a whole still remains more unequal than any single country within it.[85] And that extreme skew in global incomes helps to push humanity beyond both sides of the Doughnut. For several centuries we have been encouraged to identify ourselves foremost as nations, each one with its own economy, looking over the border or across the water at 'others'. If we take the inevitable twenty-first-century step and each consider ourselves as part of a global community too, connected in a multi-layered but interdependent economy, what possibilities for globally redistributive design might emerge?

The promised means of international redistribution was overseas development assistance, ODA, but the history of its rich-to-poor transfers is nothing short of a myopic failure in global action. In a 1970 UN resolution, high-income countries pledged to contribute 0.7% of their annual income to ODA, and to do so by 1980 at the latest. But by 2013 – over 30 years beyond that deadline – the total stood at just 0.3%, less than half of what was promised each year. Well spent, that missing finance could have delivered decades of progress in maternal health, child nutrition, and girls' education in the world's poorest communities: it would have empowered women, transformed livelihoods, boosted national prosperity, and helped to stabilise the global population at the same time.[86]

Where high-income countries have broken their promise of financial redistribution, global migrants have stepped in. Out of their earnings, the remittances they send to their families back home are now the single largest source of external finance in many low-income countries, outstripping both ODA and foreign direct investment. Those worker remittances constitute around 25% of GDP in countries like Nepal, Lesotho and Moldova, and are a vital source of resilience during domestic economic and humanitarian crises.[87] That makes migration one of the most effective ways of reducing global income inequality. But its long-term success hinges on preventing wide income inequalities within the host countries themselves, and on building community connections and social capital. Without these, local communities that have been left behind economically often resort to blaming immigrants, instead of welcoming the diversity and dynamism that their presence can bring.

High-income countries have often justified their meagre record on ODA by arguing that, rather than being well spent, too much aid gets embezzled by corrupt leaders or wasted on poorly designed projects. Rigorous evaluations show that much overseas aid is in fact highly effective in tackling poverty, but there is no denying that it is sometimes abused. What if, then, a portion of that promised ODA were channelled directly to people living in poverty in those countries instead? It would act as a basic income, giving every person access to the market as a means of providing for their needs. What's more, for the first time in history such a scheme could actually work, thanks to the rapid worldwide spread of mobile phones and the proven success of mobile banking.

Kenya has been a trailblazer in mobile banking since launching its M-PESA mobile money service in 2007. Within six years, three quarters of all Kenyan adults had used the service, including 70% of those in rural areas, and – astonishingly – over 40% of Kenya's GDP was passing through M-PESA.[88] Worldwide, 5.5 billion people are expected to be using mobile phones by 2018, and mobile banking will come as part of the package.[89] In essence, it will soon be feasible to create a phone book of the world's 'bottom billion' and to text digital cash directly to them. Contrary to concerns that a guaranteed basic income would make people lazy or even reckless, cross-country studies of cash transfer schemes show no such effect: if anything, people tend to work harder and seize more opportunities when they know they have a secure fallback.[90] When it comes to delivering a basic income to the world's poorest people, the question is no longer 'how on earth?' but 'why on earth not?'[91]

The biggest and longest experiment in piloting such a scheme is getting under way in Kenya, set up by the US-based charity GiveDirectly. For the next 10–15 years, 6,000 of the poorest people in Kenya will regularly receive a guaranteed income that is enough to meet their family's basic needs, sent via their phone. By running such an extended pilot scheme, the charity hopes to give recipients the security needed to take longer-term life-changing decisions – and to prove that a universal basic income is an idea whose time has come.[92] There's only one caution: that private incomes are no substitute for public services. The market works best in tackling inequality and poverty when it complements, rather than replaces, the state and the commons. Accompanied by free-at-the-point-of-use provision of education and primary healthcare, such a basic income would be a direct investment in the potential of every woman, man and child, significantly advancing the prospects of achieving the Doughnut's social foundation for all.

How could additional funds – on top of 0.7% ODA – be raised in the spirit of global redistribution? Through a global tax on extreme personal wealth, for starters. There are now more than 2,000 billionaires living in 20 countries from the USA, China and Russia to Turkey, Thailand and Indonesia.[93] An annual wealth tax levied at just 1.5% of their net worth would raise $74 billion each year: that alone would be enough to fill the funding gap to get every child into school and deliver essential health services in all low-income countries.[94] Match that with a global corporate tax system that treats multinational corporations as single, unified firms, and closes tax loopholes and tax havens, so boosting public revenue for public purposes worldwide.[95] Supplement these with taxes on destabilising and damaging industries, such as a global financial transactions tax to curb speculative trading, and a global carbon tax levied on all oil, coal and gas production. Yes, some of these tax proposals sound unfeasible now, but so many once-unfeasible ideas – abolishing slavery, gaining the vote for women, ending apartheid, securing gay rights – turn out to be inevitable. In the century of the planetary household, global taxes will too.

If universal access to markets is to become a twenty-first-century norm, along with universal access to public services, then so too should universal access to the global commons – particularly to Earth's life-giving systems and to the global knowledge commons.

Given what we now understand about planetary boundaries, the integrity of the living world is clearly and profoundly in the common interest of all: clean air and clean water, a stable climate, and thriving biodiversity are among the most important 'common pool' resources for all of humanity. 'The great task of the twenty-first century,' writes the ecological thinker Peter Barnes, 'is to build a new and vital commons sector that can resist enclosure and externalization by the market, protect the planet, and share the fruits of our common inheritances more equitably than is now the case.'[96] One way of achieving this, he proposes, is to create an array of Commons Trusts, each one endowed with property rights enabling it to protect and steward a particular realm of Earth's commons – be it a local watershed or the global atmosphere – to the benefit of all citizens and future generations. In order to keep the use of these commons within local or planetary ecological boundaries, each trust would cap overall use and charge its users – such as companies extracting water from aquifers or offloading greenhouse gases into the sky – and share the benefits widely.[97] Some national trusts similar to these already exist but it will be a challenge to design global-scale ones, given the vast inequalities between rich and poor people and countries: who would be required to pay, who would share in the benefits, and how could historic ecological debts be repaid? These tough issues are the very governance questions to take on once we recognise Earth's life-giving systems as humanity's common heritage.

Creating a global knowledge commons, in contrast, is more immediately feasible, in good part because it is already under way. But its potential has barely been tapped. Imagine what a worldwide network of free open-source design might mean for the community innovators who have the most to gain from it. Back in 2002, William Kamkwamba, the 14-year-old son of drought-stricken Malawian farmers, had to drop out of secondary school because his parents could no longer afford to pay the fees. He went to the local library instead, read a textbook on energy, and set out to build his own windmill, in spite of his friends' and neighbours' ridicule. A local scrapheap was his only hope for materials so, using an old tractor fan, PVC pipes, an old bicycle frame, discarded bottle tops, and a dynamo, he rigged up a 16-foot windmill and connected the wires. It actually worked, generating enough electricity to power four light bulbs and two radios in his family home. Soon there was a queue of people at the door wanting to charge up their mobile phones, and a string of journalists reporting his remarkable invention. It was five whole years later, when invited to Arusha in Tanzania to give a TED talk, that William got to use a computer for the first time. 'I had never seen the Internet,' he later recalled. 'It was amazing ... I Googled about windmills and found so much information.'[98]

Kamkwamba's ingenuity is clearly exceptional, but there are already innovators and experimenters in every community who, with access to the Internet, the knowledge commons, and a makerspace, could

William Kamkwamba and his windmills.

copy, modify and invent technologies for tackling their own communities' most pressing needs, from rainwater harvesting and passive solar housing to agricultural tools, medical equipment and, yes, wind turbines. What's still missing, however, is a dedicated global digital platform enabling them to collaborate with researchers, students, enterprises and NGOs worldwide to develop free open-source technologies.

Imagine such a peer-to-peer platform built on all the features that make for top-quality collaborative networks: 'resource recipes' listing the tools, materials and skills required to replicate each item; user ratings and reviews of every design; photographs and diagrams tracking how those designs evolve; and portals for similar communities – such as solar-rich urban slums or drought-prone villages – to learn alongside each other's errors and successes.[99]

Creating such a platform will be disruptive because, says Joshua

Pearce, 'it will become a true rival to the paradigm of technology development that has dominated civilization since the industrial revolution'.[100] But it needs start-up funding, be it from foundations, governments, the UN, or via crowdsourcing. And it needs new forms of open-source licensing too, to ensure that old-style intellectual property claims – patents, copyright and trademarks – do not encroach upon the resurgent knowledge commons.

William was offered a scholarship to study at a US university and is now a 28-year-old graduate with plans to set up a makerspace and innovation centre in Malawi for school and university students. 'Many young people are talented and have brilliant ideas,' he explains, 'yet they don't exploit the full potential of these ideas because of a dearth of organizations that can incubate them.'[101] I asked him what he thought such a digital platform for the knowledge commons might do for those future innovators back home. His answer was immediate. 'It will allow them to get creative in solving problems across Africa,' he told me, 'because they will be able to learn from one another and keep on improving the designs that they make.'[102] Widening such access to the global knowledge commons will be one of the most transformative ways of redistributing wealth this century.

Where does all of this leave Arnold's gym routine? In the 1980s, doctors were quick to warn against the 'no pain, no gain' exercise mantra, pointing out that painful workouts often lead to injury, not fitness. Economists, misled for decades by the erroneous Kuznets Curve, have taken far longer to reach the same conclusion, but it is finally hitting home. Equitable economies don't emerge after an unavoidable process of economic pain: they are created by pursuing an intentional pattern of design. As far as the economy goes, pain is out and distributive design is in, leading to a fundamental shift in the economist's mindset. It's farewell to the mythical rollercoaster ride: bring on the network.

Rather than wait (in vain) for growth to deliver greater equality, twenty-first-century economists will design distributive flow into the very structure of economic interactions from the get-go. Instead of focusing on redistributing income alone, they will also seek to redistribute wealth – be it the power to control land, money creation, enterprise, technology or knowledge – and will harness the market, the commons and the state alike to make it happen. Rather than wait for top-down reform, they will work with bottom-up networks that are already driving a revolution in redistribution. What's more, they will match this revolution in distributive economic design with an equally powerful one in regenerative economic design, as the following chapter explores.

6

CREATE TO REGENERATE

from 'growth will clean it up again'
to regenerative by design

Travelling through Europe in 2015, I met Prakash, a student from India who was studying for an advanced engineering degree in Germany. When I asked whether he had opted to learn about ecologically smart technologies, he just shook his head and replied, 'No, India has other priorities – we are not rich enough to worry about that yet.' Surprised, I pointed out that almost half of India's land is degraded, the nation's groundwater levels are falling fast, and air pollution is the worst in the world. A flicker of recognition crossed his face but he just smiled and repeated his words, 'We still have other priorities.'

In one quick conversation, Prakash summed up the economic story that has been circulating for decades: poor countries are too poor to be green. What's more, they don't need to be because economic growth will eventually clean up the very pollution that it creates, and replace the resources that it runs down. It's a story that once appeared to be backed up by data, along with an iconic diagram to embed its message. But, despite its continuing grip on the imagination of politicians and publics alike, it has turned out to be a myth, in India just as in the rest of the world. 'India has performed remarkably economically,' points out Muthukumara Mani, a World Bank senior environmental economist, 'but that's not reflected in its environmental outcomes. "Grow now, clean up later" really doesn't work.'[1]

Ecological degradation is not a luxury concern for countries to leave on one side until they are rich enough to give it their attention. Rather than wait for growth to clean it up – because it won't – it is far smarter to create economies that are regenerative by design, restoring and renewing the local-to-global cycles of life on which human well-being depends. It is time to erase the old diagram whose influence lingers on and replace it with a twenty-first-century vision of regenerative economic design.

What goes up might not come down

In the early 1990s, US economists Gene Grossman and Alan Krueger discovered a striking pattern. Studying trend data for GDP side by side with data on local air and water pollution in around 40 countries, they found that pollution first rose then fell as GDP increased, tracing out the shape of an inverted-U when plotted on the page. Given its uncanny resemblance to that famous inequality curve of Chapter 5, this new one was soon known as the Environmental Kuznets Curve.

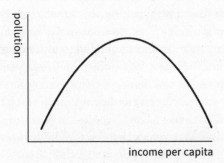

The Environmental Kuznets Curve, which suggests that growth will eventually fix the environmental problems that it creates.

Having discovered another apparent economic law of motion, the economists could not resist the urge to use statistical modelling in order to identify the level of income at which the curve magically turned. For lead contamination in rivers, they found, pollution peaked and started to fall when national income reached $1,887 per person (measured in 1985 US dollars, the standard metric of the day). What about sulphur dioxide in the air? That appeared to fall when income hit $4,053 per person. As for black smoke? Wait until GDP exceeds $6,151 per capita and it will begin to clear. Overall, they claimed, growth would start to clean up air and water pollution before countries hit the $8,000 per capita mark – equivalent to around $17,000 today.[2]

It's hard to miss the irony: just as the debunked Kuznets Curve was being ushered out of the economic limelight, its environmental cousin stepped centre stage. But Grossman and Krueger, like Kuznets before them, were careful to add a caveat to their findings. They acknowledged that they only had data for local air and water pollutants, not for concerns like global greenhouse gas emissions, biodiversity loss, soil degradation, and deforestation. They noted that national outcomes depended on the politics, technologies and economics of the day. And they pointed out that an observed correlation between economic growth and falling pollution didn't demonstrate that growth itself caused the clean-up. But, like most economists who think they have uncovered an economic law of motion, they couldn't resist drawing the conclusion that, for most environmental indicators, 'economic growth brings an initial phase of deterioration followed by a subsequent phase of improvement'.[3]

Despite those careful caveats their hypothesis soon turned into a widely cited economic mantra, repeated in policy briefings, newspaper op-eds, and economics lectures worldwide: when it comes to pollution, growth – like a well-trained child – will clean up after itself. Some, like the pro-market economist Bruce Yandle, twisted this message into the much stronger claim that 'economic growth helps to undo the damage done in earlier years. If economic growth is good for the environment, policies that stimulate growth (trade liberalisation, economic restructuring, price reform) ought to be good for the environment.'[4] Yes, 'no pain, no gain' economics was back in town, this time recommending a perverse fitness regime for the living world. If you want clean air and water, healthy forests and oceans, then here's the deal: it's got to get worse before it gets better – and growth will make it better. So grit your teeth and feel the burn.

With the curve and its equations in hand, mainstream econo-mists mocked what they called the 'alarmist cries' of environmental critics who argued that economic growth was severely degrading Earth's soils, oceans, ecosystems and climate. Still, they acknow-ledged that there was no proof of a direct link between economic growth and environmental clean-up, so they put forward three pos-sible explanations for it. First, as countries grow, they argued, their citizens can afford to start caring about the environment and so begin to demand higher standards; second, the nation's industries can afford to start using cleaner technologies; and third, those industries will shift from manufacturing to services, swapping smoke stacks for call centres.

They might sound credible at first but these explanations for the curve's rise then fall don't stand up to scrutiny. First, citizens do not have to wait for GDP growth to deliver them the desire and power to demand clean air and water. That's what Mariano Torras and James K. Boyce concluded when they matched up the very same cross-country data used to create the Environmental Kuznets Curve with measures of citizen power. Across a wide range of countries – and particularly in low-income ones – they found that environmental quality is higher where income is more equitably distributed, where more people are literate, and where civil and political rights are bet-ter respected.[5] It's people power, not economic growth per se, that protects local air and water quality. Likewise it is citizen pressure on governments and companies for more stringent standards, not the mere increase in revenue, that compels industries to switch to cleaner technologies. Third, cleaning up a nation's air and water by shifting from manufacturing to service industries doesn't eliminate those pollutants: it sends them overseas, letting someone else, somewhere else, feel the burn while those back home can import the neatly packaged finished product. That means it is a strategy for environmental clean-up that cannot be followed by all countries because eventually there will be nowhere left to outsource the pollution.

Lacking broader data, Grossman and Krueger could not investigate whether the Environmental Kuznets Curve's rise and fall held true for wider ecological impacts such as greenhouse gas emissions, groundwater depletion, deforestation, soil degradation, agrochemical use, and biodiversity loss. Nor could they assess how much of each nation's environmental impact was being incurred overseas. But thanks to advances in natural-resource-flow accounting those data are fast improving – and they tell a very different story from the one widely touted.

The extraction and processing of Earth's materials within the borders of high-income countries has indeed been falling, leading to triumphant claims across the EU and the OECD of rising resource productivity and the decoupling of GDP growth from resource use – both touted as early evidence of the 'green growth' dream. But the celebrations have come too soon. 'These trends make developed countries look more resource-efficient,' warns Tommy Wiedmann, one of the experts spearheading the analysis of international resource flows, 'but they actually remain deeply anchored to a material foundation underneath.'[6]

Recently compiled international data reveal that when a nation's global material footprint is taken into account – by adding up all of the biomass, fossil fuels, metal ores, and construction minerals used worldwide to create the products that the country imports – then the success story seems to evaporate. From 1990 to 2007, as GDP grew in high-income countries, so did their global material footprints. And not just by a little bit: the US, the UK, New Zealand and Australia all saw their footprints grow by more than 30% over that period; in Spain, Portugal and the Netherlands they grew by over 50%. Japan's footprint, meanwhile, grew by 14% and Germany's by 9%: impressively lower than the rest, but still growing.[7] Far from the promised rise and fall of the Environmental Kuznets' Curve, these data point to a disturbing rise and rise.

Calculating global material footprints is a complex business, however, and some disagree with these findings. The resource analyst Chris Goodall, for one, compiled an alternative set of data for the UK in which the nation's resource consumption – including imports – appears to have peaked and plateaued, or even started to decline.[8] But even if these alternative data turned out to be close to accurate, there would still be a problem: the UK's consumption would have peaked at an unfeasibly high level. If other countries were to follow suit – trusting that growth would eventually lead them to a similar peak and decline – it would require the resources of at least three planet Earths, pushing the global economy into extreme overshoot beyond planetary boundaries.[9] In other words, if it turns out to exist at all, then the Environmental Kuznets Curve is a mountain that humanity simply cannot afford to climb because we cannot survive its peak.

Facing up to the degenerative linear economy

It's time to put aside the search for economic laws demonstrating that growing national output will eventually deliver ecological health. Economics, it turns out, is not a matter of discovering laws: it is essentially a question of design. And the reason why even the world's richest countries are still making us all feel the burn is because the last two hundred years of industrial activity have been based upon a linear industrial system whose design is inherently degenerative. The essence of that industrial system is the cradle-to-grave manufacturing supply chain of take, make, use, lose: extract Earth's minerals, metals, biomass and fossil fuels; manufacture them into products; sell those on to consumers who – probably sooner rather than later – will throw them 'away'. When drawn in its simplest form, it looks something like an industrial caterpillar, ingesting food at one end, chewing it through, and excreting the waste out of the other end.

This ubiquitous industrial model has delivered strong profits to many businesses and has financially enriched many nations in the process. But its design is fundamentally flawed because it runs counter to the living world, which thrives by continually recycling life's building blocks such as carbon, oxygen, water, nitrogen and phosphorus. Industrial activity has broken these natural cycles apart, depleting nature's sources and dumping too much waste in her sinks. Extracting oil, coal and gas from under land and sea,

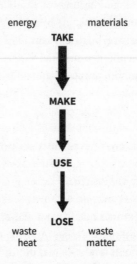

The caterpillar economy of degenerative industrial design.

burning them, and dumping carbon dioxide in the atmosphere. Turning nitrogen and phosphorus into fertiliser, then offloading the effluent – from agricultural run-off and sewage – into lakes and oceans. Uprooting forests to mine metals and minerals which, once packed into consumer gadgets, will be cast onto e-waste dumpsites, with toxic chemicals leaching out into the soil, water and air.

Economic theory recognises the potentially damaging effects – the 'negative externalities' – of such industry, and has its favoured market-based tools for addressing them: quotas and taxes. To internalise those externalities, the theory advises, put a cap on total pollution, assign property rights with quotas, and allow market trading to put a price on the right to pollute. Or impose a tax equivalent to the 'social cost' of pollution, and then let the market decide how much pollution it is worth emitting.

Such policies can have significant effect. From 1999 to 2003, Germany's eco-tax raised the price of fossil fuels used for transport, heating and electricity, while lowering payroll taxes by an equivalent amount: it cut fuel consumption by 17% and carbon emissions by 3%, increased car sharing by 70%, and created 250,000 jobs.[10] California's carbon cap-and-trade scheme, launched in 2013, aims to bring the state's greenhouse gas emissions back to 1990 levels by 2020. It still gives industry most of the quota for free, but intends to reduce the total quota and auction more of those permits over time, while using a price floor to avoid the collapse of permit prices, as occurred in Europe's equivalent carbon-trading scheme.[11]

Tiered pricing is growing in use too, ensuring that the more that people use, the more they pay. From Santa Fe, California to water-stressed cities across China, tiered pricing is used to ration water use between households of widely differing incomes. Every household pays a low rate for its initial daily supply, intended for essentials such as drinking, bathing, and washing dishes and clothes. Beyond that – whether it is for cleaning cars, irrigating lawns or filling swimming pools – further water use is charged at three or four times higher rates. As water market expert Roger Glennon explains, 'The beauty of tiered pricing is that it doesn't prevent people from using water, and it doesn't rely on government regulations. But it insists you pay more for extra water for your lawn than for basic human needs.'[12] In Durban, South Africa, where access to water is recognised as a constitutional human right, each day's essential supply is provided free to all low-income households, with pricing only kicking in beyond that level.[13]

Taxes, quotas and tiered pricing can clearly help to ease humanity's pressure on Earth's sources and sinks, but here's the trouble with believing that they will do the whole job. In practice they fall short because they are rarely set to the level required: corporations lobby hard to delay their introduction, to lower the tax rate, to increase the quota, and to get permits given for free, not auctioned. Governments, in return, too often concede, fearing that their nation will lose competitiveness – and that their political parties will lose corporate backing. These policies fall short in theory too: from a systems-thinking perspective, quotas and taxes to limit the stock and reduce the flow of pollution are indeed leverage points for changing a system's behaviour – but they are low points of leverage. Far greater leverage comes from changing the paradigm that gives rise to the system's goals.[14]

When industry is based upon the degenerative linear design of take-make-use-lose, there is only so much that price incentives can do to mitigate its depleting effects. The visionary landscape architect John Tillman Lyle clearly recognised the limits inherent in such design. 'Eventually a one-way system destroys the landscapes on which it depends,' he wrote in the 1990s. 'The clock is always running and the flows always approaching the time when they can flow no more. In its essence, this is a degenerative system, devouring the sources of its own sustenance.'[15] What's needed in its place is a paradigm of regenerative design – and that paradigm is now emerging, giving rise to a fascinating spectrum of business responses.

Can we do business in the Doughnut?

When companies first become aware of the scale of pressure that degenerative industrial design puts on Earth's planetary boundaries, what do they do? Over the past five years I have presented the concept of the Doughnut to a wide range of business leaders, from senior executives in Fortune 500 companies to the founders of community enterprises. Their responses have varied widely, reflecting the many stages that lie on the journey from degenerative to regenerative design – and they can be summed up with what I call the Corporate To Do List.

The first and oldest response is simple: *do nothing*. Why change our business model, they reason, when it is delivering strong returns today? Our responsibility is to maximise our profits so until environmental taxes or quotas are introduced to shift the incentives we face, we'll carry right on. What we are doing is (mostly) legal and if we get fined, we tend to consider it a cost of business. For decades, the majority of companies worldwide took this tack, treating sustainability as a nice-to-have that they didn't need to have because it did nothing for the share price. But times are changing fast. Many manufacturers who depend upon worldwide suppliers – such as cotton growers and coffee farmers, wine makers and silk weavers – now realise that their own product supply chains are vulnerable to the impacts of rising global temperatures and falling water tables, so recognise that doing nothing no longer seems such a smart strategy.

That's why the next-step response has become the most common: *do what pays*, by adopting eco-efficiency measures that cut costs, or boost the brand. Cutting greenhouse gas emissions and reducing industrial water use are classic efficiency measures that tend to boost company profits in the process, especially in the early stages. That said, some companies evidently believe it pays more to deceive: Volkswagen gained notoriety in 2015 when it was caught fitting

215

millions of its diesel cars with 'defeat device' software that switched their engines into a low-emissions mode during tests, so significantly under-reporting their nitrogen oxide and carbon dioxide emissions.[16] Others pursue the credentials of 'green' product branding that appeals to consumers willing to pay a premium for eco-friendly products. Motivated by this kind of green positioning, such companies benchmark their progress against industry competitors: it's a start, yes, but the most that it demonstrates is that 'we are doing more than our competitors' or 'we are doing more than we did last year'. And that is very likely to be a long way off what's needed.

The third response – getting more serious now – is to *do our fair share* in making the switch to sustainability. To their credit, companies taking this approach at least start by acknowledging the scale of change needed based on, say, the total reduction in greenhouse gas emissions, fertiliser use, or water withdrawals that is recommended by Earth-system scientists or required by national policy targets. One well-intended example comes from South Africa's Nedbank, which in 2014 committed to channel its 'fair share' of commercial financing – equivalent to $400 million per year – into investments that promote the nation's goals for 2030, such as affordable, low-carbon energy services, and sustainable clean water and sanitation for all. 'Fairshare 2030 is money working for the future we want,' says the bank's chief executive.[17] True, but it still begs the question of what the rest of the bank's money is doing. Furthermore, as anyone knows who has ever been left holding the restaurant bill once their fellow diners have chipped in with what they think is their fair share, it almost never adds up. Self-determined fair shares never quite get the job done – as the world's governments have demonstrated with their woefully inadequate, nationally-determined pledges to cut their greenhouse gas emissions.

More worryingly, 'doing our fair share' can too easily slip into 'taking our fair share'. On first encountering the Doughnut, many businesses seem to look upon its outer ring of planetary boundaries as if it were a cake to be sliced up and handed out. And, like all kids at a birthday party, they want their fair share. Still trapped in the mindset of degenerative, linear industry, the first question that many ask is: how big a slice of that ecological cake is ours? How many tonnes of carbon dioxide can we emit? How much groundwater can we withdraw? The answer is likely to be far less than they currently do, so it certainly raises the bar of ambition. But 'taking your fair share' reinforces the view that the 'right to pollute' is a resource worth competing for. And when competing over limited resources, we humans too easily start to jostle for space, lobbying policymakers and gaming the system, significantly raising the risk of transgressing the boundaries in the process.

The fourth response – and it is a true step-change in outlook – is to *do no harm*, an ambition that is also known as 'mission zero': designing products, services, buildings and businesses that aim for zero environmental impact. Examples aspiring to that goal include 'zero-energy' buildings like the Bullitt Center in Seattle which (despite that city's reputation for relentless rain) uses solar panels to generate as much energy as it uses each year. Net-zero-water factories likewise make no net withdrawals from public water supplies, such as Nestlé's dairy plant in Jalisco, Mexico, which meets all its industrial water needs by condensing the steam evaporated from the cows' milk, instead of continually extracting fresh water from the region's severely stressed groundwater reservoirs.[18]

Aiming for net-zero impact is a truly impressive departure from the business-as-usual of degenerative industrial design, and it is more impressive still if the aim is net zero not just in energy or water but in all resource-related aspects of a company's operation – a still far-off goal. It is also a sign of profound efficiency in resource use but, as the architect and designer William McDonough has put it, the avid pursuit of resource efficiency is simply not enough. 'Being less bad is not being good,' he says. 'It is being bad, just less so.'[19]

And, once you think about it, pursuing mission zero is an odd vision for an industrial revolution, as if intentionally stopping on the threshold of something far more transformative. After all, if your factory can produce as much energy and clean water as it uses, why not see if it could produce more? If you can eliminate all toxic materials from your production process, why not introduce health-enhancing ones in their place? Instead of aiming merely to 'do less bad', industrial design can aim to 'do more good' by continually replenishing, rather than more slowly depleting, the living world. Why simply take nothing when you could also give something?

That's the essence of the fifth business response: *be generous* by creating an enterprise that is regenerative by design, giving back to the living systems of which we are a part. More than an action on a to-do checklist, it is a way of being in the world that embraces bio-sphere stewardship and recognises that we have a responsibility to leave the living world in a better state than we found it.[20] It calls for creating enterprises whose core business helps to reconnect nature's cycles, and that gift as much as they can – because only generous design can bring us back below the Doughnut's ecological ceiling. For Janine Benyus, a leading thinker and doer in the field of bio-mimicry, this notion of generosity has become the design mission of a lifetime. As she told me,

> We are big-brained animals, but we are newcomers on this planet, so we are still acting like toddlers expecting Mother Nature to clean up after us. I want us to take on this design task and become full participants in every one of nature's cycles. Start with the carbon cycle – let's learn to halt our industrial 'exhale' of carbon pollution, and then, by mimicking plants, learn to 'inhale' carbon dioxide into our products and store it for centuries in rich agricultural soils. Once we've cut our teeth on the carbon cycle, let's apply what we have learned to the phosphorus, nitrogen, and water cycles, too.

To discover the essence of generous design, she suggests that we take nature as our model, measure and mentor. With nature as *model*, we can study and mimic life's cyclical processes of take and give, death and renewal, in which one creature's waste becomes another's food. As *measure*, nature sets the ecological standard by which to judge the sustainability of our own innovations: do they measure up and fit in by participating in natural cycles? And with nature as *mentor*, we ask not what we can extract, but what we can learn from its 3.8 billion years of experimentation.[21]

Each tick-box on the Corporate To Do List could be seen as a stage on the path to regenerative design: for individual companies, what matters as much as where you are now is where you are heading. But there is no need (nor indeed time) to make that value shift step by step: far more inspired is to transform – like a caterpillar into a butterfly – into generous design.

Which one is your business aiming to do?

The circular economy takes flight

Industrial manufacturing has begun the metamorphosis from degenerative to regenerative design through what has come to be known as the 'circular economy'. It is regenerative by design because it harnesses the endless inflow of the sun's energy to continually transform materials into useful products and services.[22] So bid farewell to the linear industrial economy's caterpillar as, before your eyes, it turns into a butterfly, in a diagram based on one created by the Ellen MacArthur Foundation.[23] And, just as with real butterflies, the brilliance lies in the wings.

What are the design features that enable this industrial butterfly to take flight? First, focus in on the old cradle-to-grave mentality of the linear economy that incited the twentieth century's voracious mining for minerals, drilling for oil, and burning of waste.

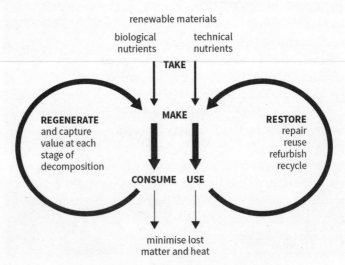

The butterfly economy: regenerative by design.

That caterpillar, the throwaway economy of take-make-use-lose, still flows from top to bottom through the centre of the diagram. But watch as it turns into a butterfly thanks to cradle-to-cradle thinking in the circular economy.[24] It runs on renewable energy – from solar, wind, wave, biomass and geothermal sources – eliminating all toxic chemicals and, crucially, eradicating waste by design. It does so by recognising that 'waste equals food': instead of heading for landfill, the leftovers from one production process – be they food scraps or scrap metal – become the source materials for the next. The key to making this work is to think of all materials as belonging to one of two nutrient cycles: *biological* nutrients such as soil, plants and animals, and *technical* nutrients such as plastics, synthetics and metals. The two cycles become the butterfly's two wings, in which materials are never 'used up' and thrown away but are used again and again and again through cycles of reuse and renewal.

On the biological wing, all nutrients are eventually consumed and regenerated through the living earth. The key to using them endlessly is to: ensure that they are harvested no faster than nature regenerates them; harness their many sources of value as they cascade through the cycles of life; and design production in ways that gift back to nature. Take coffee beans as a simple example: less than one per cent of every bean ends up in a cup of coffee and the leftover coffee grounds are rich in cellulose, lignin, nitrogen, and sugars. It would be foolish to throw such organic treasure straight on to a compost heap or, far worse, into a rubbish bin, but this happens in homes, offices and coffee shops worldwide. Coffee grounds, it turns out, make an ideal medium for growing mushrooms, and then can be used as feed for cattle, chickens and pigs, and so are returned to the soil as manure. From the humble coffee bean, imagine scaling that principle up to all food, crops and timber, and scaling it out to every home, farm, firm and institution: it would start to transform our last-century forestry and food industries into regenerative ones that

221

reap value from and then regenerate the living systems on which they depend.

On the butterfly's other wing, in contrast, products made using technical nutrients such as metals and synthetic fibres do not naturally decompose so they must be designed to be restored – through repair, reuse, refurbishment, and (as a last resort) recycling. Take mobile phones, for example, which are chock-full of gold, silver, cobalt, and rare earth metals, but are typically used for just two years. In the European Union, over 160 million mobile phones are sold annually, but in 2010 only 6% of used phones were being reused, and 9% disassembled for recycling: the remaining 85% ended up in landfill or lay defunct in the back of some drawer.[25] In a circular economy they would be designed for easy collection and disassembly, leading to their refurbishment and resale, or the reuse of all their parts. Scale those principles across all industries and you start to turn twentieth-century industrial waste into twenty-first-century manufacturing food.

It's inspired stuff, but don't get carried away on the butterfly's wings because the notion of a truly circular economy belongs with the fantasy of perpetual motion machines: a more accurate name would be the cyclical economy. No industrial loop can recapture and reuse 100% of its materials: Japan impressively recycles 98% of metal used domestically, but there's still an elusive 2% leaking from that loop. And given enough time, all technical materials – from metals to plastics – will start to rust or decay. But if we start to look upon every object, be it an eighteenth-century building or the latest smartphone, as if it were a battery storing valuable materials and energy, then we begin to focus on retaining or reinventing that stored value. And since we have the extraordinary luck of being bathed in a constant river of solar energy, we can – like all living things – be ingenious in harnessing that real-time energy to restore what we have created, and to regenerate the living world in which we thrive.

In a degenerative industrial economy, value is monetary and it is created by searching for ever-lower costs and ever-greater product sales: the typical result has been intense material throughflow. In a regenerative economy, that material throughflow is transformed into *round-flow*. But the real transformation comes from a new understanding of value. 'There is no wealth but life,' as John Ruskin wrote in 1860. His words were poetic but they were prophetic too. Economic value lies not in the throughflow of products and services but in the wealth that is their recurring source. That includes the wealth embodied in human-made assets (from tractors to houses) but also the wealth embodied in people (from their individual skills to community trust), in a thriving biosphere (from the forest floor to the ocean floor), and in knowledge (from Wikipedia to the human genome). Yet even these forms of wealth eventually dissipate: tractors rust; trees decompose; people die; ideas are forgotten. Only one form of wealth persists through time and that is the regenerative power of life, powered by the sun. Ruskin was evidently a regenerative pioneer.

Welcome to the generous city

Factories and industries can be regenerative by design and so too can urban landscapes. Janine Benyus is bringing to life her vision to create what she calls 'generous cities': human settlements that nestle within the living world. As a first step in the process, she starts by observing a city's local native ecosystem – such as the nearby forest, wetland or savannah – and records the rate at which it harvests solar energy, sequesters carbon, stores rainwater, fertilises soil, purifies the air, and more. These metrics are then adopted as the new city standard, challenging and inspiring its architects and planners to create buildings and landscapes that are 'as generous as the wildland next door'. Rooftops that grow food, gather the sun's energy, and welcome wildlife. Pavements that absorb storm water then slowly release it into aquifers. Buildings that sequester carbon dioxide, cleanse the air, treat their own wastewater, and turn sewage back into rich soil nutrients. All connected in an infrastructural web that is woven through with wildlife corridors and urban agriculture.[26] Such design possibilities arise out of regenerative, not degenerative, questions. 'Don't ask: what's my fair share to take?' Benyus explains. 'Ask: what other benefits can we layer into this so we can give some away?'[27]

Imagine if such a regenerative city were also distributive by design. Renewable energy microgrids would turn every household into an energy provider. Affordable housing connected by dedicated public transport routes would make the cheapest form of travel the fastest. Neighbourhood enterprise hubs would allow parents to be parents again by bringing the workplace and home closer together for women and men alike. And given that its life-regenerating infrastructure would be 'high-touch', as Benyus calls it, it would need people to continually tend, steward and maintain its regenerative capacity, so creating purposeful, skilful jobs in the process.

No such city can yet be found on a map of the world, but there are enterprises and projects aiming to put its design principles into practice across continents. In the Netherlands, Park 20|20 is a business park designed on 'cradle to cradle' principles, constructed with recyclable materials, an integrated energy system, a water treatment facility, and roofs that collect solar energy, store and filter water, block heat, and provide wildlife habitats.[28] In California, the company Newlight Technologies is capturing methane emissions from dairy cows, turning them into bioplastic and making products – such as bottles and office chairs – which have been independently verified as carbon-negative, sequestering greenhouse gas emissions across their entire life cycle.[29] In the arid coastal lands of South Australia, Sundrop Farms is using seawater and sunlight to grow tomatoes and capsicums. Its state-of-the-art greenhouses harness solar energy to desalinate the saltwater, create heat, and generate

How can a city be as generous as a forest?

electricity, all used to grow the crops. 'We're not just addressing an energy issue or a water issue,' says Philipp Saumweber, Sundrop's CEO, 'we are addressing both of those together to produce food from abundant resources, and to do that in a sustainable way.'[30]

Villages, towns and cities in low- and middle-income countries are embracing regenerative design principles too. Bangladesh aims to become the first solar-powered nation and is training thousands of women as solar engineers who can install, maintain and repair renewable energy systems in their own villages.[31] In Tigray, Ethiopia, over 220,000 hectares of desertified land have – astonishingly – been regenerated since 2000 thanks to farming communities that have built terraces and planted bushes and trees. They have restored once-barren hillsides to lush valleys that provide grain, vegetables and fruit for the surrounding villages and cities, while sequestering carbon, storing water, and rebuilding the soil.[32] In Kenya, social enterprises such as Sanergy are building hygienic toilets in slum districts and turning 100% of the human waste they collect into biogas and organic fertiliser for sale to local farms – improving human health and creating much-needed jobs while cutting nitrogen pollution and increasing soil fertility.[33] Likewise in Brazil, the start-up enterprise ProComposto collects organic waste from city restaurants, apartment blocks and supermarkets, turning it into fertiliser for organic farming. By saving biological materials from the landfill, the company is cutting methane emissions, enriching the soil with carbon instead, and creating jobs.[34]

These pioneering examples are inspiring but they still prompt important questions. For instance, Park 20|20's buildings are made of recyclable materials – but will they, one day, actually be recycled? Sundrop Farms' greenhouses are mostly powered by the sun but occasionally rely on a back-up gas boiler on cloudy days: could they still succeed without it?[35] If Newlight's production of plastic from methane were significantly scaled up, might it give rise to unforeseen ecological impacts? Too many village-level solar energy

226

initiatives have, to date, ended up with panels lying out of use and no one to fix them: can that trend be turned around? And can enterprises turning food waste into organic compost earn enough revenue to provide decent jobs, while doing so on the scale required? Nascent technologies and enterprises like these need to be tested and adapted as they go to scale, but they also – crucially – need to be enabled by an economic system that makes them feasible as investments, and that is where the twenty-first-century economist has a key role to play.

In search of the generous economist

Despite the potential of circular manufacturing and regenerative design, today's pioneering industrial and urban designers face a formidable challenge: working with business, finance and governments that are still trapped within the mindset and metrics of degenerative economic design. Janine Benyus knows the frustrations of this challenge at first hand. While collaborating with a large commercial land developer on designs for renovating the suburb of a major city, she proposed constructing buildings whose biomimetic living walls would sequester carbon dioxide, release oxygen, and filter the surrounding air. The developer's first response? 'But why should I provide clean air for the rest of the city?'

It's an unsurprising question, indicative of the near ubiquitous business mindset that has arisen from the design of contemporary capitalism. And that design is the opposite of generous. It is focused instead on creating just one form of value – financial – for just one interest group: shareholders. While regenerative designers now ask themselves, 'how many diverse benefits can we layer into this?', mainstream business still asks itself, 'how much financial value can we extract from this?' Of course there may be some overlap of those two ambitions – since being regenerative can sometimes be highly

227

profitable – but if that area of overlap is all that business is interested in pursuing then regenerative design will fall very far short of its potential.

This partial embrace of regenerative design by many mainstream businesses is certainly visible in the way that they have so far put circular economy thinking into practice. Corporate interest in forging 'circular advantage' is growing fast, and companies leading the pack have adopted a niche set of circular economy techniques such as: aiming for zero-waste manufacturing; selling services instead of products (like computer printing services instead of printers); and recovering their own-brand goods – ranging from tractors to laptops – for refurbishment and resale. These are excellent strategies for efficient resource reuse and they can be highly profitable too. By recovering and re-manufacturing key component parts used in their products, the construction equipment company Caterpillar has increased gross profit on those product lines by 50% while cutting water and energy use by around 90%.[36] That's impressive (surely they should rename their re-manufacturing division Butterfly?), and many other circular economy corporate initiatives are too, as far as they go.

The trouble is, they just do not go far enough, and there is a clear reason why. Shaped to fit in with existing corporate interests, circular economy strategies to date have typically been: top down, driven by large corporations; in-house, with companies seeking to establish control over their used products; opaque, thanks to patented materials and proprietary technologies; and fragmented into disconnected parts, within and across industries. That is by no means a strong foundation for building a regenerative, let alone distributive, industrial ecosystem. Take one illustration: a growing number of manufacturers are seeking to recover their used products, such as cars and clothing, in order to reclaim and reuse their parts and materials. But with the average Westerner owning more than 10,000 objects made worldwide, such an individualised approach is highly unlikely to succeed, and furthermore it would lead to highly concentrated corporate control over the economy's material round-flow.[37] Here's the nub of it:

> Regenerative industrial design can only be fully realised
> if it is underpinned by regenerative economic design

. . . and that is currently sorely missing. Making it happen calls for rebalancing the roles of the market, the commons and the state. It calls for redefining the purpose of business and the functions of finance. And it calls for metrics that recognise and reward regenerative success. Taking on *this* redesign task is surely one of the most exciting opportunities for twenty-first-century economists. And – as you would expect in a complex, evolving economy – it is a redesign process that will emerge not from textbook theories, but from the innovative experiments of those who are trying to bring it about.

The circular future is open

The glaring gap between the regenerative potential of the circular economy and its narrow efficiency-focused practice by corporations has inspired the launch of an Open Source Circular Economy (OSCE) movement. Its worldwide network of innovators, designers and activists aims to follow in the footsteps of open-source software by creating the knowledge commons needed to unleash the full potential of circular manufacturing. Why a knowledge commons? Because, as those in the OSCE movement point out, the full regenerative potential of circular production cannot be reached by individual companies seeking to make it happen all within their own factory walls: it is an illogical and unfeasible basis for creating a circular economy.

Like the biomimicry movement launched by Benyus, this movement

229

takes nature as a model to learn from: a seed in soil grows into a tree and decomposes to become soil for new trees – but a single tree cannot make this happen alone. It depends upon a rich and continual interaction of many living cycles, from fungi and insects to rainfall and sunshine, and it is the interaction of all of these that creates the forest's self-renewing ecosystem. Likewise in industry: if every tractor, refrigerator and laptop manufacturer attempts to recover, refurbish and resell all and only its own-brand products within proprietary cycles of material flow, the system-wide regenerative potential will never be achieved.[38]

Sam Muirhead, one of the instigators of the Open Source Circular Economy movement, believes that circular manufacturing must ultimately be open source because the principles behind open-source design are the strongest fit for the circular economy's needs. These principles include: modularity (making products with parts that are easy to assemble, disassemble and rearrange), open standards (designing components to a common shape and size); open source (full information on the composition of materials and how to use them); and open data (documenting the location and availability of materials). In all this, transparency is key. 'For whoever has the product at the end of its use, the recipe should be open source so anyone can see how to reuse its materials,' Muirhead told me, and since that open recipe allows anyone to improve or adapt the product to their needs, 'It means you have a distributed R&D team around the world made up of expert users like local repair shops, customisation specialists, and innovative designers. These principles give rise to a set of circular business models that work not *despite* being open source but *because* they are open source.'[39]

So what's going round in the emerging open source circular economy? Early pioneers include AXIOM, the open-source video camera for film makers, made by Apertus° (the 'O' stands for 'open'), which uses standardised components so it can be customised, reassembled, and continually reinvented by its user community.[40] Look, too, at the fast-evolving OS Vehicle – the open-source future of 100% electric cars – whose parts can be quickly assembled to make an airport buggy, a golf cart, or even a smart city car.[41]

The OS Vehicle was developed in Silicon Valley but open-source circular manufacturing is thriving in far more surprising places too. In the Togolese capital of Lomé, architect Sénamé Agbodjinou and colleagues set up Woelab in 2012, a 'low-high tech' workshop making its own design of open-source 3D printers using the component parts of defunct computers, printers and scanners that have been dumped in West Africa. 'We wanted to make our 3D printer from the resources we have at hand – and electronic waste is now practically our primary material available in Africa,' says Agbodjinou. The project is exploring the most useful local applications for 3D printing. 'Doctors have told us that when a little piece of equipment breaks, it takes at least two months for the replacement parts to come from Europe or the United States,' he explains. 'With this technology – if we can master it – we can create these parts, repair the equipment faster, and perhaps help to save a life.'[42]

These open-source innovations are impressive but still fledgling, and to many the movement may look unfeasibly utopian. So remember the 21-year-old Finnish computer student, Linus Torvalds, who in 1991 was writing the kernel of an open-source operating system – just for a hobby, he said – which quickly morphed into Linux, now the most widely used computer operating system in the world. At the time, Microsoft's CEO Steve Ballmer called Linux 'a cancer', but today even Microsoft has embraced the movement by using Linux in its own products.[43] 'The story of open-source software is a little portal to the future for us,' Muirhead told me, and he is optimistic. 'Once you put something in the commons, you can't take it away,' he explained, 'so every single day the knowledge commons grows and becomes more useful. Once people get the idea – and see its circular economy potential – they really want to create solutions for it.'[44]

That same spirit of building the knowledge commons inspired

Janine Benyus to launch the website Asknature.org, which makes the long-held secrets of nature's materials, structures and processes open-source for all – such as how a gecko clings without glue, how butterflies make pigment-free colours, and how mussels glue themselves to watery rocks. Almost two million users, from high-school design students to research scientists, have learned from and contributed to the site since it began in 2008. Every contribution to its database helps to deter individuals and companies from seeking bogus patents with false claims of novelty on innovations that nature came up with billions of years ago. Benyus's ultimate aim for Asknature.org, she explained to me, is to keep nature's genius in the public domain so that life can teach us how to build, feed, travel, power ourselves, and even manufacture in life-enhancing ways. 'With nature-inspired structural blueprints,' she said, 'we can add extraordinary function to the planet's most ubiquitous polymers such as cellulose, keratin, chitin, and lignin. These are the building blocks for the open-source circular economy.'[45]

An open-source basis for regenerative design is certainly compelling. But if mainstream business is unlikely to embrace its full potential, what kind of enterprise would be intent on making it work? There are of course many ways to design business, some of them far more regenerative than others, as visionary entrepreneurs have learned the hard way.

Redefining the business of business

'The social responsibility of business is to increase its profits,' said Milton Friedman back in 1970 and the mainstream business world willingly believed him.[46] But Anita Roddick had a different take on that. In 1976, before the words to say it had been found, she set out to create a business that was socially and environmentally regenerative by design. Opening The Body Shop in the British seaside town of Brighton, she sold natural plant-based cosmetics (never tested on animals) in refillable bottles and recycled boxes (why throw away when you can use again?) while paying a fair price to the communities worldwide that supplied cocoa butter, brazil nut oil and dried herbs. As production expanded, the business began to recycle its wastewater for using in its products, and was an early investor in wind power. Meanwhile, company profits went to The Body Shop Foundation, which gave them to social and environmental causes. In all, a pretty generous enterprise. Roddick's motivation? 'I want to work for a company that contributes to and is part of the community,' she later explained. 'If I can't do something for the public good, what the hell am I doing?'[47]

Such a values-driven mission is what the analyst Marjorie Kelly calls a company's *living purpose* – turning on its head the neoliberal script that the business of business is simply business. Roddick proved that business can be far more than that, by embedding benevolent values and a regenerative intent at the company's birth. 'We dedicated the Articles of Association and Memoranda – which in England is the legal definition of the purpose of your company – to human rights advocacy and social and environmental change,' she explained in 2005, 'so everything the company did had that as its canopy.'[48]

Today's most innovative enterprises are inspired by the same idea: that the business of business is to contribute to a thriving world. And the growing family of enterprise structures that are intentionally distributive by design – including cooperatives, not-for-profits, community interest companies, and benefit corporations – can be regenerative by design too.[49] By explicitly making a regenerative commitment in their corporate by-laws and enshrining it in their governance, they can safeguard a 'living purpose' through times of leadership change and protect it from mission creep. Indeed the most profound act of corporate responsibility for any company today is to rewrite its corporate by-laws, or articles of association, in order to redefine itself with a living purpose, rooted in regenerative and distributive design, and then to live and work by it.

Finance in service to life

A business that is built on a living purpose may have strong foundations, but without a source of finance that is aligned with its values it is unlikely to survive and thrive. Regenerative enterprise needs the support of financial partners seeking to invest long term in generating multiple kinds of value – human, social, ecological, cultural and physical – along with a fair financial return. But current finance culture is still narrowly focused on driving short-term financial value, such as through share buybacks or increasing dividends instead.

Anita Roddick certainly found this out the hard way. When The Body Shop first issued shares in 1986, she quickly encountered the clash between her regenerative-spirited enterprise and the narrow demands of shareholder finance. 'One of the biggest mistakes I made was to go public and on the stock market,' she recalled a decade later. 'I think there's a fascism attached to financial institutions, which only look at a very unimaginative bottom line. Profit is the law of business: that has to be considered, but not at the expense of human rights, environmental standards and community.'[50] Roddick's frustrations no doubt resonate with many like-minded entrepreneurs. Because whether or not a regenerative enterprise can deliver on its living purpose depends in good part on how it is financed. And the challenge of figuring that out is, of course, another great redesign opportunity waiting for the twenty-first-century economist.

One unlikely financial rethinker who is taking on this design task is John Fullerton, a former managing director at JP Morgan. He walked away from Wall Street in early 2001 on an instinct that something was profoundly wrong with the way it worked and he started reading widely. Gradually, he says, 'I came to the understanding that the economic system is actually the root cause of the ecological crisis, and that finance is what drives the economic system. So as a twenty-year finance veteran hotshot, I had some rethinking to do.'[51] Starting with eight key principles that he believes underpin all complex living systems – including: taking a holistic view of wealth; being in 'right relationship'; and seeking balance – Fullerton began using them to design what he calls 'regenerative finance' with the aim of creating finance that is in service to life.

When finance is in 'right relationship' with the whole economy, he explains, it will no longer be driving it, but rather supporting it by turning savings and credit into productive investments that deliver long-term social and environmental value. That means, first, that the global financial system as we know it needs to shrink, simplify, diversify and deleverage – a transformation that will make it more resilient in the process, rather than ever-prone to speculative bubbles and crashes. Policies for heading in that direction, suggests Fullerton, include: separating customers' deposit accounts from the speculative activities of securities firms; introducing taxes and regulation that make it unprofitable to be too big, too leveraged and too complex, and a global financial transactions tax to rein in high-frequency trading.[52]

Reining in short-term, speculative finance is a crucial start, but equally important is replacing it with long-term, investment finance. State-led development banks have an obvious role here in offering 'patient capital' for long-horizon investments such as renewable energy technologies and public transport systems. But there is a role, too, for private investors, ranging from the personal saver to institutional investors like pension funds and endowment funds. Community banks, credit unions, and ethical banks may sound like small players but they have taken the lead in this space. Take the Dutch bank Triodos, for example, whose mission – or living purpose – is 'to make money work for positive social, environmental, and cultural change', and which has over half a million customers across Europe: savers and investors, entrepreneurs and companies who share those values and aims. Or look to Florida's First Green Bank, established in the depths of the 2008 recession, which has set out to be 'a regenerative bank', and is working with the support of Fullerton and his team at the think tank Capital Institute to explore what it will take to make that happen.[53]

Finance that is in service to life, however, goes beyond redesigning investment to redesigning currency. Just as a currency's design – its creation, its character, and its intended use – can be distributive within a community, as we saw in Chapter 5, it can also be regenerative of the living world. The Belgian complementary currency guru, Bernard Lietaer, loves this kind of challenge. 'Give me a social or environmental problem,' he once told me, 'and I will design a currency to solve it.' One city in his home country took him up on that offer, inviting him to Rabot, a run-down district of Ghent. 'I was given an impossible task: the worst neighbourhood in all of Flanders,' he recounted with a twinkle in his eye, as he described the district: densely populated tower blocks housing a diverse and divided community of first-generation immigrants, surrounded by dilapidated public spaces. The challenge? 'Can we create a nice neighbourhood to live in – where people say hello to each other – and which is "greening", one of the priorities of the city?'

Lietaer's first move was to ask the residents of Rabot what they actually wanted. The resounding answer: little plots of land for growing food. So a five-hectare derelict factory site was soon converted into allotments available for rent, which was payable only in a new currency, Torekes, meaning 'little towers', named after the district's ubiquitous tower blocks. And they can be earned by volunteering to collect litter, replant public gardens, and repair public buildings, or by using the car pool and switching to green electricity. Along with paying the allotment rent, Torekes can be spent on bus travel and cinema tickets, or used in local shops to buy fresh produce and energy-efficient light bulbs, so boosting their uptake. But their social value has reached even further. 'When people see that immigrants, who tend to be blamed as polluters themselves, are helping to clean up the neighbourhood, then that is a positive signal to anyone,' notes Guy Reynebeau, head of Health and Welfare in the district. 'Such actions can't be priced, not in Euros or Torekes.'[54]

Imagine taking this concept to the next level by integrating complementary currencies at the very design stage of a generous city. Just as blood flowing throughout the human body keeps all of its organs healthy, so complementary currencies could be designed to harness the flow of human activity in ways that keep the city's infrastructure thriving. They could reward residents and enterprises for a wide range of regenerative behaviour – from collecting, sorting and recycling waste to maintaining the living walls of the city's buildings – all the while encouraging the community to shop locally and travel publicly. Complementary currencies could, in effect, help a city's inhabitants become full participants in nature's cycles, just as Benyus envisages.

Bring on the partner state

The state's role is key to ending the business-as-usual of degenerative economic design. And it has many ways to actively promote a regenerative alternative, including restructuring taxes and regulations, stepping up as a transformative investor, and empowering the dynamism of the commons.

Governments have historically opted to tax what they could, rather than what they should, and it shows. Tax windows and you'll get dark houses, as Britain discovered in the eighteenth and nineteenth centuries; tax employees and you'll head for a jobless economy, as many countries are discovering today. It is happening in part thanks to the twentieth century's legacy of perverse tax policies, which charge firms for hiring humans (through payroll taxes), subsidise them for buying robots (through tax-deductible capital investments), and levy next to nothing on the use of land and non-renewable resources. In 2012, over 50% of tax revenue raised in the EU came from taxing labour; in the United States, the percentage was even higher.[55] It's no surprise that industry's response has been to focus on increasing labour productivity – output per worker – by replacing as many workers as possible with automatons.

The long-advocated switch from taxing labour to taxing non-renewable resources can be boosted by subsidies for renewable energy and resource-efficient investments. Such measures would refocus industry's attention away from raising *labour* productivity and towards raising *resource* productivity, dramatically reducing the use of new materials and creating jobs at the same time. Refurbishing buildings instead of demolishing them and building again from scratch, for example, typically generates more jobs, comparable energy consumption, and far less use of water and new materials.[56] One recent European study of the effects of promoting a circular economy along with renewable energy and energy-efficiency measures estimated that together they would generate around 500,000 jobs in France, 400,000 in Spain, and 200,000 in the Netherlands.[57]

Taxes and subsidies can move markets, as we have seen, but the transformation from degenerative to regenerative industrial design needs to be backed by regulation too. At its most simple, it means phasing out the use of 'red list' chemicals and polluting production processes, while phasing in the use of life-friendly chemistry only, along with net-zero and net-positive industrial standards. The world's most progressive enterprises are already aiming to perform to such standards: economy-wide regulations requiring regenerative design will ultimately help to move those ambitious business practices from being a rare exception to becoming the industry norm.

Moving markets clearly matters, but it is not enough, argues economist Mariana Mazzucato. This is especially true when it comes to the clean energy revolution, a crucial power source for the regenerative economy. 'We cannot rely on the private sector to bring about the kind of radical reshaping of the economy that is required,' Mazzucato explains. 'Only the state can provide the kind of patient finance required to make a decisive shift.'[58] The Chinese government clearly shares her view of the state's role as a risk-taking partner: over the past decade it has invested billions of dollars in a portfolio of innovative renewable energy companies, supporting not just their research and development costs but demonstration and deployment too. At the same time, the Chinese Development Bank, along with state-owned utilities, is financing the world's biggest deployment to date of wind and solar photovoltaic parks.[59]

If the state can be a transformative partner in creating a regenerative economy, where is this happening? To date, it is most visible in city-scale initiatives that are dotted across the globe. One such city is Oberlin, Ohio, located in America's 'rust belt' of post-industrial decline. In 2009 the city administration teamed up with Oberlin College and the municipal light and power utilities with the goal of becoming one of America's first 'climate positive' cities by sequestering more carbon dioxide than it produces. The initiative also aims to grow 70% of the city's food locally, conserve 20,000 acres of urban green space, and revive local culture and community, creating much-needed enterprises and jobs to make it all possible. By 2015, college- and city-run buildings were powered by 90% renewable energy and a growing proportion of food for the city's university, high schools, hospitals and government offices was sourced from local growers. Cultural life is reviving too, thanks to a new performing arts centre in the city's Green Arts District, and environmental education is now built into the public school curriculum.[60] 'Our aim is full-spectrum sustainability,' says David Orr, executive director of The Oberlin Project, explaining the systems thinking behind the project's design. 'We need to recalibrate prosperity with the way that ecosystems work and what they can actually regenerate.'[61]

The era of living metrics

The shift to regenerative economic design can be monitored only if it is backed up by metrics that reflect its mission. Monetary metrics alone will inevitably fall far short of reflecting the value created in a regenerative economy: financial income is just one narrow slice of what an economy generates when its aim is to promote human prosperity in a flourishing web of life. The monopoly of monetary metrics is over: it's time for a panoply of living metrics. And instead of focusing on the throughflow of monetary value, as GDP was designed to do, the new metrics will monitor the many sources of wealth – human, social, ecological, cultural and physical – from which all value flows.

Living metrics are developing fast at many scales. Among cities, Oberlin is once again at the forefront. With its clear living purpose 'to improve the resilience, prosperity and sustainability of our community', the city has started to create the metrics it needs to monitor that goal. Oberlin's Environmental Dashboard website was set up to educate, motivate and empower the city's community in transforming its ecological impact. Public data displays in the city library, in public buildings, and online show in real time the city's water use, electricity use, and the health of its river. One July evening, as I browsed the website from my UK home over 3,500 miles away, I could track minute-by-minute Oberlin's local ecological flows: the real-time carbon emissions produced in the city per person that hour, the volume of drinking water used and of wastewater treated, and even the oxygen levels in nearby Plum Creek as the stream flowed past. [62] Real-time data are a fun and engaging way to gain community interest but many of the deeper insights come from monitoring their dynamic trends year on year.[63] Given Oberlin's ambitions, I'll bet that, once the data become available, the city will expand its Environmental Dashboard beyond the local to show

Oberlin's global material footprint, and use it to monitor its ambitious longer-term goal of full-spectrum sustainability.

If Oberlin is a leader in living metrics for cities, what of living metrics for business? Fortunately, enterprises can now escape the narrow accounting tyranny of the financial rate of return by adopting a more diverse set of key performance indicators. Several leading initiatives – such as the Economy for the Common Good, B Corp's Impact Reports, and the MultiCapital Scorecard – all offer businesses a matrix against which to score their sustainability.[64] And since the matrices are openly and independently scored, the results can empower consumers and enable governments to proactively support regenerative enterprises by rewarding high scores with, say, lower taxes and preferential public procurement.

All of these business scorecards push corporate ambition in the right direction in terms of measuring what matters but they are largely still geared to achieving 'zero impact' – such as by giving companies a climate-impact score of 100% if they achieve net-zero carbon emissions. The next leap for such business metrics is to go beyond do-no-harm sustainability towards rewarding generous design. When the living metrics for business match the ambition of Janine Benyus's Ecological Performance Standards for cities, then companies will ask themselves not simply 'how we can do no harm' but 'how can our enterprise be as generative as a giant redwood forest?' And with that leap of ambition – among businesses, among cities, and among nations – we will start to become not just harmless to nature's cycles but helpful participants in their regeneration.

'Somewhere over the rainbow, skies are blue,' sang Dorothy in *The Wizard of Oz*. It's a charming thought, and the perfect theme tune for the rainbow-shaped Environmental Kuznets Curve. Keep going, keep growing and, one day, the air will be clear, the rivers will be clean, and the desecration of the living world will cease. But evidence amassed over many years, in global data sets and in millions of people's harsh experience, has made plain that growth doesn't simply clean it up. If anything, it spreads it out: to date, as nations' economies have got larger, so too have their global material footprints, ratcheting up the pressures of climate change, water scarcity, ocean acidification, biodiversity loss, and chemical pollution. We have inherited degenerative industrial economies: our task now is to transform them into ones that are regenerative by design. There's no denying that it is an extraordinary challenge, but it's one that is inspiring the next generation of smart engineers, architects, urban planners and designers. I wish I could track down Prakash because India, and the world, needs him to be on the team.

It is clearly time for economists to leave behind the foolhardy search for economic laws of motion. Instead, step up to the design table and take a seat alongside those innovative architects, industrial ecologists and product designers who are spearheading the regenerative design revolution. There is certainly an empty seat waiting, because the economist's role here is key: to design the economic policies and institutional innovations – for enterprise and finance, for the commons and the state – that will unleash the extraordinary potential of the circular economy and regenerative design. And if it is accompanied by distributive design then we will indeed be heading towards the Doughnut's safe and just space. But since the Doughnut is, itself, a global dashboard of living metrics, what does this imply for the future of that infamous indicator, GDP: going up, going down, or going agnostic?

7

BE AGNOSTIC ABOUT GROWTH

from growth addicted to growth agnostic

Once a year I teach a class that divides friends, confronts ideologies, and challenges us all to change our minds. I get to the seminar room early, pull the chairs out of their neat rows and split the seating into two long columns divided by an aisle, rather like the seats on an airplane. As the students start arriving, they are confronted by a single question on the screen: *Is green growth possible? Yes / No.* I ask them to take a seat in answer to that question: for Yes, sit in the column by the window; for No, sit in the column by the door. And standing in the aisle is not allowed.

Those hoping to work for the big consultancy firms upon graduation move swiftly to the Yes block, some practically hugging the windowsill. Others hover in the middle, slightly panicked by the sudden public decision, and then head for the No block, wary of the reaction it may draw. Once seated, they start pointing and gawping at each other across the aisle, shocked to see their close friends so far away, stunned by the gulf in their unvoiced opinions.

As these students quickly discover, our beliefs about economic growth are almost religious: personal in nature, political in consequence, privately held, and little discussed. So as our discussions get going, I invite them to consider what it would take for them to switch sides, reminding them – with help from the poet Taylor Mali – that, 'changing your mind is one of the best ways of finding out whether or not you still have one'.[1] After the mid-class break, I suggest that they literally take a seat on the opposite side of the aisle and lean as far as possible into understanding that other perspective.

I admit it, my question is unfair because it begs so many others: growth of what, for whom, for how long – and what exactly is 'green'? Perhaps I force them to confront it anyway as a cathartic way to revisit my own struggles with the future of economic growth. Back in 2011 I was tasked by Oxfam to write a policy paper to help the organisation decide whether, in high-income countries, it should promote the concept of 'green growth', or side with those advocating 'degrowth'. I jumped at the chance because it took me back to the heart of macroeconomic thinking. But my excitement soon turned to paralysis as I dug into the debate and found that while both sides had some strong arguments, both too quickly dismissed the opposition's case, and neither had a singularly compelling answer. As I attempted to come up with a clear policy position for Oxfam despite my own deepening uncertainty, my stomach tied itself in knots and my throat became so tight that I could barely breathe. I had been immobilised by one of the most existential economic questions of our age. So I called my project manager and explained the situation. 'OK,' she said. 'What do you need – two more weeks?'

What I needed was to stop trying to answer that question head-on. If the Greek hero Perseus had been my project manager, he would have warned me against the task in the first place: he knew never to look directly into the face of the monstrous Medusa because anyone doing so would simply be turned to stone. Instead, by catching her reflection in his polished shield, he managed to creep up on the Gorgon monster and deftly chop off her head. Perhaps there's a lesson here for how to think best about the future of economic growth.

Back in Chapter 1 we booted the cuckoo goal of GDP growth out

244

of the nest, but that doesn't mean that it has simply flown from the story. Why? Here's the conundrum:

No country has ever ended human deprivation without a growing economy.
And no country has ever ended ecological degradation with one.

If the twenty-first-century goal is to get into the Doughnut by ending deprivation and degradation at the same time, what are the implications for GDP growth? Contemplating this question takes us to a new level in rethinking growth. It is one thing to move beyond using GDP as the primary indicator of a nation's economic success, but it is another thing altogether for that nation to overcome its financial, political and social addiction to GDP growth. This chapter takes on that challenge and makes the case for creating economies that are *agnostic* about growth. By agnostic I do not mean simply not caring whether GDP growth is coming or not, nor do I mean refusing to measure whether it is happening or not. I mean agnostic in the sense of designing an economy that promotes human prosperity whether GDP is going up, down, or holding steady.

Being agnostic may sound like a cop-out, an extreme case of sitting on the fence, but read on because it has radical implications. The twentieth century bequeathed to us economies that need to grow, whether or not they make us thrive, and we are now living through the social and ecological fallout of that inheritance. Twenty-first-century economists, especially those in today's high-income countries, now face a challenge that their predecessors did not have to contemplate: to create economies that make us thrive, whether or not they grow. As we will explore, becoming agnostic in this way calls for transforming the financial, political and social structures that have made our economies and societies come to expect, demand and depend upon growth.

Too dangerous to draw

If you find yourself in the company of economists and wishing for an ice-breaker, here's a fun game you can play, and all you need is a piece of paper and a pencil. Simply ask an economist to draw for you a picture of the long-term path of economic growth. If you are wondering what shape they will sketch on the page, don't rush to the textbooks to find out, because the answer isn't there. It may sound extraordinary but, despite having adopted GDP growth as the de facto goal of economic policy, the textbooks never actually depict how it is expected to evolve over the long term. Yes, there may be graphs showing various economic cycles, ranging from the 7–10-year boom and bust of business cycles to the 50–60-year waves – known as Kondratieff waves – that are due to technological innovation. But it is rare indeed to come across a graph plotting several centuries of past GDP growth, let alone a diagram suggesting what might happen in centuries ahead.

Is the answer so obvious that the textbooks need not bother? Quite the opposite. It is so challenging that they do not dare: the long-term future of GDP growth – that Medusa of economic theory – is simply too dangerous to draw because it forces economists to face up to their deepest assumptions about growth. But if you are lucky enough to find an economist willing to play this little game, you may actually come to glimpse the Gorgon's terrible form.

Handed your pencil and paper, any mainstream economist of the last half-century will most likely draw the very same image that we encountered in Chapter 1: an ever-rising line, known as the exponential growth curve, in which GDP increases by a fixed percentage (be it 2% or 9%) of its current size every period. They would, however, instinctively leave its leading tip hanging mid-air, as if in suspended animation.

The trouble for economists who produce this picture is the

246

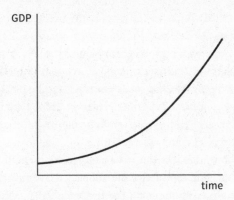

The exponential growth curve, revisited.

obvious question that is left hanging in the air with it: what happens next? There are essentially two options. Either the line keeps rising indefinitely, rapidly shooting up off the top of the page, or it must start to flatten out and eventually come to a level. For the mainstream economist, the first option is awkward, the second unconscionable, and here's why.

Unchecked exponential growth – that first option – will, by its own logic, always shoot up towards infinity, and far more quickly than we imagine. Indeed it has a well-earned reputation for creeping up on us because our brains evolved to be good at adding but infamously bad at compounding. This is not just a problem for budding mathematicians to worry about: as the nuclear physicist Al Bartlett warned, 'The greatest shortcoming of the human race is our inability to understand the exponential function.'[2] That is because if something grows exponentially – be it algae on a pond, debt in the bank, or a nation's energy use – it will get much bigger much faster than we expect. A 10% growth rate means that something will double in size every seven years. A 3% growth rate sounds far more modest but it still leads to doubling in size every 23 years.

What would that imply for GDP growth? In 2015, World GDP – also known as Gross World Product – was around $80 trillion and the global economy was growing at around 3% per year. If it continued indefinitely at that rate, the global economy would be nearly three times bigger by 2050, over ten times bigger by 2100, and – astonishingly – almost 240 times bigger by 2200. Take note: not a penny of that growth in value would be due to inflation; it is due only to the logic of compound growth.

Most economists, like the rest of us, would be hard pressed to envisage a thriving global economy of such extraordinary proportions, especially given the stress that human activity already puts on the planet, and so they may prefer to wave the implications off to the horizon. No one epitomised this approach so literally and influentially as the American economist Walt W. Rostow who, in 1960, published his seminal book, *The Stages of Economic Growth*, renowned for its dynamic theory of economic development. Every country, he claimed, must pass through five stages of growth so that it can come to 'enjoy the blessings and choices opened up by the march of compound interest'.[3] The five stages go like this:

W.W. Rostow's Five Stages of Growth
(The twentieth-century journey)

1. The traditional society
2. The preconditions for take-off
3. The take-off
4. The drive to maturity
5. The age of high mass-consumption

The journey starts with the *traditional society*, whose agricultural and artisanal techniques place a ceiling on its economic productivity. From here begins the critical process that establishes the *preconditions for take-off.* 'The idea spreads,' wrote Rostow, 'not

merely that economic progress is possible, but that economic progress is a necessary condition for some other purpose, judged to be
good: be it national dignity, private profit, general welfare, or a better life for the children.' Banks open, entrepreneurs start investing,
transport and communications infrastructure builds up, education
is tailored to suit the modern economy's needs and, crucially,
said Rostow, an effective state emerges, 'touched with a new
nationalism'.

All these changes pave the way for 'the watershed in the life of
modern societies': the *take-off* stage, in which 'growth becomes the
normal condition' as mechanised industry and commercialised
agriculture dominate the economy. 'Compound interest becomes
built, as it were, into its habits and institutional structure,' explained
Rostow, and 'both the basic structure of the economy and the social
and political structure of the society are transformed in such a way
that a steady rate of growth can be, thereafter, regularly sustained.'
That pivotal stage leads on to *the drive to maturity*, a phase in which
a wide range of modern industries can be established, regardless of
the nation's resource base. And that phase, in turn, ushers in
what Rostow named as the fifth and last stage: *the age of high
mass-consumption* in which growth delivers enough surplus income
for households to start buying durable consumer goods like sewing
machines and bicycles, kitchen gadgets and cars.

Rostow's economic plane flight is the unmissable metaphor in
this story, complete with its pre-flight procedural checks and its alti-
tude signifying the economy's growth rate. But it differs from every
other plane flight in one crucial respect: the plane never actually
lands, but cruises instead at a constant growth rate into the sunset of
consumerism. Rostow hinted at his uncertainty of what might lie
over that horizon, briefly acknowledging 'the question beyond,
where history offers us only fragments: what to do when the increase
in real income itself loses its charm?'[4] But he did not follow his
own questioning through, and for understandable reasons: it was

1960 – the year of John F. Kennedy's election bid on a promise of 5% growth – and for Rostow, a soon-to-be presidential adviser, it was wise to focus on keeping that plane in the sky, not on pondering when and how it would ever land.

The miscast star of the stage

The founding fathers of classical economic theory may never have seen airplanes or heard of GDP but they had an intuitive understanding that things that grow must eventually slow to a stop. They believed, with mixed feelings, that the end of economic growth was inevitable and they had different views on what would bring it about – or, as systems thinkers would say, on which limiting factors would ultimately counter GDP's reinforcing feedback. Adam Smith believed that every economy would eventually reach what he called a 'stationary state' with its 'full complement of riches' ultimately being determined by 'the nature of its soil, climate and situation'.[5] David Ricardo, in contrast, believed that the stationary state would be brought about by the cost of rising rents and wages squeezing capitalists to the point of near-zero profits, and he feared it would happen soon (in the early nineteenth century) if technical progress and foreign trade could not keep it at bay.[6]

Others were more optimistic: John Stuart Mill, for one, could hardly wait for the stationary state to usher in what many would now call a post-growth society. 'The increase of wealth is not boundless,' he wrote in 1848. 'A stationary condition of capital and population implies no stationary state of human improvement. There would be as much scope as ever for all kinds of mental culture, and moral and social progress; as much room for improving the art of living, and much more likelihood of it being improved, when minds ceased to be engrossed by the art of getting on.' And, as if to prove himself no fan of GDP almost a century before it was invented, he added, 'those who do not accept the present very early stage of human improvement as its ultimate type, may be excused for being comparatively indifferent to the kind of economical progress which excites the congratulations of ordinary politicians: the mere increase of production and accumulation.'[7] A full century on, John Maynard Keynes echoed Mill's sentiments, asserting (rather wishfully) that 'the day is not far off when the economic problem will take the back seat where it belongs, and the arena of the heart and the head will be occupied or reoccupied, by our real problems – the problems of life and of human relations, of creation and behaviour and religion'.[8]

So, pencil in hand, what shape would these most famous of economists have drawn in response to the ice-breaker invitation to depict the long-term path of GDP growth? If presented with the exponential curve left hanging mid-air by today's mainstream economists, they would most probably have picked up the line of its leading edge and brought it gradually to a plateau as the economy comes up against a limiting factor of one kind or another. With one sweep of the pencil, exponential growth has been subsumed as a passing phase in the

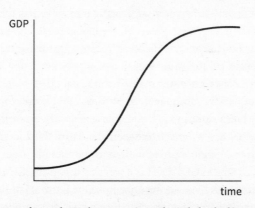

The S curve of growth. Early economists acknowledged what most of their successors have since ignored: that economic growth must eventually reach a limit.

economic journey as annual GDP has matured to become much bigger in size but no longer growing. In other words, they would have drawn what is known as 'logistic growth', or simply the S curve.

It may not feature in the textbooks but this S curve is no newcomer to the theatre of economics: it is, in fact, one of the oldest but most miscast of all actors in the play. Its shape first stepped on to the economic stage in 1838 when the Belgian mathematician Pierre Verhulst drew it to depict the trajectory of population growth, showing that populations would not increase exponentially, as the Reverend Thomas Malthus had believed, but would tend to a limit set by the availability, or carrying capacity, of resources such as food. It was a brilliant insight – worthy of an economic Oscar – but hardly anyone noticed the S curve's star-like qualities, so it got dropped from the cast list for over a century.

Left to languish backstage, the S curve's talents were spotted by ecologists, biologists, demographers and statisticians who realised that it was a strong fit for describing many processes of growth in the natural world – from a child's feet and the world's forests to bacteria in a Petri dish and tumours in a body – and so they have used it ever since. Economists, however, kept the S curve well out of the plot until 1962, when it was recast, this time as a tool for charting the diffusion of technologies, from early adopters to late laggards – a role for which it has since gained worldwide fame, especially in the marketing industry.[9] Never once did mainstream economists consider letting that same S curve audition for the leading role of long-term GDP. But its lucky break came in 1971 when the ecological economist Nicholas Georgescu-Roegen dared to write an alternative third act for the economic play. Without ever actually drawing it on the page, he boldly cast the S curve as GDP itself in a plot that brings the global economy face to face with the carrying capacity of the Earth. Mainstream economic theatre has long rejected it, but that deviant script is now influencing the new economic story that is being written.[10]

The S curve may have been a breakthrough but, like the exponential curve that lies within it, it is incomplete because it too begs the question of what happens next: when GDP growth ultimately ceases, can GDP be sustained permanently on that high plateau, or is decline inevitable? Nature's experience is at least partly reassuring. Living organisms can clearly sustain themselves – with the help of an external energy source – as mature, stable, complex systems for very long periods. A child's feet stop growing after 18 years, but can remain in perfect podiatric health for another 80, and large swathes of the Amazon rainforest have been thriving for over 50 million years. But from teenager's feet to tropical forests, nothing survives for ever. Still, that need not give us immediate cause for alarm. Life on Earth has the chance of another five billion years in its favour, at which point our star, the sun, will start to die. Earth's Holocene-like conditions could continue for another 50,000 years – as Chapter 1 described – if we humans learn to navigate the Anthropocene without pushing our planet into a far hotter, drier, and more hostile state. The economies that we create could keep on thriving – not growing, but thriving – for millennia too, if we manage them wisely.

If we now recognise that the S curve depicts a desirable long-term path for GDP growth, a far more interesting question comes into view: not 'is endless economic growth possible?' but rather, 'where are we now on the growth curve: still near the bottom or close to the top?' In fact we can play the classic children's party game, Pin the Tail on the Donkey, and invite economists to pinpoint the spot on the S curve that they think their own nation's economy has reached. The nineteenth-century British economist Alfred Marshall – he with the scissors of supply and demand – would have been a willing contestant in his day, firmly sticking his pin low on the S curve's exponential slope. 'We are moving on at a rapid pace that grows quicker every year; and we cannot guess where it will stop,' he wrote in 1890. 'There seems to be no good reason for believing that we are anywhere near a stationary state.'[11] If Marshall were here to play today, would he still hold to that view? He might well find some compelling reasons to change his mind.

World GDP has increased more than fivefold since the Great

Acceleration began in 1950 and, according to mainstream economic forecasts, it is likely to continue growing at around 3–4% per year at least in the near future.[12] But global economic growth is made up of around two hundred national economies with widely differing growth rates. Their differences range from a fast-paced 7–10% per year in low-income countries like Cambodia and Ethiopia to a lethargic 0.2% per year in high-income countries like France and Japan.[13] As a result, the donkey's tail would most likely get pinned at very different places on their national S curves.

In many low-income but high-growth countries, the domestic economy is clearly in what Rostow called the take-off stage – low down on the S curve – and, when that growth leads to investments in public services and infrastructure, its benefits to society are extremely clear. Across low- and middle-income countries (where national income is less than $12,500 per person per year) a higher GDP tends to go hand-in-hand with greatly increased life expectancy at birth, far fewer children dying before the age of five, and many more children going to school.[14] Given that 80% of the world's population live in such countries, and the vast majority of their inhabitants are under 25 years old, significant GDP growth is very much needed and it is very likely coming. With sufficient international support these countries can seize the opportunity to leapfrog the wasteful and polluting technologies of the past. And if they channel GDP growth into creating economies that are distributive and regenerative by design, they will start bringing all of their inhabitants above the Doughnut's social foundation without overshooting its ecological ceiling.

It is, however, in today's high-income but low-growth countries that the growth debate is most pressing, with some beginning to wonder whether the top of the S curve is coming within view. In many of these countries, population growth is already very low and in some – such as Japan, Italy and Germany – population size is expected to fall by 2050.[15] Meanwhile the sluggish GDP growth of recent decades in many high-income countries has infamously been accompanied by widening income inequalities. At the same time all of these countries' global ecological footprints already far exceed Earth's capacity: it would take four planets for everyone in the world to live as they do in Sweden, Canada and the US, and five planets for all to live like an Australian or Kuwaiti.[16] Does this suggest that, while aiming to get into the Doughnut, high-income countries should give up on the pursuit of GDP growth and accept that it might no longer be possible?

That is not a comfortable question to consider. As Upton Sinclair famously noted, 'It is difficult to get a man to understand something, when his salary depends on his not understanding it.'[17] Some staff at the OECD must be struggling with this now because, whether or not growth can be green and equitable, it doesn't look like growth is coming in some of the world's richest nations. The average GDP growth rate of 13 long-standing OECD member countries had fallen from over 5% in the early 1960s to under 2% by 2011.[18] Diverse reasons for this have been suggested, from shrinking and ageing populations, falling labour productivity, and an overhang of debt to widening wealth inequality, rising commodity prices, and the costs of responding to climate change.[19] Whatever the mix of reasons in each country, the declining long-term GDP growth trend raises the very real possibility that these economies could be close to the top of their S curves, with growth tailing off.

But such a possibility jars with the OECD's mission. One of the organisation's founding objectives is the pursuit of economic growth; one of its leading annual reports is entitled *Going for Growth*; and it has a flagship green growth strategy to boot. It is very hard for passengers on planes like this one – along with the World Bank, the IMF, the UN, the EU, and almost every political party worldwide – to even voice the idea that it might be time for some countries to start thinking about landing the economic plane.

That might just explain why the OECD quietly tweaked a recent long-term growth forecast to make its message more palatable to its members. In 2014, the organisation published a long-run projection of global economic growth through to 2060, showing 'mediocre' prospects for the global economy, and with annual growth rates in member countries such as Germany, France, Japan and Spain falling to just 1%, punctuated by years of 0%. What the forecast hid in the small print of its model, however, is that this mediocre outlook was achieved in good part by assuming that global greenhouse gas emissions would double by 2060, including a 20% increase coming from the OECD's own members.[20] The promise of even slight GDP growth was secured only at the cost of accepting catastrophic climate change: talk about crushing the nest in order to feed the cuckoo.

Since then, however, leading economists in the OECD and in major financial institutions have been choosing their words carefully when discussing future growth prospects. In early 2016, Mark Carney, governor of the Bank of England, warned that the global economy risked being trapped in a 'low growth, low inflation, low interest rate equilibrium'.[21] The Bank for International Settlements – effectively the central banks' central bank – concurred, noting that 'the global economy seems unable to return to sustainable and balanced growth . . . the road ahead is quite narrow'.[22] The IMF meanwhile advised that, 'our projections continue to be progressively less optimistic over time . . . policymakers should not ignore the need to prepare for possible adverse outcomes'.[23] The OECD itself agreed that the world was in a 'low-growth trap' with growth 'flat' in high-income countries.[24] And the influential US economist Larry Summers declared that we have entered 'the age of secular stagnation'.[25] It sounds suspiciously as if some economies might be approaching the top of their S curves.

Can we keep on flying?

Set in this context, the debate over the future of GDP growth in today's high-income countries is polarised between the 'keep-on-flying' advocates of green growth and the 'prepare-for-landing' advocates of post-growth economics. Disagreement between the two sides appears to hinge on technical questions. Will the cost of solar power fall low enough to provide abundant renewable energy? How resource-efficient can the circular economy become? And how much economic growth will the digital economy deliver? In fact, as I discovered, the real source of disagreement goes far deeper and is more political than technical.

A few months after my immobilising encounter with the Medusa, I went along to a university reunion and bumped into one of my former economics professors. After a quick catch-up on families and careers, I asked if he thought GDP growth was possible for ever. 'Yes!' he instantly declared. 'It has to be!' I was taken aback, not just by the force of his conviction, but by the reasoning behind it. He was sure that economic growth was possible for ever because it *had* to be possible for ever. That fleeting exchange started to beckon me back towards the Gorgon monster. What made him think that endless GDP growth had to be possible? What would happen if it wasn't? And why – most alarmingly – had we not addressed either of these questions in my four years of economics degrees?

From then on, I started listening more closely for the deeper beliefs that underpin positions on both sides of this debate and I began to hear the source of their differences. To make those differences clear, imagine all those in the debate seated as passengers on opposite sides of the aisle in Rostow's airplane. In essence, the beliefs that divide many of them come down to this:

The keep-on-flying passengers:
economic growth is still necessary – and so it must be possible.

The prepare-for-landing passengers:
economic growth is no longer possible – and so it cannot be necessary.

Both sides are on to something here, but both tend to be unduly optimistic in the conclusions they draw, so let's explore their arguments.

The keep-on-flying passengers are clear on one thing: that economic growth is a social and political necessity in every country. 'If growth were to be abandoned as an objective of policy,' wrote the economist Wilfred Beckerman in 1974, 'democracy too would have to be abandoned . . . the costs of deliberate non-growth, in terms of the political and social transformation that would be required in society, are astronomical.'[26] Beckerman's influential book *In Defense of Economic Growth* was a scathing response to the Club of Rome's *Limits to Growth* report and it became an instant pro-growth classic. His belief in the political necessity of growth is still shared by many economists and public commentators today. As Benjamin Friedman argues in *The Moral Consequences of Economic Growth,* it is not *high* incomes but *ever-growing* incomes that foster 'greater opportunity, tolerance of diversity, social mobility, commitment to fairness and dedication to democracy'.[27] The economist Dambisa Moyo agrees. 'If growth wanes,' she warned a TED audience in 2015, 'the risk to human progress and the risk to social and political instability rises and societies become dimmer, coarser, and smaller.'[28]

Since economic growth is deemed a political necessity by the keep-on-flying crowd – no matter how wealthy a country already is – it is no surprise to hear them argue that further growth in high-income countries is possible because it is coming and it can be made environmentally sustainable. First, growth is on the way, argue technology optimists such as Erik Brynjolfsson and Andrew McAfee: thanks to the exponential growth in digital processing power, we are entering the 'second machine age', in which the fast-rising productivity of robots will drive a new wave of GDP growth.[29]

What's more, argue green growth advocates such as the UN, World Bank, IMF, OECD and EU, future growth can become green by decoupling GDP from ecological impacts. In other words, while

GDP continues to grow over time, its associated resource use – such as freshwater use, fertiliser use, and greenhouse gas emissions – can fall at the same time. But how much decoupling is enough for growth to be green on the scale required to get into the Doughnut? It's a tall order, and (like many things) is best shown in a picture.

The diagram shows GDP growing over time, accompanied by three very different possible pathways of resource use. When GDP grows faster than resource use does – due, for example, to water and energy efficiency measures – it is known as *relative* decoupling – and this is the kind of 'green growth' that is the focus in many low-income countries today. But in high-income countries – where consumption levels have long exceeded what Earth can sustain – it would clearly be by no means enough. Any further GDP growth in these countries

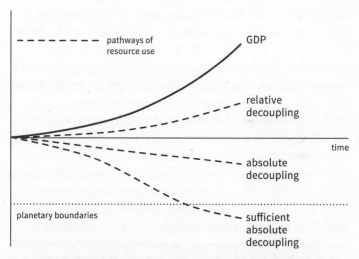

The challenge of decoupling. If GDP is to continue growing in high-income countries, its associated resource use must fall not just relatively or absolutely but sufficiently absolutely to move back within planetary boundaries.

would at least need to be accompanied by *absolute* decoupling so that resource use falls in absolute terms as GDP rises.

When it comes to carbon dioxide emissions – the key to tackling climate change – many high-income countries, including Australia and Canada, have so far failed to achieve any absolute decoupling. But others appear to have shown that it is possible – at least some of the time – even when taking account of emissions embedded in the nation's imports. According to available international data, between 2000 and 2013 Germany's GDP grew by 16% while its consumption-based CO_2 emissions fell by 12%. Likewise, the UK's GDP grew by 27% while emissions fell by 9%, and GDP in the US grew by 28% while emissions fell by 6%.[30]

If these data are accurate then this is a striking break with the past – and yet it is still far from enough. Despite achieving a degree of absolute decoupling, these countries' emissions are not falling nearly fast enough. Some leading climate scientists calculate that high-income countries' emissions now need to be falling at a rate of at least 8–10% per year in order to help bring the global economy back within planetary boundaries.[31] But in reality they have been falling at most by 1–2% per year. Highlighting this gap calls for setting a more relevant standard, *sufficient* absolute decoupling – sufficient because it is on the scale needed to get back within planetary boundaries – and it is a distinction that is too often missing in the green growth debate.

So can sufficient absolute decoupling be compatible with an ever-growing GDP? According to the keep-on-flying crowd, yes, in three broad ways. First, by rapidly shifting energy supply away from fossil fuels and into renewables such as solar, wind and hydro – a trend that is being sped along by the fast-falling cost of renewables, especially solar photovoltaics. Second, by creating a resource-efficient circular economy whose material throughflow becomes a round-flow within the capacity of Earth's sources and sinks. And third by expanding the 'weightless' economy made possible by digital products and services, in which 'mind not matter, brain not brawn, ideas not things' drive future GDP growth.[32] It's important to note, however, that the decoupling required would not be a one-off phase: if GDP were to keep on growing, then the rate of decoupling would have to more than keep pace with it, year on year on year.

Is the keep-on-flying crowd sure that these measures can deliver enough decoupling in high-income countries to make growth as green as it needs to be? Many acknowledge that the scale of the challenge is extremely daunting but still believe it is possible, particularly since most governments have barely started introducing the policies needed to bring it about. In other words, according to economists Alex Bowen and Cameron Hepburn, 'It is too early to rule out absolute decoupling.'[33]

Others, however, are privately less certain. I have had many conversations with representatives from government, academia, international agencies, and business to try to get to the source of their apparent conviction in the green growth vision that is now ubiquitously embedded in their job titles, imprinted on their business cards, and written into their organisational strategies. One conversation with a senior adviser to the UN summed up the unspoken uncertainty for me. During a break at a recent green growth conference, I asked him whether he really believed that green growth – on a scale sufficiently green to bring us back within planetary boundaries – was possible in the world's richest countries. As the other delegates started filing back into the conference room, he lingered behind and replied in a hushed voice, 'I don't know, no one does, but we have to say it is to keep everyone on board.' I admired his off-the-record honesty, but wished there were more space on the record in those very conferences for such doubts to be voiced because they certainly need airing.

Those seated on the other side of the aisle – the prepare-for-landing passengers – are quick to air those doubts publicly because they believe that in high-income countries green-enough growth is simply not feasible. Far from being too early to rule decoupling out, it is too late to rely on the belief that it will happen. If sufficient action were taken to move back within planetary boundaries, they argue, it would be unrealistic to believe that it could be accompanied by continual growth. And to understand why, we must revisit long-standing assumptions about what drives GDP growth in the first place.

Back in the 1950s Robert Solow, father of economic growth theory, attempted to pin down exactly what had caused the US economy to grow over the past half-century. His seminal growth model – based on the same theoretical foundations as the Circular Flow diagram – assumed it would be due to the productivity gains arising from labour and capital working ever more effectively together. But when he plugged US data into the model's equations, to his surprise he found that capital invested per worker explained a mere 13% of the American economy's growth over the previous 40 years, and he was forced to ascribe the unexplained remaining 87% to 'technical change'.[34] It was an embarrassingly large residual, leading his contemporary Moses Abramovitz, whose own calculations were turning up similarly large explanatory gaps, to admit that this residual was effectively a 'measure of our ignorance about the causes of economic growth'.[35]

Economists have been chasing after better explanations of GDP growth ever since, seeking to discover the contents of that mysterious residual. The answer would probably have been spotted decades ago if Bill Phillips had simply opted for a different power source to keep the water pumping round his MONIAC machine. If he had run it not off electricity but off pedal power – complete with a panting student cranking the bike pedals round during every demonstration – it would have been far harder for him and his fellow economists to overlook the role played by an external source of energy in keeping the economy going. Alternatively, if either Phillips or Solow had seen the economic big picture – summed up in Chapter

2's Embedded Economy diagram – then their economic models might well have incorporated the answer from the get-go.

In 2009 physicist Robert Ayres and ecological economist Benjamin Warr decided to construct a new model of economic growth. To the classic duo of labour and capital they added a third factor of production: energy, or, more precisely, exergy, the proportion of total energy that can be harnessed for useful work, instead of being lost as waste heat. And when they applied this three-factor model to data on twentieth-century growth in the US, UK, Japan and Austria, they found that it could explain the vast majority of economic growth in each of the four countries: Solow's mystery residual, long assumed to reflect technological progress, turned out to reflect the increasing efficiency with which energy is converted into useful work.[36]

The implication? The last two centuries of extraordinary economic growth in high-income countries are largely due to the availability of cheap fossil fuels. It makes sense when you break it down: the energy contained in a single gallon of oil is equivalent to 47 days of hard human labour, making current global oil production equivalent to the daily work of billions of invisible slaves.[37] What then are the implications for GDP in the post-fossil-fuel future that we must create? 'We have to anticipate the possibility that economic growth will slow down or even turn negative,' warn Ayres and Warr. 'In short, future GDP growth is not only not guaranteed, it is more than likely to end within a few decades.'[38]

What, though, of the promise of renewable energy? Its price may be falling fast but – like all stocks in a system – solar, wind and hydro capacity take time to install. Many in the prepare-for-landing crowd believe it cannot be installed fast enough to match the economy's demand for energy, especially if fossil fuels are phased out at the speed required. What's more, in comparison to the easy-to-access oil, coal and gas reserves of the twentieth century, a far larger proportion of renewable energy that is generated must be used by the energy industry itself simply to generate more – as is the case for energy from sources such as shale gas and tar sands. Some analysts believe the economic implications are stark. 'It is time to re-examine the pursuit of economic growth at all costs,' concludes US energy economist David Murphy; 'we should expect the economic growth rates of the next 100 years to look nothing like those of the last 100 years.'[39]

Furthermore, some in the prepare-for-landing crowd doubt that the weightless economy can be as dematerialised as its name implies, given the material- and energy-intensive infrastructure that underpins the coming digital revolution.[40] Others, meanwhile, doubt that the weightless economy will contribute as much to GDP growth as the growth optimists expect. A wide array of online products and services like software, music, education and entertainment are already available almost for free because, thanks to the Internet, they can be created and reproduced at near-zero marginal cost. Analysts such as Jeremy Rifkin believe that today's emerging horizontal networks of renewable energy generation and 3D printing are set to amplify this trend. If they do, it could result in a great deal of economic value that was once sold at a profit in the marketplace being shared for low or no cost in the collaborative commons.

The sharing economy is also growing, in which the culture of ownership – with every household equipped with its own washing machine and car – is giving way to a culture of access, with households sharing laundry facilities and renting cars by the hour from a local car club. Rather than go shopping for new clothes, books and children's toys, a growing number of people are swapping – or 'swishing' – them with friends and neighbours.[41] In such an economy, plenty of economic value will still be generated through the products and services that people enjoy, but far less of that total value will flow through market transactions. The implication of these various trends for GDP growth? 'The steady decline of GDP in the coming years,' concludes Rifkin, 'is going to be increasingly attributable to the change-over to a vibrant new economic paradigm that measures economic value in totally new ways.'[42]

It's an intriguing point, but does it make a difference to the future of economic growth? After all, some in the keep-on-flying crowd suggest, what ultimately matters for human well-being is the total value of economic activity, regardless of whether or not it is captured through market transactions in GDP. That may be true for households, where the value of caring work is given and received directly with no money changing hands (and so is already missing from standard GDP accounts). It is also true for those engaged in the commons who reap economic value as they co-create it – whether it is the value generated by irrigating their rice paddies or by collaborating online in open-source design, again with no money changing hands.

But whether or not economic value gets monetised through the market does matter a good deal to finance, to business, and to government. Financiers only make a return – by extracting interest, rent or dividends – on economic value that has a market value. Business can only capture value as revenue and profit when that value has been monetised in sales. And governments find it far easier to levy taxes for public revenue on economic value that is exchanged through the market. All three of these – finance, business and government – are structured to expect and depend upon a growing monetary income: if GDP is no longer set to grow even though total economic value may well continue to do so, then those expectations need to change profoundly.

For those in the prepare-for-landing crowd, the upshot of all these trends is that green growth in high-income countries is nowhere on the horizon: it is time to go green without growth instead. But this is where they tend to be over-optimistic themselves: certain that endless GDP growth is not possible, some are too quick in concluding that it therefore cannot be necessary, and point to the so-called Easterlin Paradox as evidence that higher incomes do not make us happier anyway.

The US economist Richard Easterlin found that between 1946

and 1974, GDP per capita grew significantly in the US but the population's self-reported levels of happiness – on a scale of 0 to 10 – remained flat, and even fell in the 1960s.[43] Those findings have since been called into question by studies that find self-reported happiness continuing to rise as income rises, albeit ever more slowly the richer a country becomes.[44] But even if we were to accept Easterlin's data at face value, the fact that people's self-assessed happiness stayed flat while their income rose is no proof that happiness would still stay level if incomes flatlined. What's more, when wages for the worse-off stagnate, immigrants are all too quickly blamed, as has happened in many high-income countries in recent years, fuelling xenophobia and social strife. Our societies, like our economies, have evolved to expect growth and have come to depend upon it: it seems we do not yet know how to live without it.

No wonder Martin Wolf, one of the UK's most respected financial journalists, wrote with palpable unease in 2007 when he took the rare step of leaning across the debating aisle to agree with the prepare-for-landing crowd about the economic implications of cutting global carbon emissions. 'If there are limits to emissions, there may also be limits to growth,' he acknowledged in his *Financial Times* column. 'But if there are indeed limits to growth, the political underpinnings of our world fall apart. Intense distributional conflicts must then re-emerge – indeed, they are already emerging – within and among countries.'[45] Such a view of GDP growth – that it is still necessary but no longer possible – is clearly a deeply uncomfortable one to hold. These are the words of a man daring to face the Medusa.

Are we there yet?

Whether our economic airplane can keep on cruising, or is about to stall mid-air, one thing is evident: it is currently heading for a destination that we do not want to reach, one that is degenerative and deeply divisive. If we reorient ourselves to the economic destination that we do want – an economy that is regenerative and distributive by design – then new questions about growth come to the fore. What might happen to GDP as we transition towards that destination? And what is GDP likely to do once we get there? It is not possible to predict definitively one way or the other whether GDP will go up or down in high-income countries as they create regenerative and distributive economies that engage the household, market, commons and state alike.

Getting there calls for many sectoral transformations, including a strong contraction of industries such as mining, oil and gas, industrial livestock production, demolition and landfill, and speculative finance, offset by a rapid and lasting expansion of long-term investment in renewable energy, public transport, commons-based circular manufacturing, and retrofit buildings. It calls for investing in the sources of wealth – natural, human, social, cultural and physical – from which all value flows, whether it is monetised or not. And it opens up opportunities for rebalancing the roles of the market, the state and the commons as means of provisioning for our needs.

Combine these uncertain shifts and it is by no means clear what will happen to the total value of products and services that are bought and sold in the economy. It might go up and then down. It might go down and then up. Or it might come to oscillate around a steady size. We simply cannot be certain of how GDP will respond and evolve as we make this unprecedented transition into the Doughnut's safe and just space, or how it will behave once we are thriving there. And that is precisely why we have a problem. Because over the past couple of centuries, just as Rostow spelled out, capitalist economies have restructured their laws, institutions, policies and values so that they are geared to expect, demand and depend upon

continual GDP growth. Let's revisit that conundrum we find ourselves facing:

We have an economy that needs to grow, whether or not it makes us thrive.
We need an economy that makes us thrive, whether or not it grows.

What does this mean for the economic airplane ride? If Rostow
were still alive, and no longer an aspiring presidential adviser but a
concerned fellow citizen on this flight, perhaps he'd offer to update
his theory, realising that the story cannot end with the plane cruising for ever into the sunset of growth. As much as having the ability
to fly, this plane must have the ability to land: the capacity to thrive
when growth comes to an end. So he might just agree to amend his
book like this:

W.W. Rostow's six stages of growth
(the twenty-first-century update)

1. The traditional society
2. The preconditions for take-off
3. The take-off
4. The drive to maturity
5. ~~The age of high mass-consumption~~
5. Preparation for landing
6. Arrival

Of course it would be a revolution in mainstream economics simply for Rostow to propose these new chapter headings. It would be
another revolution altogether for him – and us – to know what to
write in those two missing chapters of the flight manual, because
such a controlled descent has never been attempted. Every real
passenger jet comes equipped to make a safe landing: wing flaps to

create drag and slowdown without stalling; landing gear with sturdy wheels and shock absorbers for that moment of touchdown; and brakes and reverse thrust for bringing the plane to a smooth stand-still. But the economic airplanes that Rostow so admired in the 1960s were not built to land: in fact their institutions were locked on autopilot, expecting to cruise at around 3% growth for ever, and have been attempting to do so ever since.

Attempting to sustain GDP growth in an economy that may actually be close to maturing can drive governments to take desperate and destructive measures. They deregulate – or rather *re*regulate – finance in the hope of unleashing new productive investment, but end up unleashing speculative bubbles, house price hikes, and debt crises instead. They promise business that they will 'cut red tape', but end up dismantling legislation that was put in place to protect workers' rights, community resources and the living world. They privatise public services – from hospitals to railways – turning public wealth into private revenue streams. They add the living world into the national accounts as 'ecosystem services' and 'natural capital', assigning it a value that looks dangerously like a price. And, despite committing to keep global warming 'well below 2°C', many such governments chase after the 'cheap' energy of tar sands and shale gas, while neglecting the transformational public investments needed for a clean-energy revolution. These policy choices are akin to throwing precious cargo off a plane that is running out of fuel, rather than admitting that it may soon be time to touch down.

Learning how to land

What would it mean to prepare high-income economies for landing so that they could touch down safely and become thriving, growth-agnostic economies when the time was right? The clue lies in

Rostow's preconditions for take-off, the key stage during which, he wrote, 'each of the major characteristics of the traditional society was altered in such ways as to permit regular growth: its politics, social structure, and (to a degree) its values, as well as its economy'.[46] Preparing for landing, then, calls for taking the economy out of that growth autopilot and redesigning the financial, political and social structures that have turned growth into what Rostow called 'the normal condition'. It will be tricky, of course, because economists have not had the training, let alone the experience, to land this plane and create economies that thrive whether or not they grow. But some innovative economic thinkers have started to put their minds to the task by asking, in the words of the ecological economist Peter Victor, can we 'go slower by design, not disaster'? Or even – in the name of agnosticism – what would it take to design an economy that can handle GDP growth without hankering after it, deal with it without depending upon it, embrace it without exacting it?

It has been a long flight: is it time to land?

As ever, the core ideas of systems thinking set out in Chapter 4 will be a useful tool. GDP growth, like all growth, arises out of a reinforcing feedback loop, and it will eventually come up against a limit – a balancing feedback – that will most probably emerge from the larger system in which the economy is embedded. Based on the evidence available to date, it looks as if that limit lies in the carrying capacity of the living world. Must this encounter lead to collapse, or could we pre-empt that future by transforming the economy from ever-growing on an unstable trajectory to ever-oscillating within a stable range? What advice would a systems thinker offer?

We have already followed Donella Meadows's wise advice to go for high leverage points like changing the goal, by booting out the cuckoo of GDP growth and aiming for the Doughnut instead. Other powerful leverage points include finding ways to weaken growth's reinforcing feedback loops while strengthening balancing ones instead. Looked at through this lens, it becomes clear that many innovations in economic thinking are aiming to do just this, as we will see below. Most striking is that many of the policies proposed for enabling an economy to be growth-agnostic are also ones that could help drive it towards being distributive and regenerative by design.

How, then, are today's high-income economies locked into dependency on GDP growth, and how could they learn to thrive with or without it? Few economists have bothered – or dared – to ask these questions in public until now. Herman Daly was an early pioneer in the 1970s but his prescient call for creating 'steady state' economies fell on reluctant political ears. Today, an increasing number of governments in high-income countries face very real prospects of low or no GDP growth over the coming decades and, for the first time, some are quietly asking if economists have ideas about how to embrace that reality. Support for such thinking is emerging from the most unexpected of places, such as the influential mainstream US economist Kenneth Rogoff, whose career has spanned the IMF, the US Federal Reserve and Harvard University. 'In a period of great economic uncertainty,' he wrote in 2012, 'it may seem inappropriate to question the growth imperative. But then again, perhaps a crisis is exactly the occasion to rethink the longer-term goals of global economic policy.'[47]

Let's take up the opportunity of this prolonged crisis and start identifying the various ways – financial, political and social – in which today's high-income economies, and others following their path, are locked into and addicted to pursuing GDP growth. From there we can start to ask what it would take to cut loose, and whether there are innovations under way that illustrate some possible options. There are, of course, no easy answers. It will take some decades of experiments and experience to come up with smart solutions given that this problem has been brewing for so long – which is precisely why it deserves far more attention and analysis now. Consider what follows, then, as an initial attempt to sketch the 'Preparation for Landing' pages that have long been missing from the economist's flight manual.

Financially addicted: what's to gain?

Let's start at the heart of the matter: with the financial addiction to growth. Because every decision in the world of finance revolves around one underlying question: what's the rate of return? That question is prompted by the search for 'gain', the driving motive of the capitalist economy since it took off in Britain in the nineteenth century. 'The mechanism which the motive gain set in motion,' wrote Karl Polanyi in the 1940s, 'was comparable in effectiveness only to the most violent outburst of religious fervor in history. Within a generation the whole human world was subjected to its undiluted influence.'[48] Polanyi was far from the first to realise that the pursuit of gain opened the door to endless accumulation: he got the idea from Marx, who described capital as 'money which begets money' and 'has therefore no limits'.[49] Marx in turn got the idea from Aristotle who, recall from Chapter 1, distinguished *economics*, which he saw as the noble art of managing the household, from *chrematistics*, the pernicious art of accumulating wealth. 'Money was intended to be used in exchange, but not to increase at interest,' he wrote in 350 BCE; '. . .of all modes of getting wealth this is the most unnatural.'[50]

The search for gain – which drives shareholder returns, speculative trading, and interest-bearing loans – lodges dependency upon continual GDP growth deep within the financial system. For John Fullerton, the banker who walked away from Wall Street, here lies the source of the problem. 'We've reached the logical conclusion of this expansionist economic paradigm,' he says. 'Unless we can achieve magical decoupling we have an exponential function on a closed system planet . . . yet the finance system has no in-built plateau, it can't "mature" – and none of the experts in finance are even thinking about this.'[51]

That is why Fullerton and his colleague Tim MacDonald started thinking about ways for regenerative enterprises to escape the constant pressure to grow from shareholders. They came up with the concept of Evergreen Direct Investing (EDI), which delivers acceptable and resilient financial returns from mature low- or no-growth enterprises. Instead of paying profit-based dividends to shareholders, the enterprise pays out a share of its income stream to investors in perpetuity. This set-up enables a profitable but non-growing business to attract stable investment from wealth stewards with a long-term view, such as pension funds.[52] 'EDI allows an enterprise to behave like a tree,' Fullerton explained to me. 'Once it is mature, it stops growing and bears fruit – and the fruit are just as valuable as the growth was.'[53]

The pressure for shareholder returns is, however, just one manifestation of how financial gain drives growth. Indeed this expectation of gain is so ingrained that we hardly notice its most unusual feature: it runs counter to the fundamental dynamic of our world. Given time, tractors rust, crops rot, smartphones break, and buildings crumble. But money? Money accumulates for ever, thanks to interest. No wonder it has become a commodity itself, and hence is so underinvested in creating the productive assets – from renewable energy systems to circular manufacturing processes – that are needed to underpin a regenerative economy.

What kind of currency, then, could be aligned with the living world so that it promoted regenerative investments rather than pursuing endless accumulation? One possibility is a currency bearing *demurrage*, a small fee incurred for holding money, so that it tends to lose rather than gain in value the longer it is held. The fact that demurrage is an unfamiliar term shows how accustomed we are to the ever-rising financial escalator that we ride – like knowing the idea of 'up' but not 'down', 'more' but not 'less'. But demurrage is a word worth knowing because it could just feature in the financial future.

The concept was first proposed by Silvio Gesell, a German-Argentinian businessman whose 1906 book *The Natural Economic Order* advocated introducing a paper currency accompanied by stamps that must be bought and periodically affixed to it to ensure its continued validity. Today the same effect could be achieved far more simply with electronic currency that incurred a charge for being held over time, so curtailing the use of money as a store of ever-accumulating value. Only money that 'goes out of date like a newspaper, rots like potatoes, rusts like iron' would be willingly handed over for objects that similarly decay, argued Gesell: ' . . . we must make money worse as a commodity if we wish to make it better as a medium of exchange'.[54]

These ideas sound outlandish and impracticable on first hearing but they have proven very practical in the past. Paper-based demurrage was successfully used in city-scale complementary currencies in 1930s Germany and Austria to reinvigorate the local economy, and it was almost introduced across the US in 1933. But in each case, the national government shut the initiative down, evidently threatened by its bottom-up success and the loss of state control over the power to create money. Keynes, however, was impressed by Gesell – who he called 'an unduly neglected prophet' – and was drawn to his proposal because of its proven ability to reboot spending in the economy, the priority of the Depression era.[55]

Imagine, then, if a demurrage-bearing currency could be designed so that, instead of boosting consumption today, it boosted regenerative investments in tomorrow. It would transform the landscape of financial expectations: in essence, the search for *gain* would be replaced by the search to *maintain* value. And one of the best ways to preserve the long-term value of stored wealth would be to invest it in long-term regenerative activity such as a reforestation scheme.[56] Banks would consider lending to enterprises promising a near-zero return on investment if it were preferable to the cost of holding money: that would bode well for regenerative and distributive enterprises delivering social and natural wealth along with a modest financial return. And it would, crucially, help to release the economy from the expectation of endless accumulation, and hence the financial addiction to growth.

Demurrage may seem quite alien to modern financial markets, but it is not so far removed from negative interest rates, which effectively charge those who are holding money in savings. These negative rates have become part of the contemporary financial landscape, being used for emergency measure by Japan, Sweden, Denmark, Switzerland, and the European Central Bank since 2014. These countries' aims have been diverse – to resurrect GDP growth, to manage exchange rates, and to raise inflation – but between them they have bust the myth that interest rates cannot fall below zero.

Of course the idea of designing demurrage into currency raises many challenging questions for a financial system, such as its implications for inflation and exchange rates, for capital flows and pension funds, and its balance between stimulating consumption and boosting investment. But these are just the kinds of question that are now well worth exploring in the process of reinventing finance so that it is in service to thriving – rather than ever-growing – economies.

And, as the use of negative interest rates has shown in recent years, it is striking just how quickly the unfeasibly radical can become the feasibly practical.

Politically addicted: hope, fear and power

What of the ubiquitous political lock-in to growth? As we saw in Chapter 1, in the mid twentieth century, pursuing national income growth quietly shifted from being a policy option to a political necessity. Three reasons stand out among the politician's concerns: hope for raising revenue without raising taxes; fear of the unemployment line; and the power that resides in the G20 family photo.

Hope for raising revenue without raising taxes. Governments depend upon public funds for investing in public goods but they are infamously loath to raise taxes. No wonder so many pin their hopes instead on unending GDP growth, since it promises to deliver an ever-growing stream of tax revenue without the need for a high rate of tax. How could this political addiction be overcome to make low- or no-growth economies fiscally viable?

First, reframe the purpose of taxes to help build social consensus for the kind of higher-tax, higher-returns public sector that has been a proven success in many Scandinavian countries. And remember, the verbal framing expert George Lakoff advises, to choose your words wisely: don't oppose *tax relief* – talk about *tax justice*. Likewise, the notion of public *spending* is often used by those who oppose it to evoke a never-ending outlay. Public *investment*, on the other hand, focuses on the public goods – such as high-quality schools and effective public transport – that underpin collective well-being.[57]

Second, end the extraordinary injustice of tax loopholes, offshore havens, profit shifting, and special exemptions that allow many of the world's richest people and largest corporations – from Amazon

276

to Zara – to pay negligible tax in the countries in which they live and do business. At least $18.5 trillion is hidden by wealthy individuals in tax havens worldwide, representing an annual loss of more than $156 billion in tax revenue, a sum that could end extreme income poverty twice over.[58] At the same time, transnational corporations shift around $660 billion of their profits each year to near-zero tax jurisdictions such as the Netherlands, Ireland, Bermuda and Luxembourg.[59] The Global Alliance for Tax Justice is among those focused on tackling this, campaigning worldwide for greater corporate transparency and accountability, fair international tax rules, and progressive national tax systems.[60]

Third, shifting both personal and corporate taxation away from taxing income streams and towards taxing accumulated wealth – such as real estate and financial assets – will diminish the role played by a growing GDP in ensuring sufficient tax revenue. Of course progressive tax reforms like these can quickly encounter pushback from the corporate lobby, along with claims of state incompetence and corruption. This only reinforces the importance of strong civic engagement in promoting and defending political democracies that can hold the state to account.

Fear of the unemployment line. Humans are ingenious: we are good at making more out of what we've got, or making the same from less. When Henry Ford introduced the moving assembly line in his Michigan automobile factory in 1913, car production rose fivefold almost overnight; if there had not been a growing market for his Model T car, he would have needed far fewer workers. In an expanding economy workers laid off by one business can hope to find jobs elsewhere, but when economy-wide demand does not keep up with productivity growth the result is widespread unemployment. As history has repeatedly demonstrated, that can quickly lead to xenophobia, intolerance and fascism. It was the Great Depression's endless unemployment lines that convinced John Maynard Keynes to focus on full employment as the economy's goal in the 1930s, and the answer, he believed, was continual GDP growth. A century on from the Model T revolution, however, robots have taken over much more than car production. It is simply no longer feasible to expect GDP growth rates to keep pace with the anticipated scale of lay-offs due to automation, which only reinforces the case for introducing a basic income for all. But other changes can also improve the distribution of paid work in a growth-agnostic economy.

Keynes anticipated that, as technology increased labour productivity, the typical working week would shorten: he famously predicted that a 15-hour week would suffice in the twenty-first century, and society would endeavour 'to make what work there is still to be done as widely shared as possible'.[61] He got that wrong, at least up to this point, but time could still prove him right. He would certainly have been among the first to back a proposal by the UK's New Economics Foundation to shorten the standard paid working week in high-income countries from above 35 hours to just 21 hours as a means of tackling both unemployment and overwork.[62] It would, of course, be a challenging transition that could not happen without transforming the economics of employment. 'We will need to get rid of perverse incentives in tax and insurance systems,' explains Anna Coote, the social policy expert behind the proposal, 'so that employers are encouraged rather than penalized for taking on more workers.'[63]

Such initiatives for a shorter working week are all the more likely to happen if the employers are the workers themselves: from the Great Depression to the 2008 financial crisis, worker-owned cooperatives have proven more adept at preventing lay-offs: they tend to share reduced working hours between all members instead – an excellent example of an adaptive employment response in the face of fluctuating demand.[64] But there are ways to transform employment in traditional companies too. The widely recommended shift from taxing labour to taxing resource use would simultaneously draw human ingenuity away from making more stuff with fewer people towards repairing and remaking more things with less stuff, while employing more people too. Such policies would certainly help to make economies more distributive and regenerative, but could these policies also help economies to become growth-agnostic when it comes to providing sufficient employment? What other adjustments might be required? This is just where more innovative experiments and research are needed.

Power in the G20 family photo. Every year, when the leaders of the world's most powerful nations meet at the G20 summit, an official group photograph is taken. I like to think of it as the G20 family photo, remembering that, just as in many modern families, its membership may occasionally be rearranged. No wonder every political leader jealously guards their spot in that picture as a sign of their nation's geopolitical power. In his influential 1989 book, *The Rise and Fall of the Great Powers*, historian Paul Kennedy concluded that it is the relative, not absolute, wealth of nations that determines their power on the world stage.[65] The rivalry between the USA and the USSR that was set in motion in the 1950s has become an unrelenting geopolitical race for all: keep growing to hold on to your spot in the family picture, or you'll be bumped out of the frame by the next emerging powerhouse.

This is an international collective action conundrum and hence a tough growth addiction to tackle. Systems thinkers would suggest that one way out of this bind is to diversify and 'start a new game' with alternative measures of success. If a successful economy is one that thrives in balance, then that success will be reflected not in the metric of money but in metrics that reflect human prosperity in a flourishing web of life. Some well-known initiatives have taken this route. The UN's Human Development Index, which ranks countries in terms of human health and education along with income per person, was created in 1990 precisely to start countering the sole use of

GDP. Others like the Happy Planet Index, the Inclusive Wealth Index, and the Social Progress Index are now also aiming to create an alternative international family picture in which the biggest-GDP nations do not automatically appear centre frame. Other strategic initiatives have sought to bypass national rivalry by championing city-to-city collaboration instead. The C40 network, for instance, now connects more than 80 of the world's megacities in a shared commitment to tackle climate change. Home to over 550 million people and 25% of World GDP, these cities – and their economic vision – will be profoundly influential far beyond their city limits.[66]

New games help, but the compulsion of the old GDP game holds its grip because GDP brings both global market power and global military power. This geopolitical lock-in demands far more strategic attention. 'An economic race for global power is certainly an understandable rationale for focusing on long-term growth,' argues Kenneth Rogoff, 'but if such competition is really a central justification for this focus, then we need to re-examine standard macroeconomic models, which ignore this issue entirely.'[67] Beyond merely rewriting macroeconomic models, however, this lock-in highlights the need for innovative thinkers in international relations to turn their attention to strategies that could help to usher in a future of growth-agnostic global governance.

Socially addicted: something to aspire to

Lastly, how are we socially locked in, addicted to, and stuck on GDP growth? Through the culture of consumerism and the tensions created by inequality, which in turn are rooted in the need for something to aspire to.

Despite being far richer than kings of old, we are too easily trapped on a treadmill of consumerism, continually searching for identity, connection and self-transformation through the things that we buy. Keeping up with the Joneses has us forever chasing the promise of that next purchase. As we saw in Chapter 3, Freud's nephew Edward Bernays realised that his uncle's psychotherapy opened up a very lucrative world of retail therapy. His method of persuasion – tastefully named 'public relations' – transformed marketing world-wide and, over the course of the twentieth century, embedded consumer culture as a way of life. As the media theorist John Berger put it in his book, *Ways of Seeing*, 'publicity is not merely an assembly of competing messages: it is a language in itself which is always being used to make the same general proposal . . . it proposes to each of us that we transform ourselves, and our lives, by buying something more'.[68]

Do we have a chance of shaking off this twentieth-century inheritance? In an attempt to do so, some governments, such as in Sweden, Norway and Quebec, have banned advertising to children under 12 (leaving the adult subconscious as fair game), while cities such as Grenoble and São Paolo have banned the 'visual pollution' of street billboards. But the simultaneous boom in targeted online advertising, backed up by high-tech consumer research, has taken personalised marketing into a far more sophisticated and invasive realm. Meanwhile, advertising has secured its role – in the street, in schools, on social media, and in the news media – as a major income source for local governments, and for free website services and news outlets, creating an uneasy financial dependence of the state and the digital commons upon the endless enticements of the market. Reversing consumerism's financial and cultural dominance in public and private life is set to be one of the twenty-first century's most gripping psychological dramas.

Society is also said to be addicted to GDP growth because it eases the tension of wide social inequalities. An ever-growing GDP is often claimed to be essential because it creates a 'positive sum economy' in which everyone can become better off.[69] When the economic pie is growing, the argument goes, the wealthy are more likely to accept redistributive taxes that invest in public services because it can be done without cutting into their take-home income. Others, however, believe continual GDP growth is essential for the very opposite reason: because it serves to permanently defer the need for redistribution. In the words of Henry Wallich, governor of the US Federal Reserve in the 1970s, 'Growth is a substitute for equality of income. So long as there is growth there is hope, and that makes large income differentials tolerable.'[70]

Whether growth is seen as the key to redistribution, or the key to forever avoiding it, its social importance is rooted in a basic conviction. I once found myself in a workshop discussing new economic thinking with a leading figure in complexity economics. He talked about promoting GDP growth in high-income countries as if it were an obvious necessity. When I questioned him about it, his answer was simple. 'We have a deep-seated drive for growth,' he said. 'People need something to aspire to.'

I agree: people need something to aspire to. But is an ever-growing income really the best aspiration on offer? It was Alfred Marshall, back in Chapter 3, who endowed rational economic man with insatiable wants and desires. Thanks to Edward Bernays, that particularly seems to be the case among the WEIRD ones today – people in Western, educated, industrial, rich, democratic countries that are now the homelands of consumer society. Yet anthropologists can name both historical and contemporary examples of traditional societies that have lived by a principle of sufficiency instead, such as the Cree in northern Manitoba in the nineteenth century whose response to European traders defied economists' expectations. In the hope of acquiring more furs, the Europeans offered them higher prices: in response the Cree brought fewer furs to the trading post, since a smaller number were now needed to obtain the goods that they wanted in exchange.[71]

If Bernays were here and willing to help try creating or recovering a similar sense of material sufficiency in WEIRD societies, which deep human values would he attempt to trigger? What might we aspire to instead, if not more possessions? 'Wherever and whenever we are excessive in our lives it is the sign of an as yet unknown deprivation,' argues the psychoanalyst Adam Phillips. 'Our excesses are the best clue we have to our own poverty, and our best way of concealing it from ourselves.'[72] When it comes to consumerism, perhaps the poverty that we aim to conceal lies in our neglected relationships with each other and with the living world. The psychotherapist Sue Gerhardt would certainly agree. 'Although we have relative material abundance, we do not in fact have emotional abundance,' she writes in her book, *The Selfish Society*. 'Many people are deprived of what really matters.'[73]

There are many views on what really matters to us in life – from using our talents and helping others, to standing up for what we believe in. Drawing on a wide array of psychological research, the New Economics Foundation has distilled the findings down to five simple acts that are proven to promote well-being: *connecting* to the people around us, *being active* in our bodies, *taking notice* of the world, *learning* new skills, and *giving* to others.[74] Perhaps these are first steps towards the kind of moral and social progress that Mill was imagining as he looked forward to a time when people who were no longer engrossed in the art of getting on would aspire instead to the art of living.

This brief sketch of how to prepare the economic plane for landing has touched on many addictions to growth that have become financially, politically and socially ingrained in many nations' institutions, policies and culture. It is, of course, overwhelming to contemplate them all at once – just as every novice pilot is no doubt overwhelmed on first learning how to use a plane's landing equipment. But that equipment can be mastered, and not one of the growth addictions outlined above is inherently insurmountable. If there is one task that merits the attention of the twenty-first-century economist, it is this: to come up with economic designs that would enable nations coming towards the end of their GDP growth to learn to thrive without it.

Welcome to the arrivals lounge

If we can master the art of landing the plane – creating an economy that enables us to thrive, whether or not it grows – what happens on arrival? I have no doubt that the next generation of economic innovators will be best placed to fill in those still-blank pages of the manual, so I will add just two thoughts.

First, if Rostow were indeed a fellow passenger on this flight, I think he would realise upon landing that an airplane is not actually the best metaphor to describe GDP's future journey: it lacks the agility needed to lift up, touch down, lift up, touch down in response to ever-changing conditions. Flying was the novel way to travel in Rostow's day: his book came out just five years after the first passenger jet flight so no wonder he was drawn to it as an economic metaphor. But introduce him to twenty-first-century water sports and I reckon he would set his heart on kite surfing as a far better metaphor for the future of GDP. A skilled kite surfer rides her surfboard across the rolling waves while catching the wind in her kite, and she must continually adjust – bending, dipping, and twisting her body – to maintain that dynamic interplay of the wind and the waves. That is just how GDP should come to move in the twenty-first century, with the value of products and services sold each year bobbing and dipping in response to the constantly evolving economy.

Second, whatever else happens on arrival, I will bet one thing: that John Maynard Keynes and John Stuart Mill will be there waiting to greet us, ready to get to work on figuring out the economics – and the philosophy and politics too – of the art of living in a distributive, regenerative, growth-agnostic Doughnut economy. The destination will certainly not be what they had expected, but they will recognise our dilemmas. What better pair of original thinkers could we hope to have on the team?

WE ARE ALL ECONOMISTS NOW

Doughnut Economics sets out an optimistic vision of humanity's common future: a global economy that creates a thriving balance thanks to its distributive and regenerative design. Such an aspiration may seem foolish, even naive, given the intertwined crises of climate change, violent conflict, forced migration, widening inequalities, rising xenophobia, and endemic financial instability that we face. Watch or read the daily news and the possibility of breakdown – social, ecological, economic and political – feels very real. Humanity's glass can easily look half empty. Follow those fears through and you can quickly find yourself turning to the economics of collapse and survival which, like all powerful frames, could help to make those very outcomes self-fulfilling.

But there are enough people who still see the alternative, the glass-half-full future, and are intent on bringing it about. I count myself amongst them. Ours is the first generation to properly understand the damage we have been doing to our planetary household, and probably the last generation with the chance to do something transformative about it. And we know full well, as an international community, that we have the technology, know-how and financial means to end extreme poverty in all of its forms should we collectively choose to make that happen.

Think, then, of the students heading to universities worldwide to study economics every year. Many of them will have chosen this subject because they too see the glass half full and passionately want to be part of better managing humanity's shared home in the interests of all. And they believe – as I did – that mastering the mother tongue of public policy is the best way to skill themselves up for the task. Those students deserve the most enlightened economics education possible, whether in words, equations or pictures, and I believe it starts with the seven ways of thinking set out in this book.

The twenty-first-century task is clear: to create economies that promote human prosperity in a flourishing web of life, so that we can thrive in balance within the Doughnut's safe and just space. It starts with recognising that every economy – local to global – is embedded within society and within the living world. It also means recognising that the household, the commons, the market and the state can all be effective means of provisioning for our many needs and wants, and they tend to work best when they work together. By deepening our understanding of human nature we can create institutions and incentives that reinforce our social reciprocity and other-regarding values, rather than undermine them. Once we accept the economy's inherent complexity, we can shape its ever-evolving dynamics through smart stewardship. That opens up the possibility of turning today's divisive and degenerative economies into ones that are distributive and regenerative by design. And it invites us to become agnostic about growth, creating economies that enable us to thrive, whether or not they are growing.

This book has set out just seven ways to think (and draw) like a twenty-first-century economist; there are no doubt many more. But I am convinced that these seven are the best way to start erasing the old economic graffiti that has for so long occupied our minds. Still, even these seven will keep on evolving because we have only just begun drawing their pictures, sensing their patterns, and understanding their interplay. And the politics won't go away either. Given the diverse technological, cultural, economic and political routes that could take us into the Doughnut, there will be many possible ways of distributing the costs and benefits, power and risk, within and between countries and communities. That makes the political process of adjudicating between alternative policies as important as ever.[1]

Storming the citadels

Many of the most exciting insights driving new economic thinking seem to be emerging from every quarter but economics departments themselves. There are of course some important exceptions to that, but they are too rare. So many of the transformative ideas are originating in other fields of thought such as psychology, ecology, physics, history, Earth-system science, geography, architecture, sociology, and complexity science. Economic theory would be wise to embrace what these other perspectives have to offer. In the dance of the intellects, it is time for economics to step back from soloing in the limelight and join the troupe instead. Less Lord of the Dance and more maypole dance, more actively interweaving its theories with insights arising in other disciplines.

The smartest economists have always understood the importance of such intellectual maypole dancing. John Stuart Mill believed that his 1848 book *Principles of Political Economy* was acclaimed in his own day because it treated political economy, 'not as a thing in itself, but as a fragment of a greater whole; a branch of social philosophy, so interlinked with all the other branches that its conclusions, even in its own peculiar province, are only true conditionally, subject to interference and counteraction from causes not directly within its scope'.[2] John Maynard Keynes would clearly have danced round this maypole too. 'The master-economist must possess a rare *combination* of gifts,' he wrote. 'He must be mathematician, historian, statesman, philosopher . . . He must study the present in the light of the past for the purposes of the future. No part of man's nature or his institutions must be entirely outside his regard.'[3] Some prominent contemporary economists echo this view, such as Joseph Stiglitz, who has advised prospective students to 'study economics, but study it with skepticism and study it within the broader context'.[4]

So is intellectual maypole dancing gaining equal popularity in the citadels – the university economics departments themselves? This question inspired me to track down Yuan Yang, the disillusioned economics student who helped to launch a protest movement and whose story opened this book. Nearly a decade on – incongruous though it may sound – she is now a Beijing correspondent for the *Financial Times*, the UK's most prestigious financial newspaper, at the same time as being co-chair of trustees of Rethinking Economics, the international student network that she helped to launch, which is demanding a revolution in economics education. How did she come to straddle two such different worlds? On completing her Master's degree, Yuan turned down a place on a PhD programme because she was convinced that she would learn more about the real economy by working as an economic journalist than she ever would by studying in an economics department. And so she reports on issues at the forefront of China's fast-changing economy, from the large-scale loss of jobs in coal and steel industries to the rise of Beijing as the world's capital for billionaires.

At the same time, Yuan has helped to take Rethinking Economics from strength to strength. Since it was founded in 2013, this student-led movement has built a broad coalition, teaming up with employers who are likewise frustrated by the vast gap between what their graduate recruits understand and the workings of the real economy. The movement has won the support of the wider public too. 'When we travel around the UK giving talks we meet people on the train who ask what we are doing,' Yuan told me.'When we say we think the economists have got it wrong, they immediately know what we are talking about. The financial crisis has turned economics – this strange and awkward profession – into an issue of public discussion and debate.'

To counter the narrow curricula on offer, students at universities worldwide have held teach-ins, set up reading groups, helped to design massive open online courses, or MOOCs, and lobbied their own professors to revamp and diversify the curricula that they are being taught. A few universities, say the students, have embraced their call for a pluralistic education – including Kingston and Greenwich in the UK, Siegen in Germany, Paris 7 and 13 in France, and Aalborg in Denmark. They are bringing economic history and the history of economics back on to the syllabus, updating their macroeconomic models to include the financial sector, and introducing critiques from more diverse schools of thought such as feminist, ecological, behavioural, institutional and complexity economics.

The least responsive universities to date, say the students, have been the most prestigious ones, such as Harvard and the London School of Economics. 'The highest-ranked departments don't want to do anything that would risk losing their place in the league tables,' Yuan told me. 'Their high scores come from publishing research in what are known as the "top" journals, but those journals simply maintain the status quo.' What's more, the league-topping universities set a norm that others follow, with universities in China, India, Brazil and elsewhere training up students to get a place on their elite graduate courses. This intellectual inertia at the top has left Yuan far from satisfied. 'We have to storm the citadels,' she told me, 'we can't just build our camps outside. You can have as many extra-curricular reading groups and MOOCs as you like but unless the university accepts that what you are doing is economics then it's not seen as economics. In the end, we don't just want to talk about the narrowness of the current teaching, we want to change it.'

Her words made me recall just how much Paul Samuelson

relished being the one who got to define what is and is not seen as good economics. Remember his gleeful claim as textbook author knowing that 'the first lick is the privileged one, impinging on the beginner's *tabula rasa* at its most impressionable state'. The *tabula rasa* – or blank slate – is how he saw the novice student's mind. So to today's economics students I would simply say this: be watchful over the ideas that others try to sketch upon your mind. Look out for the words, be wary of the equations, but most of all pay attention to the pictures, especially the most fundamental ones, because they go in deep without your even realising it. What's more, don't let anyone make the extraordinary presumption that, whether 18 or 81, your *tabula* is *rasa*, your economic slate blank. It has in fact been etched with experience from birth, starting with years of nurture in the core economy, backed up by the dependence of every one of us on the living world. And each of us plays multiple roles in the economy throughout our lives, whether as citizen, worker, consumer, entrepreneur, saver or commoner. So don't let anyone try to wipe your slate clean: draw on its rich bank of experience as a personal reference point for sense-checking the economic theories that are put before you – including the ones in this book, of course.

Economic evolution: one experiment at a time

Yuan's frustration with the privileged position still given to old economic theory is palpable. 'Many university departments – such as sociology or political science – teach their students to think in different ways about the economy,' she told me, 'but only people who study neoclassical economic theory in economics departments go out into the world labelled as "economists", with all the power that the label grants them. We have to break down the power of the expert which is concentrated in that title and make it mean lots of different things.'[5]

One promising way of redefining the meaning of 'economist' is to look to those who have gone beyond new economic thinking to new economic doing: the innovators who are evolving the economy one experiment at a time. Their impact is already reflected in the take-off of new business models, in the proven dynamism of the collaborative commons, in the vast potential of digital currencies, and in the inspiring possibilities of regenerative design. As Donella Meadows made clear, the power of self-organisation – the ability of a system to add, change and evolve its own structure – is a high leverage point for whole system change. And that unleashes a revolutionary thought: it makes economists of us all.

If economies change by evolving then every experiment – be it a new enterprise model, complementary currency, or open-source collaboration – helps to diversify, select and amplify a new economic future. We all have a hand in shaping that evolution because our choices and actions are continually remaking the economy and not merely through the products that we do or don't buy. We remake it by: moving our savings to ethical banks; using peer-to-peer complementary currencies; enshrining living purpose in the enterprises that we set up; exercising our rights to parental leave from work; contributing to the knowledge commons; and campaigning with political movements that share our economic vision.

Of course these innovations face the challenge of attempting to grow and thrive within economies that are still heavily dominated by last century's economic thinking and doing. Enterprises that are committed to generous industrial design may sometimes struggle when positioned side by side with last-century businesses that are merely intent on maximising shareholder returns. It cannot be easy to launch a complementary currency if you think the government's first response will be to arrest you. Regenerative finance must feel like an ambitious pitch to clients who are used to focusing on short-term returns. Designing a building that gives back to the city is a tough sell if your client's first reaction is going to be, 'But why would I do that?' Yet from Bangla Pesa's community traders in Kenya and Woelab's recycled 3D printers in Togo to Newlight's plastic-from-methane in California and the worldwide potential of peer-to-peer digital currencies, economic innovators are clearly succeeding in reshaping the economy's evolution, making it distributive and regenerative, design by design.

'Be the change you want to see in the world' is Gandhi's most famous phrase, and in terms of remaking the economy, today's economic innovators are doing him proud. But with all due respect, I want to riff on Gandhi's theme. When it comes to new economic thinking, *draw* the change you want to see in the world too. By combining the well-known power of verbal framing with the hidden power of visual framing, we can give ourselves a far better chance of writing a new economic story – the one that we so desperately need for a safe and just twenty-first century.

It's easy to get started. Just pick up a pencil and draw.

APPENDIX: THE DOUGHNUT AND ITS DATA

The Doughnut of social and planetary boundaries is a simple visualisation of the dual conditions – social and ecological – that underpin collective human well-being. The social foundation demarks the Doughnut's inner boundary, and sets out the basics of life on which no one should be left falling short. The ecological ceiling demarks the Doughnut's outer boundary, beyond which humanity's pressure on Earth's life-giving systems is in dangerous overshoot. Between the two sets of boundaries lies the ecologically safe and socially just space in which humanity can thrive.

The social foundation comprises 12 social dimensions that are derived from the social priorities specified in the United Nation's 2015 Sustainable Development Goals. Table 1 sets out the variables and data used to gauge and illustrate the extent of humanity's shortfall in these 12 areas.

Table 1. The social foundation and its indicators of shortfall

Dimension	Illustrative Indicators (percent of global population unless otherwise stated)	%	Year
Food	Population undernourished	11	2014–16
Health	Population living in countries with under-five mortality rate exceeding 25 per 1,000 live births	46	2015
	Population living in countries with life expectancy at birth of less than 70 years	39	2013
Education	Adult population (aged 15+) who are illiterate	15	2013
	Children aged 12–15 out of school	17	2013
Income and Work	Population living on less than the international poverty line of $3.10 a day	29	2012
	Proportion of young people (aged 15–24) seeking but not able to find work	13	2014
Water and Sanitation	Population without access to improved drinking water	9	2015
	Population without access to improved sanitation	32	2015
Energy	Population lacking access to electricity	17	2013
	Population lacking access to clean cooking facilities	38	2013
Networks	Population stating that they are without someone to count on for help in times of trouble	24	2015
	Population without access to the Internet	57	2015
Housing	Global urban population living in slum housing in developing countries	24	2012
Gender Equality	Representation gap between women and men in national parliaments	56	2014
	Worldwide earnings gap between women and men	23	2009
Social Equity	Population living in countries with a Palma ratio of 2 or more (the ratio of the income share of the top 10% of people to that of the bottom 40%)	39	1995–2012
Political Voice	Population living in countries scoring 0.5 or less out of 1.0 in the Voice and Accountability Index	52	2013
Peace and Justice	Population living in countries scoring 50 or less out of 100 in the Corruption Perceptions Index	85	2014
	Population living in countries with a homicide rate of 10 or more per 100,000	13	2008–13

Sources: FAO, World Bank, WHO, UNDP, UNESCO, UNICEF, OECD, IEA, Gallup, ITU, UN, Cobham and Sumner, ILO, UNODC, and Transparency International. All percentages are rounded to the nearest integer.

The ecological ceiling comprises the nine planetary boundaries proposed by an international group of Earth-system scientists led by Johan Rockström and Will Steffen. These nine critical processes are:

Climate change. When greenhouse gases such as carbon dioxide, methane and nitrous oxide are released into the air, they enter the atmosphere and amplify Earth's natural greenhouse effect, trapping more heat within the atmosphere. This results in global warming, whose effects include rising temperatures, more frequent extremes of weather, and sea level rise.

Ocean acidification. Around one quarter of the carbon dioxide emitted by human activity is eventually dissolved in the oceans, where it forms carbonic acid and decreases the pH of the surface water. This acidity reduces the availability of carbonate ions that are an essential building block used by many marine species for shell and skeleton formation. This missing ingredient makes it hard for organisms such as corals, shellfish and plankton to grow and survive, thus endangering the ocean ecosystem and its food chain.

Chemical pollution. When toxic compounds, such as synthetic organic pollutants and heavy metals, are released into the biosphere they can persist for a very long time, with effects that may be irreversible. And when they accumulate in the tissue of living creatures, including birds and mammals, they reduce fertility and cause genetic damage, endangering ecosystems on land and in the oceans.

Nitrogen and phosphorus loading. Reactive nitrogen and phosphorus are widely used in agricultural fertilisers but only a small proportion of what is applied is actually taken up by crops. Most of the excess runs off into rivers, lakes and oceans, where it causes algae blooms that turn the water green. These blooms can be toxic and they kill off other aquatic life by starving it of oxygen.

Freshwater withdrawals. Water is essential for life and is widely used by agriculture, industry and households. Excessive withdrawals of water, however, can impair or even dry up lakes, rivers and aquifers, damaging ecosystems and altering the hydrological cycle and climate.

Land conversion. Converting land for human use – such as turning forests and wetlands into cities, farmland and highways – depletes Earth's carbon sinks, destroys rich wildlife habitats, and undermines the land's role in continually cycling water, nitrogen and phosphorus.

Biodiversity loss. A decline in the number and variety of living species damages the integrity of ecosystems and accelerates species extinction. In doing so it increases the risk of abrupt and irreversible changes to ecosystems, reducing their resilience and undermining their capacity to provide food, fuel and fibre, and to sustain life.

Air pollution. Micro-particles, or aerosols, emitted into the air – such as smoke, dust and pollutant gases – can damage living organisms. Furthermore, they interact with water vapour in the air and so affect cloud formation. When emitted in large volumes these aerosols can significantly alter regional rainfall patterns, including shifting the timing and location of monsoon rains in tropical regions.

Ozone layer depletion. Earth's stratospheric ozone layer filters out ultraviolet radiation from the sun. Some human-made chemical substances, such as chlorofluorocarbons (CFCs) will, if released, enter the stratosphere and deplete the ozone layer, exposing Earth and its inhabitants to the sun's harmful UV rays.

Table 2 sets out the indicators and data used to gauge the current extent of overshoot of these planetary boundaries.

298

Table 2. The ecological ceiling and its indicators of overshoot

Earth-System Pressure	Control Variable	Planetary Boundary	Current Value and Trend
Climate change	Atmospheric carbon dioxide concentration, parts per million (ppm)	At most 350ppm	400ppm and rising (worsening)
Ocean Acidification	Average saturation of aragonite (calcium carbonate) at the ocean surface, as a percentage of pre-industrial levels	At least 80% of pre-industrial saturation levels	Around 84% and falling (intensifying)
Chemical Pollution	No global control variable yet defined	—	—
Nitrogen and Phosphorus Loading	Phosphorus applied to land as fertiliser, millions of tons per year	At most 6.2 million tons per year	Around 14 million tons per year and rising (worsening)
	Reactive nitrogen applied to land as fertiliser, millions of tons per year	At most 62 million tons per year	Around 150 million tons per year and rising (worsening)
Freshwater Withdrawals	Blue water consumption, cubic kilometres per year	At most 4,000 km^3 per year	Around 2,600 km^3 per year and rising (intensifying)
Land Conversion	Area of forested land as a proportion of forest-covered land prior to human alteration	At least 75%	62% and falling (worsening)
Biodiversity Loss	Rate of species extinction per million species per year	At most 10	Around 100–1,000 and rising (worsening)
Air Pollution	No global control variable yet defined	—	—
Ozone Layer Depletion	Concentration of ozone in the stratosphere, in Dobson Units	At least 275 DU	283 DU and rising (improving)

Source: Steffen et al. (2015b).

NOTES

Who Wants to be an Economist?

1. Autisme-economie (17 June 2000) 'Open letter from economic students'. http://www.autisme-economie.org/article142.html
2. Delreal, J. (2011) 'Students walk out of Ec 10 in solidarity with "Occupy"', *The Harvard Crimson* 2 November 2011. http://www.thecrimson.com/article/2011/11/2/mankiw-walkout-economics-10/
3. International Student Initiative for Pluralism in Economics (2014) 'An international student call for pluralism in economics', available at: http://www.isipe.net/open-letter/
4. Harrington, K. (2015) 'Jamming the economic high priests at the AEA', 7 January 2015, http://kickitover.org/jamming-the-economic-high-priestsat-the-aea/
5. Kick It Over (2015) Kick It Over Manifesto, http://kickitover.org/kick-it-over/manifesto/
6. Roser, M. (2016) *Life Expectancy*, published online at OurWorldInData.org. Retrieved from https://ourworldindata.org/life-expectancy/
7. UNDP (2015) *Human Development Report 2015*. New York: United Nations, p. 4.
8. World Food Programme (2016) *Hunger*. https://www.wfp.org/hunger
9. World Health Organization (2016) *Children: reducing mortality*, published online at http://www.who.int/mediacentre/factsheets/fs178/en/
10. ILO (2015) *Global Employment Trends for Youth 2015*., Geneva: ILO.
11. Hardoon, D., Fuentes, R. and Ayele, S. (2016) *An Economy for the 1%: how privilege and power in the economy drive extreme inequality and how this can be stopped*. Oxfam Briefing Paper 210, Oxford: Oxfam International.

12. Climate Action Tracker (2016) *Climate Action Tracker*, published online at http://climateactiontracker.org/

13. Global Agriculture (2015) *Soil Fertility and Erosion*, published online at http://www.globalagriculture.org/report-topics/soil-fertility-and-erosion.html and UNDESA (2014) *International Decade for Action 'Water for Life' 2005–2015*, published online at http://www.un.org/waterforlifedecade/scarcity.shtml

14. FAO (2010) *State of the World Fisheries and Aquaculture* (SOFIA), FAO Fisheries Department, http://www.fao.org/docrep/013/i1820e/i1820e01.pdf and Ellen McArthur Foundation (2016) *The New Plastics Economy: rethinking the future of plastics*, published online at https://www.ellenmacarthurfoundation.org/publications/the-new-plastics-economy-rethinking-the-future-of-plastics

15. United Nations (2015) *World Population Prospects: The 2015 Revision*. New York: UN, p. 1.

16. PwC (2015) *The World in 2050: Will the shift in global economic power continue?* Published online at https://www.pwc.com/gx/en/issues/the-economy/assets/world-in-2050-february-2015.pdf

17. OECD Observer (2015) *An Emerging Middle Class*, published online at http://www.oecdobserver.or/news/fullstory.php/aid/3681/An_emerging_middle_class.html

18. Michaels, F.S. (2011) *Monoculture: How One Story Is Changing Everything*. Canada: Red Clover Press, pp. 9 and 131.

19. Keynes, J.M. (1961) *The General Theory of Employment, Interest and Money*. London: Macmillan, p. 383.

20. von Hayek, Friedrich (10 December 1974) 'Friedrich von Hayek'. Banquet Speech. The Nobel Foundation. http://www.nobelprize.org/nobel_prizes/economic-sciences/laureates/1974/hayek-speech.html

21. Brander, L. and Schuyt, K. (2010) 'Benefits transfer: the economic value of the world's wetlands', TEEBcase available at TEEBweb.org, and Centre for Food Security (2015); 'Sustainable pollination services for UK crops', University of Reading, available at: https://www.reading.ac.uk/web/FILES/food-security/CFS_Case_Studies_-_Sustainable_Pollination_Services.pdf

22. Toffler, A. (1970) *Future Shock*. London: Pan Books, pp. 374–5.

23. Berger, J. (1972) *Ways of Seeing*. London: Penguin. p. 7.

24. Thorpe, S., Fize, D. and Marlot, C. (6 June 1996) 'Speed of processing in the human visual system', *Nature* 381, pp. 520–522

25. Kringelbach, M. (2008) *The Pleasure Center: Trust Your Animal Instincts*. Oxford: Oxford University Press, pp. 86–87.

26. Burmark, L. *Why Visual Literacy?* Burmark Handouts, available at: http://tcpd.org/Burmark/Handouts/WhyVisualLit.html

27. Rodriguez, L. and Dimitrova, D. (2011) 'The levels of visual framing', *Journal of Visual Literacy* 30: 1, pp. 48–65.

28. Christianson, S. (2012) *100 Diagrams That Changed the World*. London: Salamander Books.

29. Marshall, A. (1890) *Principles of Economics*. London: Marshall, Preface, pp.10 and 11. http://www.econlib.org/library/Marshall/marP0.html#Preface

30. Parker, R. (2002) *Reflections on the Great Depression*. Cheltenham: Edward Elgar, p. 25.

31. Samuelson, P. (1997) 'Credo of a lucky textbook author', *Journal of Economic Perspectives* 11: 2, pp. 153–160.

32. Samuelson, P. (1948) *Economics: An Introductory Analysis*, 1st edn. New York: McGraw-Hill.p. 264, cited in Giraud, Y. (2010) 'The changing place of visual representation in economics: Paul Samuelson between principle and strategy, 1941–1955', *Journal of the History of Economic Thought* 32: 2, pp. 1–23.

33. Frost, G. (2009) Nobel-winning economist Paul A. Samuelson dies at age 94. MIT News 13 December 2009. http://newsoffice.mit.edu/2009/obit-samuelson-1213

34. Samuelson, P. 'Foreword', in Saunders, P. and Walstad, W., *The Principles of Economics Course: A Handbook for Instructors*. New York: McGraw Hill, 1990, p. ix

35. Schumpeter, J. (1954) *History of Economic Analysis*. London: Allen & Unwin, p. 41.

36. Kuhn, T. (1962) *The Structure of Scientific Revolutions*. London: University of Chicago Press, p. 46.

37. Goffmann, E. (1974) *Frame Analysis: An Essay on the Organization of Experience*. New York: Harper & Row.

38. Keynes, J.M. (1961) *The General Theory of Employment, Interest and Money*. London: Macmillan & Co., p. viii.

39. Box, G. and Draper, N. (1987) *Empirical Model Building and Response Surfaces*. New York: John Wiley & Sons, p. 424.

40. Lakoff, G. (2014) *The All New Don't Think of an Elephant*. White River Junction, VT: Chelsea Green.

41. Tax Justice Network, www.taxjustice.net and Global Alliance for Tax Justice, www.globaltaxjustice.org

1. Change the Goal

1. 'G20 summit: leaders pledge to grow their economies by 2.1%', BBC News, 16 November 2014, available at http://www.bbc.co.uk/news/world-australia-30072674

2. 'EU "unhappy" climate change is off G20 agenda', *The Australian*, 3 April 2014, available at http://www.theaustralian.com.au/national-affairs/climate/eu-un happy-climate-change-is-off-g20-agenda/story-e6frg6xf-1226873127864

3. Steuart, J. (1767) *An Inquiry into the Principles of Political Economy*, https://www.marxists.org/reference/subject/economics/steuart/

4. Smith, A. (1776) *An Inquiry into the Nature and Causes of the Wealth of Nations*, Book 4.

5. Mill, J.S. (1844) 'On the definition of political economy', in *Essays on Some Unsettled Questions of Political Economy*, http://www.econlib.org/library/Mill/mlUQP5.html

6. Spiegel, H.W. (1987) 'Jacob Viner (1892–1970)', in Eatwell, J., Milgate, M. and Newman, P. (eds) (1987) *The New Palgrave: A Dictionary of Economics*, Vol. IV London: Macmillan, pp. 812–814.

7. Robbins, L. (1932) *Essay on The Nature and Significance of Economic Science*. London: Macmillan.

8. Mankiw, G. (2012) *Principles of Economics*, 6th edn. Delhi: Cengage Learning.

9. Lipsey, R. (1989) *An Introduction to Positive Economics*. London: Weidenfeld & Nicolson, p. 140, and Begg, D. et al. (1987) *Economics*. Maidenhead: McGraw-Hill, p. 90.

10. Fioramenti, L. (2013) *Gross Domestic Product: The Politics Behind the World's Most Powerful Number*. London: Zed Books, pp. 29–30.

11. Arndt, H. (1978) *The Rise and Fall of Economic Growth*. Chicago: University of Chicago Press, p. 56.

12. OECD Convention 1961. Article 1(a).

13. Lakoff, G. and Johnson, M. (1980) *Metaphors We Live By*. Chicago: University of Chicago Press, pp. 14–24.

14. Samuelson, P. (1964) *Economics*, 6th edn. New York: McGraw-Hill, cited in Arndt, H. (1978) *The Rise and Fall of Economic Growth*. Chicago: University of Chicago Press, p. 75.

15. Kuznets, S. (1934) *National Income 1929–1932*, 73rd US Congress, 2nd session, Senate document no. 124 (7)

16. Meadows, D. (1999) 'Sustainable Systems'. Lecture at the University of Michigan, 18 March 1999, https://www.youtube.com/watch?v=HMmChiLZZHg

17. Kuznets, S. (1962) 'How to judge quality', in Croly, H. (ed.), *The New Republic*, 147: 16, p. 29.

18. Ruskin, J. (1860) *Unto This Last*, Essay IV 'Ad valorem', section 77.

19. Schumacher, E.F. (1973) *Small Is Beautiful*. London: Blond & Briggs, and Max-Neef, M. (1991) *Human Scale Development*. New York: Apex Press.

20. Shaikh, N. (2004) *Amartya Sen: A More Human Theory of Development*. Asia Society, available at: http://asiasociety.org/amartya-sen-more-human-theory-development

21. Sen, A. (1999) *Development as Freedom*. New York: Alfred A. Knopf, p. 285.

22. Stiglitz, J.E, Sen, A. and Fitoussi. J-P. (2009) *Report by the Commission on the Measurement of Economic Performance and Social Progress*, Paris, p. 9. http://www.stiglitz-sen-fitoussi.fr/documents/rapport_anglais.pdf

23. United Nations (2015) Sustainable Development Goals, available at https://sustainabledevelopment.un.org/?menu=1300

24. Steffen, W. et al. (2015) 'The trajectory of the Anthropocene: the Great Acceleration', *Anthropocene Review* 2: 1, pp. 81–98.

25. International Geosphere-Biosphere Programme (2015) 'Planetary dashboard shows "Great Acceleration" in human activity since 1950', press release 15 January 2015, available at: http://www.igbp.net/news/pressreleases/pressreleases/planetary dashboardshowsgreataccelerationinhumanactivitysince1950.5.950c2fa1495db7 081eb42.html

26. This graph is adapted from Young, O. R. and Steffen, W. (2009) 'The Earth System: sustaining planetary life-support systems', pp. 295–315 in Chapin, III, F.S., Kofinas, G.P. and Folke, C. (eds), *Principles of Ecosystem Stewardship: Resilience-Based Natural Resource Management in a Changing World*. New York: Springer.

27. Diamond, J. (2002) 'Evolution, consequences and future of plant and animal domestication', *Nature* 418, pp. 700–707.

28. Berger, A. and Loutre, M.F. (2002) 'An exceptionally long interglacial ahead?' *Science* 297, p. 1287.

29. Steffen,W. et al. (2011) 'The Anthropocene: from global change to planetary stewardship', *AMBIO* 40, pp. 739–761.

30. Folke, C. et al. (2011) 'Reconnecting to the biosphere', *AMBIO* 40, p. 719.

31. WWF (2014) *Living Planet Report*. Gland: WWF International.

32. Personal communication with Katherine Richardson, 10 May 2016.

33. Heilbroner, R. (1970) 'Ecological Armageddon', *New York Review of Books*, 23 April. http://www.nybooks.com/articles/archives/1970/apr/23/ecological-armageddon/

34. Ward, B. and Dubos, R. (1973) *Only One Earth*. London: Penguin Books.

35. Friends of the Earth (1990) Action plan for a sustainable Netherlands, available at http://www.iisd.ca/consume/fjeld.html

36. Gudynas, E. (2011) 'Buen Vivir: today's tomorrow', *Development* 54: 4, pp. 441–447. http://www.palgrave-journals.com/development/journal/v54/n4/full/dev 201186a.html

37. Government of Ecuador (2008), Constitution of Ecuador, Article 71. http://therightsofnature.org/wp-content/uploads/pdfs/Rights-for-Nature-Articles-in-Ecuadors-Constitution.pdf

38. Rockström, J. *The Great Acceleration*. Lecture 3 in Planetary Boundaries and Human Opportunities online course, https://www.sdsnedu.org/learn/planetary-boundaries-and-human-opportunities-fall-2014

39. Sayers, M. and Trebeck, K. (2014) *The Scottish Doughnut: a safe and just operating space for Scotland*. Oxford: Oxfam GB; Sayers, M. (2015) *The Welsh Doughnut: a framework for environmental sustainability and social justice*. Oxford: Oxfam GB; Sayers, M. (2015) *The UK Doughnut: a framework for environmental sustainability and social justice*. Oxford: Oxfam GB; and Cole, M. (2015) *Is South Africa Operating in a Safe and Just Space? Using the doughnut model to explore environmental sustainability and social justice*. Oxford: Oxfam GB.

40. Dearing, J. et al. (2014) 'Safe and just operating spaces for regional social-ecological systems', *Global Environmental Change*, 28, pp. 227–238.

41. City Think Space (2012), *Kokstad & Franklin Integrated Sustainable Development Plan* (15), available at: https://issuu.com/city_think_space/docs/kisdp_final_report

42. Dorling, D. (2013) *Population 10 Billion*. London: Constable, pp. 303–308.

43. Chancel, L. and Piketty, T. (2015) *Carbon and Inequality: From Kyoto to Paris*. Paris: Paris School of Economics.

44. Institute of Mechanical Engineers (2013) *Global Food: Waste Not, Want Not*. London: Institute of Mechanical Engineers, https://www.imeche.org/policy-and-press/reports/detail/global-food-waste-not-want-not

45. Jackson, T. (2010) 'An Economic Reality Check'. TED Talk, available at https://www.ted.com/talks/tim_jackson_s_economic_reality_check/transcript?language=en

46. Secretariat of the Convention on Biological Diversity (2012) *Cities and Biodiversity Outlook*, Montreal, available at: https://www.cbd.int/doc/health/cbo-action-policy-en.pdf, p. 19.

2. See the Big Picture

1. Palfrey, S. and Stern, T. (2007) *Shakespeare in Parts*. Oxford: Oxford University Press.

2. Shakespeare, W. (1623) *Mr William Shakespeares comedies, histories and tragedies*, First folio, available at http://firstfolio.bodleian.ox.ac.uk/, p. 19.

3. Harford, T. (2013) *The Undercover Economist Strikes Back*. London: Little, Brown, pp. 8–14.

4. Sterman, J. D. (2002) 'All models are wrong: reflections on becoming a systems scientist', *System Dynamics Review* 18: 4, p. 513.

5. The Mont Pelerin Society website available at https://www.montpelerin.org/

6. Stedman Jones, D. (2012) *Masters of the Universe: Hayek, Friedman and the Birth of Neoliberal Politics*. Woodstock: Princeton University Press, pp. 8–9.

7. Klein, N. (2007) *The Shock Doctrine*. London: Penguin.

8. Smith, A. (1776) *An Inquiry into the Nature and Causes of the Wealth of Nations*, Book 1, Chapter 2, available at http://geolib.com/smith.adam/won1-02.html.

9. Fama, E. (1970) 'Efficient capital markets: a review of theory and empirical work', *Journal of Finance* 25: 2, pp. 383–417.

10. Ricardo, D. (1817) *On the Principles of Political Economy and Taxation*, in Piero Sraffa (ed.), *Works and Correspondence of David Ricardo*, Vol. I, Cambridge: Cambridge University Press, 1951, p. 135.

11. Friedman, M. (1962) *Capitalism and Freedom*. Chicago: University of Chicago Press.

12. Hardin, G. (1968) 'The tragedy of the commons', *Science* 162: 3859.

13. Interview with Margaret Thatcher by Douglas Keay, *Woman's Own*, 23 September 1987, http://www.margaretthatcher.org/document/106689

14. Simon, J. and Kahn, H. (1984) *The Resourceful Earth: a response to Global 2000*. Oxford: Basil Blackwell.

15. Friedman, M. (1978) 'The Role of Government in a Free Society'. Lecture given at Stanford University, available at https://www.youtube.com/watch?v=LucOUSpTB3Y

16. Diagram inspired by Daly, H. (1996) *Beyond Growth*. Boston: Beacon Press, p. 46; Bauwens, M. (2014) 'Commons Transition Plan', available at http://p2pfoundation.net/Commons_Transition_Plan, and Goodwin, N. et al. (2009) *Microeconomics in Context*. New York: Routledge, pp. 350–359

17. Ricardo, D. (1817) *On the Principles of Political Economy and Taxation*, Ch. 2, http://www.econlib.org/library/Ricardo/ricP.html

18. Schabas, M. (1995) 'John Stuart Mill and concepts of nature', *Dialogue*, 34: 3, p. 452.

19. Gaffney, M. and Harrison, F. (1994) *The Corruption of Economics*. London: Shepheard-Walwyn.

20. Wolf, M. (2010) 'Why were resources expunged from neo-classical economics?' *Financial Times*, 12 July 2010. http://blogs.ft.com/martin-wolf-exchange/tag/resources/

21. Green, T. (2012) 'Introductory economics textbooks: what do they teach about sustainability?', *International Journal of Pluralism and Economics Education*, 3: 2, pp. 189–223.

22. Daly, H. and Farley, J. (2011) *Ecological Economics*. Washington: Island Press, p. 16.

23. Daly, H. (1990) 'Toward some operational principles of sustainable development', *Ecological Economics*, 2, pp. 1–6.

24. IPCC (2013) *Climate Change 2013: The Physical Science Basis. Contributions of Working Group I to the Fifth Assessment Report of the Intergovernmental Panel on Climate Change*. Cambridge: Cambridge University Press.

25. Putnam, R. (2000) *Bowling Alone: The Collapse and Revival of American Community*. New York: Simon & Schuster, p. 19.

26. Putnam, R. (2000) *Bowling Alone*, p. 290.

27. 'Election day will not be enough': an interview with Howard Zinn, by Lee, J. and Tarleton, J. *The Indypendent*, 14 November 2008, available at: http://howardzinn. org/election-day-will-not-be-enough-an-interview-with-howard-zinn/

28. Marçal, K. (2015) *Who Cooked Adam Smith's Dinner?* London: Portobello.

29. Folbre, N. (1994) *Who Pays for the Kids?* London: Routledge.

30. Coote, A. and Goodwin,. N. (2010) *The Great Transition: Social Justice and the Core Economy*. nef working paper 1. London: New Economics Foundation.

31. Coote, A. and Franklin, J. (2013) *Time On Our Side: Why We All Need a Shorter Working Week*. London: New Economics Foundation.

32. Toffler, A. (1998) 'Life Matters'. Interview by Norman Swann, Australian Broadcasting Corporation, 5 March 1998. http://www.ghandchi.com/ iranscope/Anthology/Alvin_Toffler98.htm

33. Razavi, S. (2007) *The Political and Social Economy of Care in a Development Context*. Gender and Development Programme Paper no. 3, Geneva: United Nations Research Institute for Social Development. http://www.unrisd. org/80256B3C005BCCF9/(httpAuxPages)/2DBE6A93350A7783C12573240036 D5A0/$file/Razavi-paper.pdf

34. Salary.com (2014) 2014 Mother's Day Infographics. http://www.salary.com/ how-much-are-moms-worth-in-2014/slide/13/

35. Fälth, A. and Blackden, M. (2009) *Unpaid Care Work*, UNDP Policy Brief on Gender Equality and Poverty Reduction, Issue 01, New York: UNDP, available at http://www.undp.org/content/dam/undp/library/gender/Gender%20 and%20Poverty%20Reduction/Unpaid%20care%20work%20English.pdf

36. Chang, H.J. (2010) *23 Things They Don't Tell You About Capitalism*. London: Allen Lane, p. 1.

37. Block, F. and Somers, M. (2014) *The Power of Market Fundamentalism: Karl Polanyi's critique*. London: Harvard University Press, pp. 20–21.

38. Ostrom, E. (1999) 'Coping with tragedies of the commons', *Annual Review of Political Science* 2, pp. 493–535.

39. Rifkin, J. (2014) *The Zero Marginal Cost Society*. New York: Palgrave Macmillan, p. 4.

40. Milton Friedman Speaks. Lecture 4: 'The Role of Government in a Free Society', Stanford University, 1978, available at: https://www.youtube.com/watch?v=LucOUSpTB3Y

41. Samuelson, P. (1980) *Economics*, 11th edn. New York: McGraw-Hill, p. 592.

42. Mazzucato, M. (2013) *The Entrepreneurial State*. London: Anthem Press.

43. Chang, H.J. (2010) *23 Things They Don't Tell You About Capitalism*. London: Allen Lane , p. 136.

44. Acemoglu, D. and Robinson, J. (2013) *Why Nations Fail: The Origins of Power, Prosperity and Poverty*. London: Profile Books.

45. Goodman, P. (2008) 'Taking a hard new look at Greenspan legacy', *New York Times*, 8 October 2008. http://www.nytimes.com/2008/10/09/business/economy/09greenspan.html?pagewanted=all

46. Raworth, K. (2002) *Trading Away Our Rights: women workers in global supply chains*. Oxford: Oxfam International.

47. Chang, H-J. (2010) *23 Things They Don't Tell You About Capitalism*, London: Allen Lane.

48. Ferguson, T. (1995) *Golden Rule: The Investment Theory of Party Competition and the Logic of Money-Driven Political Systems*. London: University of Chicago Press, p. 8.

49. BBC News 2 April 2014. 'US Supreme Court strikes down overall donor limits'. http://www.bbc.co.uk/news/world-us-canada-26855657

50. Hernandez, J. (2015) 'The new global corporate law', in *The State of Power 2015*. Amsterdam: The Transnational Institute. https://www.tni.org/files/download/tni_state-of-power-2015.pdf

3. Nurture Human Nature

1. Morgan, M. (2012) *The World in the Model*. Cambridge: Cambridge University Press, pp. 157–167.

2. Smith, A. (1776) *An Inquiry into the Nature and Causes of the Wealth of Nations*, Book 1, Chapters 2.1 and 2.2. Reprint edn 1994, New York: Modern Library.

3. Smith, A. (1759) *The Theory of Moral Sentiments*, Part I, Section 1, Chapter 1, available at http://www.econlib.org/library/Smith/smMS.html

4. Mill, J.S. (1844) *Essays on Some Unsettled Questions of Political Economy*, V.38 and V.46, www.econlib.org/library/Mill/mlUQP5.html#Essay V. 'On the Definition of Political Economy'.

5. Devas, C.S. (1883) *Groundwork of Economics*, Longmans, Green and Company, pp. 27 and 43.

6. Jevons, W.S. (1871) *The Theory of Political Economy* (III.47). http://www.econlib.org/library/YPDBooks/Jevons/jvnPE.html

7. Morgan, M. (2012) *The World in the Model*. Cambridge: Cambridge University Press, pp. 145–147.

8. Marshall, A. (1890) *Principles of Economics*, Book 3, Chapter 2.1. http://files.libertyfund.org/files/1676/Marshall_0197_EBk_v6.0.pdf

9. Knight, F. (1999) *Selected Essays by Frank H. Knight, Volume 2*. Chicago: University of Chicago Press, p. 18.

10. Friedman, M. (1966) *Essays in Positive Economics*. Chicago: University of Chicago Press, p. 40.

11. Morgan, M. (2012) *The World in the Model*. Cambridge: Cambridge University Press, p. 157.

12. Frank, B. and Schulze, G.G. (2000) 'Does economics make citizens corrupt?' *Journal of Economic Behavior and Organization* 43, pp. 101–113.

13. Frank, R., Gilovich, T. and Regan, D. (1993) 'Does studying economics inhibit cooperation?' *Journal of Economic Perspectives* 7: 2 (pp. 159–171) and Wang, L., Malhotra, D. and Murnighan, K. (2011) 'Economics Education and GreedAcademy of Management Learning and Education, 10: 4, pp. 643–660.

14. Frank, R., Gilovich, T. and Regan, T. (1993) 'Does studying economics inhibit cooperation?' *Journal of Economic Perspectives* 7: 2, pp. 159–171.

15. Frank, R. 1988. *Passions within Reason*. New York: W.W. Norton, p. xi.

16. MacKenzie, D. and Millo, Y. (2003) 'Constructing a market, performing theory: the historical sociology of a financial derivatives exchange', *American Journal of Sociology* 109: 1, cited in Ferraro, F., Pfeffer, J. and Sutton, R. (2005) 'Economics language and assumptions: how theories can become self-fulfilling', *Academy of Management Review* 30: 1, pp. 8–24.

17. Molinsky, A., Grant, A. and Margolis, J. (2012) 'The bedside manner of homo economicus: how and why priming an economic schema reduces compassion', *Organizational Behavior and Human Decision Processes* 119: 1, pp. 27–37.

18. Bauer, M. et al. (2012) 'Cuing consumerism: situational materialism undermines personal and social well-being', *Psychological Science* 23, pp. 517–523.

19. Shrubsole, G. (2012) 'Consumers outstrip citizens in the British media', *Open Democracy UK*, 5 March 2012.

20. Lewis, J. et al. (2005) *Citizens or Consumers? What the Media Tell Us About Political Participation*, cited in Shrubsole, G. (2012) 'Consumers outstrip citizens in the British media', *Open Democracy UK*, 5 March 2012.

21. Henrich, J., Heine, S. and Norenzayan, A. (2010) 'The weirdest people in the world?', *Behavioural and Brain Sciences* 33: 2/3, pp. 61–83.

22. Jensen, K., Vaish, A. and Schmidt, M. (2014) 'The emergence of human prosociality: aligning with others through feelings, concerns, and norms', *Frontiers in Psychology* 5, p. 822. http://journal.frontiersin.org/article/10.3389/fpsyg.2014.00822/full

23. Bowles, S. and Gintis, H. (2011) *A Cooperative Species: Human Reciprocity and Its Evolution*. Princeton, NJ: Princeton University Press, p. 20.

24. Helbing, D. (2013) 'Economics 2.0: the natural step towards a self-regulating, participatory market society', *Evolutionary and Institutional Economics Review*, 10: 1, pp. 3–41.

25. Kagel, J. and Roth, A. (1995) *The Handbook of Experimental Economics*, Princeton, NJ: Princeton University Press pp. 253–348, cited in Beinhocker, E. (2007) *The Origin of Wealth*, London: Random House, p. 120.

26. Henrich, J. et al. (2001) 'In search of Homo Economicus: behavioral experiments in 15 small-scale societies', *Economics and Social Behavior*, 91: 2, pp. 73–78.

27. Bernays, E. (2005) *Propaganda,* New York: Ig Publishing, pp. 37–38.

28. Edward L. Bernays video interview on the Beech-Nut Packing Co., available at https://www.youtube.com/watch?v=6vFz_FgGvJI, and on 'Torches of Freedom', available at: https://www.youtube.com/watch?v=6pyyP2chM8k

29. Ryan, R. and Deci, E. (1999) 'Intrinsic and extrinsic motivations: classic definitions and new directions', *Contemporary Educational Psychology* 25, pp. 54–67.

30. Schwartz, S. (1994) 'Are there universal aspects in the structure and content of human values?', *Journal of Social Issues* 50: 4, pp.19–45.

31. Veblen, T. (1898) 'Why is economics not an evolutionary science?', *Quarterly Journal of Economics* 12: 4, pp. 373–397.

32. Salganik, M., Sheridan Dodds, P. and Watts, D. (2006) 'Experimental study of inequality and unpredictability in an Artificial Cultural Market', *Science* 311, p. 854.

33. Ormerod, P. (2012) 'Networks and the need for a new approach to policymaking', in Dolphin, T. and Nash, D. (eds), *Complex New World*, London: IPPR, pp. 28–29.

34. Stiglitz, J. (2011) 'Of the 1%, for the 1%, by the 1%', *Vanity Fair* May. http://www.vanityfair.com/news/2011/05/top-one-percent-201105

35. Ormerod, P. (2012), 'Networks and the need for a new approach to policymaking', in Dolphin, T. and Nash, D. (eds), *Complex New World.* London: IPPR, p. 30.

36. Wikipedia (2016) *List of Cognitive Biases.* https://en.wikipedia.org/wiki/List_of_cognitive_biases

37. Thaler, R. and Sunstein, C. (2009) *Nudge: Improving Decisions About Health, Wealth and Happiness.* London: Penguin, p. 6.

38. Marewzki, J. and Gigerenzer, G. (2012), 'Heuristic decision making in medicine', *Dialogues in Clinical Neuroscience,* 14: 1, pp. 77–89.

39. *The Economist* (2014) Q&A: Gerd Gigerenezer 28 May 2014. http://www.economist.com/blogs/prospero/2014/05/qa-gerd-gigerenzer

40. Bacon, F. (1620) *Novum Organon,* CXXIX, available at: http://www.constitution.org/bacon/nov_org.htm

41. Leopold, A. (1989) *A Sand County Almanac.* New York: Oxford University Press, p. 204.

42. Scharmer, O. (2013) 'From ego-system to eco-system economies', *Open Democracy,* 23 September 2013. https://www.opendemocracy.net/transformation/otto-scharmer/from-ego-system-to-eco-system-economies

43. Henrich, J., Heine, S. and Norenzayan, A. (2010) 'The weirdest people in the world?', *Behavioural and Brain Sciences* 33: 2/3, pp. 61–83.

44. Arendt, H. (1973) *Origins of Totalitarianism.* New York: Harcourt Brace Jovanovich, p. 287.

45. Fall 2005 Commencement Address by Chief Oren Lyons, Berkeley College of Natural Resources, 22 May 2005, available at: https://nature.berkeley.edu/news/2005/05/fall-2005-commencement-address-chief-oren-lyons

46. Eisenstein, C. (2011) *Sacred Economics: Money, Gift and Society in the Age of Transition.* Berkeley: Evolver Books, p. 159.

47. Jo Cox, Maiden speech in Parliament, 3 June 2015, Parliament TV, available at: www.theguardian.com/politics/video/2016/jun/16/labour-mp-jo-cox-maiden-speech-parliament-video

48. Winter, C. (2014) 'Germany reaches new levels of greendom, gets 31 percent of its electricity from renewables', *Newsweek* 14 August 2014. http://www.bloomberg.com/news/articles/2014-08-14/germany-reaches-new-levels-of-greendom-gets-31-percent-of-its-electricity-from-renewables

49. Titmuss, R. (1971) *The Gift Relationship: From Human Blood to Social Policy.* New York: Pantheon Books.

50. Barrera–Osorio, F. et al. (2011) 'Improving the design of conditional transfer programs: evidence from a randomized education experiment in Colombia', *American Economic Journal: Applied Economics,* 3: 2, pp. 167–195.

51. Sandel, M. (2012) *What Money Can't Buy: The Moral Limits of Markets*. London: Allen Lane.

52. Gneezy, U. and Rustichini, A. (2000) 'A fine is a price', *Journal of Legal Studies*, 29, pp. 1–17.

53. Sandel, M. (2012) *What Money Can't Buy: The Moral Limits of Markets*. London: Allen Lane.

54. Bauer, M. et al. (2012) 'Cueing consumerism: situational materialism undermines personal and social well-being', *Psychological Science* 23: 517.

55. Kerr, J. et al. (2012) 'Prosocial behavior and incentives: evidence from field experiments in rural Mexico and Tanzania', *Ecological Economics* 73, pp. 220–227.

56. García-Amado, L.R., Ruiz Pérez, M. and Barrasa García, S. (2013) 'Motivation for conservation: assessing integrated conservation and development projects and payments for environmental services in La Sepultura Biosphere Reserve, Chiapas, Mexico', *Ecological Economics* 89, pp. 92–100.

57. Rode, J., Gómez-Baggethun, E. and Krause, T. (2015), 'Motivation crowding by economic incentives in conservation policy: a review of the empirical evidence', *Ecological Economics* 117, pp. 270–282.

58. Wald, D., et al. (2014) 'Randomized trial of text messaging on adherence to cardiovascular preventive treatment, *Plos ONE* 9, p. 12.

59. Pop-Eleches, C. et al. (2011) 'Mobile phone technologies improve adherence to antiretroviral treatment in resource-limited settings: a randomized controlled trial of text message reminders', *AIDS* 25: 6, pp. 825–834.

60. iNudgeyou (2012) 'Green nudge: nudging litter into the bin', 16 February 2012 http://inudgeyou.com/archives/819 and Webster, G. (2012) 'Is a "nudge" in the right direction all we need to be greener?', CNN 15 February 2012. http://edition.cnn.com/2012/02/08/tech/innovation/green-nudge-environment-persuasion/index.html

61. Ayers, J. et al. (2013) 'Do celebrity cancer diagnoses promote primary cancer prevention?', *Preventive Medicine* 58: pp. 81–84.

62. Beaman, L. et al. (2012) 'Female leadership raises aspirations and educations attainment for girls: a policy experiment in India', *Science* 335: 6068, pp. 582–586.

63. Bolderdijk, J. et al. (2012) 'Comparing the effectiveness of monetary versus moral motives in environmental campaigning', *Nature Climate Change*, 3, pp. 413–416.

64. Bjorkman, M. and Svensson, J. (2009) 'Power to the people: evidence from a randomized field experiment on community-based monitoring in Uganda', *Quarterly Journal of Economics* 124:2, pp. 735–769.

65. Crompton, T. and Kasser, T. (2009) *Meeting Environmental Challenges: The Role of Human Identity.* Godalming, Surrey: WWF. http://assets.wwf. org.uk/downloads/meeting_environmental_challenges___the_role_of_human_ identity.pdf

66. Montgomery, S. (2015) *The Soul of an Octopus.* London: Simon & Schuster.

4. Get Savvy with Systems

1. Jevons, S. (1871) *The Theory of Political Economy* (vii), http://www.econlib.org/ library/YPDBooks/Jevons/jvnPE.html

2. Walras, L. (1874, 2013) *Elements of Pure Economics.* London: Routledge, p. 86.

3. Jevons, W. S. (1871) *The Theory of Political Economy* (1.17), available at http:// www.econlib.org/library/YPDBooks/Jevons/jvnPE

4. Arrow, K. and Debreu, G. (1954) 'Existence of an equilibrium for a competitive economy', *Econometrica* 22, pp. 265–290.

5. Keen, S. (2011) *Debunking Economics.* London: Zed Books, pp. 56–63.

6. Solow, R. (2003) 'Dumb and Dumber in Macroeconomics'. Speech given in honour of Joseph Stiglitz's 60th birthday, available at http://textlab.io/ doc/927882/dumb-and-dumber-in-macroeconomics-robert-m.-solow-so

7. Solow, R. (2008) 'The state of macroeconomics', *Journal of Economic Perspectives* 22: 1, pp. 243–249.

8. Weaver, W. (1948) 'Science and complexity', *American Scientist* 36, p. 536.

9. Colander, D. (2000) 'New millennium economics: how did it get this way, and what way is it?', *Journal of Economic Perspectives* 14: 1, pp. 121–132.

10. Sterman, J. D. (2000) *Business Dynamics: Systems Thinking and Modeling for a Complex World.* New York: McGraw-Hill, pp. 13-14.

11. Gal, O. (2012) 'Understanding global ruptures: a complexity perspective on the emerging middle crisis', in Dolphin, T. and Nash, D. (eds), *Complex New World.* London: IPPR, p. 156.

12. Meadows, D. (2008) *Thinking In Systems: A Primer.* White River Junction, VT: Chelsea Green, p. 181.

13. Keen, S. (2011) *Debunking Economics.* London: Zed Books, p. 184.

14. Marx, K. (1867) *Capital*, Vol. I, Chapter 25, Section 1, available at http://www. econlib.org/library/YPDBooks/Marx/mrxCpA.html

15. Veblen, T. (1898), 'Why is economics not an evolutionary science?' *Quarterly Journal of Economics*, 12: 4 (pp. 373–397; at p. 373.

16. Marshall, A. (1890) *Principles of Economics.* London: Macmillan, available at http://www.econlib.org/library/Marshall/marP.html

17. Keynes, J.M. (1923) *A Tract on Monetary Reform*, p. 80, in *The Collected Writings of John Maynard Keynes*, Vol. IV, 1977 edn. London: Palgrave Macmillan.

18. Schumpeter, J. (1942) *Capitalism, Socialism and Democracy*. New York: Harper & Row.

19. Robinson, J. (1962) *Essays in the Theory of Economic Growth*. London: Macmillan, p. 25.

20. Hayek, F. (1974) 'The Pretence of Knowledge'. Lecture to the memory of Alfred Nobel, 11 December 1974, available at http://www.nobelprize.org/nobel_prizes/economic-sciences/laureates/1974/hayek-lecture.html

21. Daly, H. (1992) *Steady State Economics*. London: Earthscan, p. 88.

22. Sterman, J. D. (2012) 'Sustaining sustainability: creating a systems science in a fragmented academy and polarized world', in Weinstein, M.P. and Turner, R.E. (eds), *Sustainability Science: The Emerging Paradigm and the Urban Environment*. New York: Springer Science, p. 24.

23. Soros, G. (2009) 'Soros: a general theory of reflexivity', *Financial Times*, 26 October 2009. http://www.ft.com/cms/s/2/0ca06172-bfe9-11de-aed2-00144feab49a.html#axzz3dtwpK5o2

24. Holodny, E. (2016) 'Isaac Newton was a genius but even he lost millions in the stock market', 20 January 2016, Businessinsider.com, available at http://uk.businessinsider.com/isaac-newton-lost-a-fortune-on-englands-hottest-stock-2016-1?r=US&IR=T

25. Keen, S. *Rethinking Economics Kingston 2014*, 19 November 2014. https://www.youtube.com/watch?v=dR_75cdCujI

26. Brown, G. (1999), Speech to the Labour Party Conference, 27 September 1999. http://news.bbc.co.uk/1/hi/uk_politics/458871.stm

27. Bernanke, B. (2004) 'The Great Moderation'. Remarks at the meeting of the Eastern Economic Association, Washington, DC, 20 February 2004. http://www.federalreserve.gov/boarddocs/speeches/2004/20040220/

28. Minsky, H. (1977) 'The Financial Instability Hypothesis: an interpretation of Keynes and an alternative to Standard Theory', *Challenge*, March–April 1977, pp. 20–27.

29. Haldane, A. (2009) 'Rethinking the Financial Network'. Speech given at the Financial Student Association, Amsterdam, 28 April 2009. http://www.bankofengland.co.uk/archive/Documents/historicpubs/speeches/2009/speech386.pdf

30. Brown, G. (2011) Speech made at the Institute for New Economic Thinking, Bretton Woods, New Hampshire, 11 April 2011. http://www.bbc.co.uk/news/business-13032013

31. Personal communication with Steve Keen, 3 October 2015.

32. Sraffa, P. (1926) 'The laws of returns under competitive conditions', *Economic Journal* 36, p. 144.

33. Murphy, S., Burch, D. and Clapp, J. (2012) *Cereal Secrets: the world's largest grain traders and global agriculture.* Oxfam Research Reports, Oxford: Oxfam International, available at:. https://www.oxfam.org/sites/www.oxfam.org/files/rr-cereal-secrets-grain-traders-agriculture-30082012-en.pdf

34. Protess, B. (2011) '4 Wall Street banks still dominate derivatives trade', *New York Times* 22 March 2011. http://dealbook.nytimes.com/2011/03/22/4-wall-st-banks-still-dominate-derivatives-trade/

35. Pilon, M. (2015) 'Monopoly's Inventor: the progressive who didn't pass Go', *New York Times*, 13 February 2015, available at: http://www.nytimes.com/2015/02/15/business/behind-monopoly-an-inventor-who-didnt-pass-go.html

36. Epstein, J. and Axtell, R. (1996) *Growing Artificial Societies.* Washington, DC: Brookings Institution Press; Cambridge, MA: MIT Press.

37. Beinhocker, E. (2007) *The Origin of Wealth.* London: Random House, p. 86.

38. Milanovic, B. (2014) http://www.lisdatacenter.org/wp-content/uploads/Milanovic-slides.pdf

39. Kunzig, R. (2009) *The Big Idea: The Carbon Bathtub.* National Geographic, December 2009. http://ngm.nationalgeographic.com/big-idea/05/carbon-bath

40. Sterman, J. D. (2010) 'A Banquet of Consequences'. Presentation at MIT System Design and Management Conference, 21 October 2010. www.youtube.com/watch?v=yMNElsUDHXA

41. Sterman, J. D. (2010) 'A Banquet of Consequences'. Presentation at MIT System Design and Management Conference, 21 October 2010. www.youtube.com/watch?v=yMNElsUDHXA

42. Diamond, J. (2003) 'Why Do Societies Collapse?' TED Talk, February 2003, available at: https://www.ted.com/talks/jared_diamond_on_why_societies_collapse?language=en

43. Diamond, J. (2005) *Collapse: How Societies Choose to Fail or Survive.* London: Penguin.

44. Meadows, D. et al. (1972) *The Limits to Growth.* New York: Universe Books, and Meadows, D. et al. (2005) *Limits to Growth: The 30-Year Update.* London: Earthscan.

45. Jackson, T. and Webster, R. (2016) *Limits Revisited: a review of the limits to growth debate*, The All Party Parliamentary Group on Limits to Growth, Surrey: University of Surrey, available at: http://limits2growth.org.uk/wp-content/uploads/2016/04/Jackson-and-Webster-2016-Limits-Revisited.pdf

46. Liu, E. and Hanauer, N. (2011) *The Gardens of Democracy.* Seattle: Sasquatch Books, pp. 11 and 87.

47. Beinhocker, E. (2012) 'New economics, policy and politics', in Dolphin, T. and Nash, D. (eds), *Complex New World*. London: Institute for Public Policy Research, pp. 142–144.

48. Ostrom, E. (2012) 'Green from the grassroots'. *Project Syndicate* 12 June 2012. http://www.project-syndicate.org/commentary/green-from-the-grassroots

49. Meadows, D. (1999) *Leverage Points: Places to Intervene in a System*. Hartland, VT: Sustainability Institute, p. 1. http://donellameadows.org/archives/leverage-points-places-to-intervene-in-a-system/

50. Lovins, H. (2015) *An Economy in Service to Life*, available at: http://nat capsolutions.org/projects/an-economy-in-service-to-life/#.V3RD5ZMrLIE

51. DeMartino, G. (2012) 'Professional Economic Ethics: why heterodox economists should care'. Paper given at World Economic Association Conference, February–March 2012.

52. DeMartino, G. (2011) *The Economist's Oath*. Oxford: Oxford University Press, pp. 142–150.

53. Meadows, D. (2009) *Thinking in Systems*. London: Earthscan, pp. 169–170.

5. Design to Distribute

1. Cingano, F. (2014) *Trends in Income Inequality and its Impact on Economic Growth'*. OECD Social, Employment and Migration Working Papers, no. 163, OECD publishing, available at: http://dx.doi.org/10.1787/5jxrjncwxv6j-en

2. Jiang, Y. et al. (2016) *Basic Facts About Low-income Children*. National Center for Children in Poverty, available at: http://www.nccp.org/publications/pub_1145.html, and The Trussell Trust (2016) 'Foodbank use remains at record high', 15 April 2016, available at: https://www.trusselltrust.org/2016/04/15/foodbank-use-remains-record-high/

3. Sumner, A. (2012) *From Deprivation to Distribution: Is Global Poverty Becoming a Matter of National Inequality?'* IDS Working Paper no. 394., Sussex: IDS, available at: http://www.ids.ac.uk/files/dmfile/Wp394.pdf

4. Persky, J. (1992) 'Retrospectives: Pareto's law', *Journal of Economic Perspectives* 6: 2, pp. 181–192.

5. Kuznets, S. (1955) 'Economic growth and income inequality', *American Economic Review*, 45: 1, pp. 1–28.

6. Kuznets, S. (1954) Letter to Selma Goldsmith, US Office of Business Economics, 15 August 1954, Papers of Simon Kuznets, Harvard University Archives, HUGFP88.10 Misc. Correspondence, Box 4. http://asociologist.com/2013/03/21/on-the-origins-of-the-kuznets-curve/

7. Kuznets, S. (1955) 'Economic growth and income inequality', *American Economic Review*, 45: 1, pp. 1–28.

8. Lewis, W. A. (1976) 'Development and distribution', in Cairncross, A. and Puri, M. (eds), *Employment, Income Distribution, and Development Strategy: Problems of the Developing Countries*. New York: Holmes & Meier, pp. 26–42.

9. World Bank (1978) *World Development Report*, Washington, DC: World Bank, p. 33.

10. Krueger, A. (2002) 'Economic scene: when it comes to income inequality, more than just market forces are at work', *New York Times*, 4 April 2002, available at: http://www.nytimes.com/2002/04/04/business/economic-scene-when-it-comes-income-inequality-more-than-just-market-forces-are.html?_r=0

11. Piketty, T. (2014) *Capital in the Twenty-First Century*. Cambridge, MA: Harvard University Press.

12. Ostry, J. D. et al. (2014) Redistribution, inequality and growth. IMF Staff discussion note, February 2014, p. 5. https://www.imf.org/external/pubs/ft/sdn/2014/sdn1402.pdf

13. Quinn, J. and Hall, J. (2009) 'Goldman Sachs vice-chairman says "learn to tolerate inequality"', *Daily Telegraph* 21 October 2009. http://www.telegraph.co.uk/finance/recession/6392127/Goldman-Sachs-vice-chairman-says-Learn-to-tolerate-inequality.html

14. Lucas, R. (2004) *The Industrial Revolution: Past and Future*, 2003 Annual Report Essay, The Federal Reserve Bank of Minneapolis, available at: https://www.minneapolisfed.org/publications/the-region/the-industrial-revolution-past-and-future

15. Ossa, F. (2016) 'The economist who brought you Thomas Piketty sees "perfect storm" of inequality ahead', *New York Magazine*, 24 March 2016, available at: http://nymag.com/daily/intelligencer/2016/03/milanovic-millennial-on-millennial-war-is-next.html

16. Newsnight interview with Tony Blair and Jeremy Paxman, 4 June 2001, http://news.bbc.co.uk/1/hi/events/newsnight/1372220.stm

17. Wilkinson, R. and Pickett, K. (2009) *The Spirit Level*. London: Penguin.

18. Wilkinson, R. and Pickett, K. (2014) '*The Spirit Level* authors: why society is more unequal than ever', *Guardian*, 9 March 2014, available at: https://www.theguardian.com/commentisfree/2014/mar/09/society-unequal-the-spirit-level

19. West, D. (2014) Billionaires: Darrell West's reflections on the Upper Crust. http://www.brookings.edu/blogs/brookings-now/posts/2014/10/watch-rural-dairy-farm-writing-billionaires-political-power-great-wealth

20. Gore, A. (31 October 2013). 'The Future: six drivers of global change'. Lecture given at the Oxford Martin School. http://www.oxfordmartin.ox.ac.uk/videos/view/317

21. Islam, N. (2015) *Inequality and Environmental Sustainability*, UN DESA Working Paper no. 145 ST/ESA/2015/DWP/145, available at: http://www.un.org/esa/desa/papers/2015/wp145_2015.pdf

22. Datta, Se. et al. (2015) 'A behavioural approach to water conservation: evidence from a randomized evaluation in Costa Rica', *Ideas* 42. http://www.ideas42.org/wp-content/uploads/2015/04/Belen-Paper-Final.pdf and Ayres, I., Raseman, S. and Shih, A. (2009) *Evidence from Two Large Field Experiments that Peer Comparison Can Reduce Residential Energy Usage*, National Bureau of Economic Research, Working Paper 15386. http://www.nber.org/papers/w15386

23. Boyce, J. K. et al. (1999) 'Power distribution, the environment, and public health: a state-level analysis', *Ecological Economics* 29, pp. 127–140.

24. Holland, T. et al. (2009) 'Inequality predicts biodiversity loss', *Conservation Biology* 23: 5, pp. 1304–1313.

25. Kumhof, M. and Rancière, R. (2010) *Inequality, Leverage and Crises*, IMF Working Paper WP/10/268, Washington, DC: IMF.

26. Ostry, J. D. et al. (2014) Redistribution, inequality and growth. IMF Staff discussion note, February 2014. p. 5. https://www.imf.org/external/pubs/ft/sdn/2014/sdn1402.pdf

27. Ostry, J. (2014) 'We do not have to live with the scourge of inequality', *Financial Times*, 3 March 2014, available at: http://www.ft.com/cms/s/0/f551b3b0-a0b0-11e3-a72c-00144feab7de.html#axzz4AsgUK8pa

28. Goerner, S. (2015) *Regenerative Development: The Art and Science of Creating Durably Vibrant Human Networks*, Connecticut: Capital Institute, available at: http://capitalinstitute.org/wp-content/uploads/2015/05/000-Regenerative-Devel-Final-Goerner-Sept-1-2015.pdf

29. Goerner, S. et al. (2009) 'Quantifying economic sustainability: implications for free-enterprise theory, policy and practice', *Ecological Economics* 69, p. 79.

30. The Asia Floor Wage, available at http://asia.floorwage.org/

31. Pizzigati, S. (2004) *Greed and Good*. New York: Apex Press, pp. 479–502.

32. The Mahatma Gandhi National Rural Employment Guarantee Act 2005. http://www.nrega.nic.in/netnrega/home.aspx

33. Basic Income Earth Network (BIEN) http://www.basicincome.org/

34. Alperovitz, G. (2015) *What Then Must We Do?* White River Junction, VT: Chelsea Green, p. 26.

35. Landesa, http://www.landesa.org/resources/suchitra-deys-story/

36. 'Educating the People', *Ottawa Free Trader*, 7 August 1914, p. 3.

37. Mill, J. S. (1848) *Principles of Political Economy*, Book V, Chapter II, 28, available at: http://www.econlib.org/library/Mill/mlP.html

38. George, H. (1879) *Progress and Poverty*, New York: Modern Library, Book VII, Chapter 1.

39. Thompson, E.P. (1964) *The Making of the English Working Class*. New York: Random House, p. 218.

40. Land Matrix, available at: www.landmatrix.org

41. Pearce, F. (2016) *Common Ground: securing land rights and safeguarding the earth*. Oxford: Oxfam International.

42. Ostrom, E. (2009) 'A general framework for analyzing sustainability of social-ecological systems', *Science* 325, p. 419.

43. Ostrom, E. (2009) 'Beyond markets and states: polycentric governance of complex economic systems'. Nobel Prize lecture, 8 December 2009. http://www.nobel prize.org/nobel_prizes/economic-sciences/laureates/2009/ostrom_lecture.pdf

44. Ostrom, E., Janssen. M. and Anderies, J. (2007) 'Going beyond panaceas', *Proceedings of the National Academy of Sciences* 104: 39, pp. 15176–15178.

45. Greenham, T. (2012) 'Money is a social relationship' TEDx Leiden, 29 November 2012, available at: https://www.youtube.com/watch?v=f1pS1emZP6A

46. Ryan-Collins, J. et al. (2012) *Where Does Money Come From?* London: New Economics Foundation.

47. Bank of England Interactive Database, Table C, 'Further analyses of deposits and lending', series: 'Industrial analysis of sterling monetary financial institutions lending to UK residents: long runs', available at: http://www.bankofengland. co.uk/boeapps/iadb/index.asp?first=yes&SectionRequired=C&HideNums=-1& ExtraInfo=false&Travel=NIxSTx

48. Hudson, M. and Bezemer, D. (2012) 'Incorporating the rentier sectors into a financial model', *World Economic Review* 1, p. 6.

49. Benes, J. and Kumhof, M. (2012) *The Chicago Plan Revisited*. IMF Working Paper 12/202. https://www.imf.org/external/pubs/ft/wp/2012/wp12202.pdf

50. Keynes, J. M. (1936) *General Theory of Employment, Interest and Money*, Chapter 24.

51. Ryan-Collins, J. et al. (2013) *Strategic Quantitative Easing: Stimulating Investment to Rebalance the Economy*. London: New Economics Foundation.

52. Blyth, M., Lonergan, E. and Wren-Lewis, S., 'Now the Bank of England needs to deliver QE for the people'. *Guardian*, 21 May 2015.

53. Murphy, R. and Hines, C. (2010) 'Green quantitative easing: paying for the economy we need', Norfolk: Finance for the Future, available at: http://www. financeforthefuture.com/GreenQuEasing.pdf

54. Greenham, T. (2012) 'Money is a social relationship', TEDx Leiden, 29 November 2012, available at: https://www.youtube.com/watch?v=f1pS1emZP6A

55. Grassroots Economics (2016), 'Community currency', available at: http://grassrootseconomics.org/community-currencies

56. Ruddick, W. (2015) 'Kangemi-Pesa Launch Prep & More Currency News', Grassroots Economics, available at: http://www.grassrootseconomics.org/kangemi-pesa-launch-prep

57. www.zeitvorsorge.ch/

58. Strassheim, I. (2014) 'Zeit statt Geld fürs Alter sparen', *Migros-Magazin*, 1 September 2014. www.zeitvorsorge.ch/#!/DE/24/Medien.htm

59. DEVCON1 (2016) Transactive Grid: a decentralized energy management system. Presentation at Ethereum Developer Conference, 9–13 November 2015, London, available at: https://www.youtube.com/watch?v=kq8RPbFz5UU

60. Seaman, D. (2015) 'Bitcoin vs. Ethereum explained for NOOBZ', published 30 November 2015, available at: https://www.youtube.com/watch?v=rEJKLFH8q5c

61. Trades Union Congress (2012) *The Great Wages Grab*. London: TUC. https://www.tuc.org.uk/sites/default/files/tucfiles/TheGreatWagesGrab.pdf

62. Mishel, L. and Shierholz, H. (2013) *A Decade of Flat Wages*. EPI Briefing Paper no. 365, Washington, DC: Economic Policy Institute. http://www.epi.org/files/2013/BP365.pdf

63. Miller, J. (2015) *German wage repression*, Dollars & Sense blog. September 2015. http://dollarsandsense.org/archives/2015/0915miller.html

64. International Labour Organization (2014) *Global Wage Report*. Geneva: ILO. http://www.reuters.com/article/2014/12/04/us-employment-wages-ilo-idUSKCN0JI2JP20141204

65. Kelly, M. (2012) *Owning our Future: The Emerging Ownership Revolution*. San Francisco: Berrett-Koehler, p. 18.

66. International Cooperative Alliance (2014), *World Cooperative Monitor*. Geneva: ICA, available at: http://www.euricse.eu/publications/world-cooperative-monitor-report-2014/#

67. John Lewis (2011) The John Lewis Partnership Bond, available at: http://www.partnershipbond.com/content/jlbond/about.html

68. Cited in Kelly, M. (2012) *Owning our Future: The Emerging Ownership Revolution*. San Francisco: Berrett-Koehler, p. 12.

69. Kelly, M. (2012) *Owning our Future*, p. 212.

70. Rikfin, J. (2014) *The Zero Marginal Cost Society*. New York: Palgrave Macmillan, p. 204.

71. Brynjolfsson, E. and McAfee, A. (2012) 'Jobs, productivity and the Great Decoupling', *New York Times*, 11 December. http://www.nytimes.com/2012/12/12/opinion/global/jobs-productivity-and-the-great-decoupling.html?_r=0

72. Brynjolfsson, E. and McAfee, A. (2015) 'Will humans go the way of horses?' *Foreign Affairs*, July/August. https://www.foreignaffairs.com/articles/2015-06-16/will-humans-go-way-horses

73. World Economic Forum (2016) *The Future of Jobs*, available at: http://reports.weforum.org/future-of-jobs-2016/

74. Zuo, M. (2016) 'Rise of the robots: 60,000 workers culled from just one factory as China's struggling electronics hub turns to artificial intelligence', *South China Morning Post*, 21 May 2016, available at: http://www.scmp.com/news/china/economy/article/1949918/
rise-robots-60000-workers-culled-just-one-factory-chinas

75. Brynjolfsson, E. and McAfee, A. (2015) 'Will humans go the way of horses?' *Foreign Affairs*, July/August. https://www.foreignaffairs.com/articles/2015-06-16/will-humans-go-way-horses

76. Brynjolfsson and McAfee (2015) 'Will humans go the way of horses?'

77. Mazzucato, M. (2013) *The Entrepreneurial State*. London: Anthem Press, pp. 188–91.

78. M. Frumkin, (1945) 'The origin of patents', *Journal of the Patent Office Society*, 27: 3, p. 143.

79. Schwartz, J. (2009) 'Cancer patients challenge the patenting of a gene', *New York Times*, 12 May, available at: http://www.nytimes.com/2009/05/13/health/13patent.html

80. Stiglitz, J. (2012) *The Price of Inequality*. London: Allen Lane, p. 202.

81. The Open Building Institute, available at http://openbuildinginstitute.org/

82. Jakubowski, M. (2012) 'The Open Source Economy'. Talk given at Connecting For Change: Bioneers by the Bay conference, the Marion Institute, 28 October 2012, available at: https://www.youtube.com/watch?v=MIIzogiUHFY

83. Pearce, J. (2015) 'Quantifying the value of open source hardware development', *Modern Economy*, 6, pp. 1–11.

84. Bauwens, M. (2012) *Blueprint for P2P Society: The Partner State and Ethical Society*, http://www.shareable.net/blog/blueprint-for-p2p-society-the-partner-state-ethical-economy

85. Lakner, C. and Milanovic, B. (2015) 'Global income distribution: from the fall of the Berlin Wall to the Great Recession', *The World Bank Economic Review*, pp. 1–30.

86. OECD (2014) *Detailed Final 2013 Aid Figures Released by OECD/DAC*. http://www.oecd.org/dac/stats/final2013oda.htm

87. OECD (2015) 'Non-ODA flows to developing countries: remittances', available at: http://www.oecd.org/dac/stats/beyond-oda-remittances.htm

88. Financial Inclusion Insights (2015) *Kenya: Country Context.* http://finclusion. org/country-pages/kenya-country-page/

89. Statistica (2015) *Mobile Phone User Penetration as a Percentage of the Population Worldwide, 2012 to 2018.* http://www.statista.com/statistics/470018/mobile-phone-user-penetration-worldwide/

90. Banerjee, A. et al. (2015) *Debunking the Stereotype of the Lazy Welfare Recipient: Evidence from Cash Transfer Programs Worldwide.* HKS Working Paper no. 76, available at: http://papers.ssrn.com/sol3/papers. cfm?abstract_id=2703447 and Gertler, P., Martinez, S. and Rubio-Codina, M. (2006) *Investing Cash Transfers to Raise Long-term Living Standards.*', World Bank Policy Research Working Paper no. 3994, Washington, DC: World Bank, available at: http://www1.worldbank.org/prem/poverty/ie/dime_papers/ 1082.pdf

91. Global Basic Income Foundation, *What Is a Global Basic Income?* http:// www.globalincome.org/English/Global-Basic-Income.html

92. Faye, M. and Niehaus, P. (2016) 'What if we just gave poor people a basic income for life? That's what we are about to test', *Slate*, 14 April 2016, available at: http://www.slate.com/blogs/moneybox/2016/04/14/universal_basic_income_ this_nonprofit_is_about_to_test_it_in_a_big_way.html

93. Hurun Global Rich List 2015. http://www.hurun.net/en/articleshow. aspx?nid=9607

94. Seery, E. and Caistor Arendar, A. (2014) *Even It Up: Time to End Extreme Inequality.* Oxford: Oxfam International, p. 17.

95. ICRICT (2015) Declaration of the Independent Commissions for the Reform of International Corporate Taxation. www.icrict.org

96. Barnes, P. (2003) 'Capitalism, the Commons and Divine Right'. 23rd Annual E.F. Schumacher Lectures, Schumacher Center for a New Economics, available at: http://www.centerforneweconomics.org/publications/lectures/barnes/peter/ capitalism-the-commons-and-divine-right

97. Barnes, P. (2006) *Capitalism 3.0: A Guide to Reclaiming the Commons.* Berkeley: Berrett-Koehler.

98. Sheerin, J. (2009) 'Malawi windmill boy with big fans', BBC News, http://news. bbc.co.uk/1/hi/world/africa/8257153.stm

99. Pearce, J. et al. (2012) 'A new model for enabling innovation in appropriate technology for sustainable development', *Sustainability: Science, Practice and Policy*, 8: 2, pp. 42–53.

100. Pearce, J. (2012) 'The case for open source appropriate technology', *Environment, Development and Sustainability*, 14: 3, p. 430.

101. Kamkwamba, W. (2014) 'Updates from the past two years', 6 October 2014, William Kamkwamba's blog, available at: http://williamkamkwamba.typepad.com/williamkamkwamba/2014/10/updates-from-the-last-two-years.html

102. Personal email correspondence with William Kamkwamba, 19 October 2015.

6. Create to Regenerate

1. Mallet, V. (2013) 'Environmental damage costs India $80bn a year', *Financial Times* 17 July 2013, http://www.ft.com/cms/s/0/0a89f3a8-eeca-11e2-98dd-00144feabdc0.html#axzz3qz7R0UIf

2. Grossman, G. and Krueger, A. (1995) 'Economic growth and the environment', *Quarterly Journal of Economics*, 110: 2, pp. 353–377.

3. Grossman and Krueger (1995) 'Economic growth and the environment', p. 369.

4. Yandle, B. et al. (2002) *The Environmental Kuznets Curve: A Primer*. The Property and Environment Research Centre Research Study 02. http://www.macalester.edu/~wests/econ231/yandleetal.pdf

5. Torras, M. and Boyce, J.K. (1998) 'Income, inequality, and pollution: a reassessment of the environmental Kuznets curve', *Ecological Economics* 25, pp. 147–160.

6. Wiedmann, T. O. et al. (2015) 'The material footprint of nations', *Proceedings of the National Academy of Sciences* 112: 20, pp. 6271–6276.

7. UNEP (2016) *Global Material Flows and Resource Productivity: A Report of the International Resource Panel*, available at: http://www.uneplive.org/material#.V1rkAeYrLIG

8. Goodall, C. (2012) *Sustainability*. London: Hodder & Stoughton.

9. Global Footprint Network (2016) 'National Footprint Accounts', available at: http://www.footprintnetwork.org/en/index.php/GFN/page/footprint_data_and_results/

10. Heinrich Böll Foundation (2012) 'Energy transition: environmental taxation', available at: http://energytransition.de/2012/10/environmental-taxation/

11. California Environmental Protection Agency (2016) 'Cap-and-Trade Program', available at: http://www.arb.ca.gov/cc/capandtrade/capandtrade.htm

12. Schwartz, D. 'Water pricing in two thirsty cities: in one, guzzlers pay more, and use less', *New York Times* 6 May 2015. http://www.nytimes.com/2015/05/07/business/energy-environment/water-pricing-in-two-thirsty-cities.html?_r=0

13. ''Most progressive water utility in Africa' wins 2014 Stockholm Industry Water Award', SIWI press release, available at: http://www.siwi.org/prizes/winners/2014-2.html

14. Meadows, D. (1997) *Leverage Points: Places to Intervene in a System*. The Donella Meadows Institute, available at: http://donellameadows.org/archives/leverage-points-places-to-intervene-in-a-system/

15. Lyle, J. T. (1994) *Regenerative Design for Sustainable Development*. New York: John Wiley & Sons, p. 5.

16. Hotten, R. (2015) 'Volkswagen: the scandal explained', BBC News, available at: http://www.bbc.co.uk/news/business-34324772

17. 'Nedbank Fair Share 2030 starts with Targeted Lending of R6 billion', 3 March 2014, Nedbank, available at: https://www.nedbank.co.za/content/nedbank/desktop/gt/en/news/nedbankstories/fair-share-2030/2014/nedbank-fair-share-2030-starts-with-targeted-lending-of-r6-billion.html

18. Nestlé (2014) 'Nestlé opens its first zero water factory expansion in Mexico', 22 October 2014. http://www.wateronline.com/doc/nestle-zero-water-factory-expansion-mexico-0001

19. McDonough, W. (2015) 'Upcycle and the atomic bomb', interview in *Renewable Matter* 06–07, Milan: Edizioni Ambiente, p. 12.

20. Andersson, E. et al. (2014) 'Reconnecting cities to the Biosphere: stewardship of green infrastructure and urban ecosystem services', *AMBIO* 43: 4, pp. 445–453.

21. Biomimicry 3.8 (2014), 'Conversation with Janine', http://biomimicry.net/about/biomimicry/conversation-with-janine/

22. Webster, K. (2015) *The Circular Economy: A Wealth of Flows*. Isle of Wight: Ellen McArthur Foundation.

23. Ellen McArthur Foundation (2012) *Towards the Circular Economy*, Isle of Wight: Ellen McArthur Foundation, available at: http://www.ellenmacarthurfoundation.org/assets/downloads/publications/Ellen-MacArthur-Foundation-Towards-the-Circular-Economy-vol.1.pdf

24. Braungart, M. and McDonough, W. (2009) *Cradle to Cradle: Remaking the Way We Make Things*. London: Vintage Books.

25. Ellen MacArthur Foundation (2012) *In-depth: mobile phones*. http://www.ellenmacarthurfoundation.org/circular-economy/interactive-diagram/in-depth-mobile-phones

26. Benyus, J. (2015) 'The generous city', *Architectural Design* 85: 4, pp. 120–121.

27. Personal communication with Janine Benyus, 23 November 2015.

28. Park 20|20 http://www.park2020.com/

29. Newlight Technologies, www.newlight.com/company

30. Sundrop Farms www.sundropfarms.com and Sundrop Farms ABC Landline Coverage, 20 April 2012 https://www.youtube.com/watch?v=KCup_B_RHM4

31. Arthur, C. (2010) 'Women solar entrepreneurs transforming Bangladesh'. http://www.renewableenergyworld.com/articles/2010/04/women-solar-entrepreneurs-transforming-bangladesh.html

32. Vidal, J. (2014) 'Regreening program to restore one-sixth of Ethiopia's land', *Guardian*, 30 October 2014, available at: http://www.theguardian.com/environment/2014/oct/30/regreening-program-to-restore-land-across-one-sixth-of-ethiopia

33. Sanergy http://saner.gy/

34. ProComposto http://www.procomposto.com.br

35. Margolis, J. (2012) 'Growing food in the desert: is this the solution to the world's food crisis?', *Guardian*, 24 November 2012, available at: https://www.theguardian.com/environment/2012/nov/24/growing-food-in-the-desert-crisis

36. Lacy, P. and Rutqvist, J. (2015) *Waste to Wealth: The Circular Economy Advantage*. New York: Palgrave Macmillan, pp. 79–80.

37. Muirhead, S. and Zimmermann, L. (2015) 'Open Source Circular Economy', The Disruptive Innovation Festival 2015.

38. Open Source Circular Economy: mission statement. https://oscedays.org/open-source-circular-economy-mission-statement/

39. Personal communication with Sam Muirhead, 27 January 2016.

40. Apertus° https://www.apertus.org/

41. OSVehicle https://www.osvehicle.com/

42. Sénamé Kof Agbodjinou and the W. Afate 3D printer at NetExplo 2015. https://www.youtube.com/watch?v=ThTRqfhMLcA and My Africa Is talks Woelab and the e-waste 3D printer. http://www.myafricais.com/woelab_3dprinting/

43. Greene, T. (2001) 'Ballmer: "Linux is a cancer"', http://www.theregister.co.uk/2001/06/02/ballmer_linux_is_a_cancer/, and Finley, K. (2015) 'Whoa. Microsoft is using Linux to run its cloud', http://www.wired.com/2015/09/microsoft-using-linux-run-cloud/

44. Personal communication with Sam Muirhead, 27 January 2016.

45. Asknature.org and personal communication with Janine Benyus, 31 May 2016.

46. Friedman, M. (1970) 'The social responsibility of business is to increase its profits', *New York Times Magazine*, 13 September. http://umich.edu/~thecore/doc/Friedman.pdf

47. Satya.com (2005) 'A Dame of big ideas: the Satya interview with Anita Roddick', http://www.satyamag.com/jan05/roddick.html

48. Satya.com (2005) 'A Dame of big ideas'.

49. Benefit Corporation, http://benefitcorp.net/ and CIC Association, http://www.cicassociation.org.uk/about/what-is-a-cic

50. Satya.com (2005) 'A Dame of big ideas: the Satya interview with Anita Roddick', http://www.satyamag.com/jan05/roddick.html

51. John Fullerton's speech at the launch of *Regenerative Capitalism*. https://www.youtube.com/watch?v=6KDv06YOjxw

52. Fullerton, J. (2015) *Regenerative Capitalism*. Greenwich, CT: The Capital Institute.

53. Capital Institute (2015) *A Year in the Life of a Regenerative Bank*. http://regenerativebankproject.capitalinstitute.org/

54. Herman, G. (2011) 'Alternative currency has great success: Rabot loves Torekes', *Nieuwsblad*, 30 April 2011, http://www.nieuwsblad.be/cnt/f839i9vt

55. The Ex'Tax Project (et al.) (2014) *New Era. New Plan. Fiscal reforms for an inclusive, circular economy.* http://ex-tax.com/files/4314/1693/7138/The_Extax_Project_New_Era_New_Plan_report.pdf

56. Crawford, K. et al. (2014) *Demolition or Refurbishment of Social Housing? A review of the evidence.* London: UCL Urban Lab and Engineering Exchange, available at: http://www.engineering.ucl.ac.uk/engineering-exchange/files/2014/10/Report-Refurbishment-Demolition-Social-Housing.pdf

57. Wijkman, A. and Skanberg, K. (2015) *The Circular Economy and Benefits for Society.* Club of Rome, available at: http://www.clubofrome.org/wp-content/uploads/2016/03/The-Circular-Economy-and-Benefits-for-Society.pdf

58. Mazzucato, M. (2015) 'What we need to get a real green revolution', 10 December 2015, http://marianamazzucato.com/2015/12/10/what-we-need-to-get-a-real-green-revolution/

59. Mazzucato, M., Semieniuk, G. and Watson, J. (2015) *What Will It Take To Get Us a Green Revolution?* SPRU Policy Paper, University of Sussex. https://www.sussex.ac.uk/webteam/gateway/file.php?name=what-will-it-take-to-get-us-a-green-revolution.pdf&site=264

60. The Oberlin Project. http://www.oberlinproject.org/

61. 'David Orr: The Oberlin Project', at The Garrison Institute, February 2012. https://www.youtube.com/watch?v=K5MNI9k0wWU

62. Oberlin College (2016) Environmental Dashboard at environmentaldashboard.org

63. Meadows, D. (1998) *Indicators and Information Systems for Sustainable Development.* Vermont: The Sustainability Group, available at: http://www.comitatoscientifico.org/temi%20SD/documents/@@Meadows%20SD%20indicators.pdf

64. Economy for the Common Good https://old.ecogood.org/en B Corps https://www.bcorporation.net/ and the MultiCapital Scorecard http://www.multicapitalscorecard.com/

7. Be Agnostic about Growth

1. Mali, T. (2002) 'Like Lily like Wilson', in *What Learning Leaves*, Newtown, CT: Hanover Press.

2. Al Bartlett, http://www.albartlett.org

3. Rostow, W.W. (1960), *The Stages of Economic Growth: A Non-Communist Manifesto.* Cambridge: Cambridge University Press, p. 6.

4. Ibid., p. 16.

5. Smith, A. (1776) *An Inquiry into the Nature and Causes of the Wealth of Nations,* Book I, Chapter 9, p. 14. http://geolib.com/smith.adam/won1-09.html

6. Ricardo, D. (1817) *On the Principles of Political Economy and Taxation*, Chapter 4 (6.29). http://www.econlib.org/library/Ricardo/ricP.html

7. Mill, J. S. (1848) *Principles of Political Economy*, Book IV, Chapter VI, 6. http://www.econlib.org/library/Mill/mlP.html#Bk.IV,Ch.VI

8. Keynes, J.M. (1945) *First Annual Report of the Arts Council (1945–46).* London: Arts Council.

9. Rogers, E. (1962) *Diffusion of Innovations.* New York: The Free Press.

10. Georgescu-Roegen, N. (2013) *The Entropy Law and the Economic Process.* Cambridge, MA: Harvard University Press.

11. Marshall, A. (1890) *Principles of Economics.* London: Macmillan, Book IV, Chapter VII.7. http://www.econlib.org/library/Marshall/marP.html#

12. IMF (2016) 'World Economic Outlook Update', January 2016, available at: http://www.imf.org/external/pubs/ft/weo/2016/update/01/

13. World Bank (2016) GDP growth (annual %), 2011–2015. http://data.worldbank.org/indicator/NY.GDP.MKTP.KD.ZG

14. Jackson, T. (2009) *Prosperity without Growth*. London: Earthscan, pp. 56–58.

15. United Nations (2015) *World Population Prospects: The 2015 Revision.* New York: UN, p. 26, available at: https://esa.un.org/unpd/wpp/publications/files/key_findings_wpp_2015.pdf

16. Global Footprint Network (2015) *Footprint for Nations* (2011 data). http://www.footprintnetwork.org/en/index.php/GFN/page/footprint_for_nations/

17. Sinclair, U. (1935) *I, Candidate for Governor – and How I Got Licked.* Oakland: University of California Press, 1994 repr., p.109.

18. Bonaiuti, M. (2014) *The Great Transition.* London: Routledge (Figure 3.1).

19. Gordon, R. (2014) *The Demise of US Economic Growth: Restatement, Rebuttals and Reflections.*, NBER Working Paper no. 19895, February 2014, available at: http://www.nber.org/papers/w19895, and Jackson, T. and Webster, R. (2016)

Limits Revisited, A Report for the All Party Parliamentary Group on Limits to Growth, available at: http://limits2growth.org.uk/revisited/

20. OECD (2014) *Policy Challenges for the Next 50 Years*. OECD Economic policy paper no. 9, Paris: OECD, p. 11.

21. Carney, M. (2016) 'Redeeming an Unforgiving World', speech by Mark Carney at the 8th Annual Institute of International Finance G20 Conference, Shanghai, 26 February 2016, available at: http://www.bankofengland.co.uk/publications/Pages/speeches/2016/885.aspx

22. Borio, C. (2016) 'The movie plays on: a lens for viewing the global economy' Bank for International Settlements presentation at the FT Debt Capital Markets Outlook, London 10 February 2016, available at: http://www.bis.org/speeches/sp160210_slides.pdf

23. Obsfeld, M. (2016) 'Global growth: too slow for too long', *IMFdirect*, 12 April 2016, available at: https://blog-imfdirect.imf.org/2016/04/12/global-growth-too-slow-for-too-long/

24. OECD (2016) 'Global economy stuck in low-growth trap: policymakers need to act to keep promises, OECD says in latest Economic Outlook', 1 June 2016, available at: http://www.oecd.org/newsroom/global-economy-stuck-in-low-growth-trap-policymakers-need-to-act-to-keep-promises.htm

25. Summers, L. (2016) 'The age of secular stagnation', *Foreign Affairs*, 15 February.

26. Beckerman, W. (1972) *In Defense of Economic Growth*. London: Jonathan Cape, pp. 100–101.

27. Friedman, B. (2006) *The Moral Consequence of Economic Growth*. New York: Vintage Books, p. 4.

28. Moyo, D. (2015) 'Economic growth has stalled. Let's fix it'. TED Global, Geneva. https://www.ted.com/talks/dambisa_moyo_economic_growth_has_stalled_let_s_fix_it?language=en

29. Brynjolfsson, E. and MacAfee, A. (2014) *The Second Machine Age*. New York: W.W. Norton & Co.

30. Carbon Brief (2016) 'The 35 countries cutting the link between economic growth and emissions', 5 April 2016, available at: https://www.carbonbrief.org/the-35-countries-cutting-the-link-between-economic-growth-and-emissions. GDP data from the World Bank are given in constant local currency and consumption-based emissions data are from the Global Carbon Project's CDIAC database.

31. Anderson, K. and Bows, A. (2011) 'Beyond "dangerous" climate change: emissions scenarios for a new world', *Philosophical Transactions of the Royal Society A*, 369, pp. 20–44.

32. Bowen, A. and Hepburn, C. (2012) *Prosperity With Growth: Economic Growth, Climate Change and Environmental Limits*, Centre for Climate Change Economic and Policy Working Paper no. 109, and Brynjolfsson, E. (2013) 'The key to growth? Race with the machines', TED Talk, February 2013. https://www.ted.com/talks/erik_brynjolfsson_the_key_to_growth_race_em_with_em_the_machines?language=en

33. Bowen, A. and Hepburn, C. (2012) *Prosperity with Growth: Economic Growth, Climate Change and Environmental Limits*, Centre for Climate Change Economic and Policy Working Paper no. 109, p. 20.

34. Solow, R. (1957) 'Technical change and the aggregate production function', *Review of Economics and Statistics* 39: 3, p. 320.

35. Abramovitz, M. (1956) 'Resource and output trends in the United States since 1870', *American Economic Review*, 46: 2, p. 11.

36. Ayres. R. and Ayres, E. (2010) *Crossing the Energy Divide: Moving from Fossil Fuel Dependence to a Clean Energy Future*. Upper Saddle River, NJ: Wharton School Publishing, p. 14.

37. Let the Sun Work (2015) 'The energy in a barrel of oil', available at: http://letthesunwork.com/energy/barrelofenergy.htm

38. Ayres, R. and Warr, B. (2009) *The Economic Growth Engine*. Cheltenham: Edward Elgar, pp. 297, 309.

39. Murphy, D.J. (2014) 'The implications of the declining energy return on investment of oil production', *Philosophical Transactions of the Royal Society* 372, p. 16.

40. Semieniuk, G. (2014) 'The digital revolution's energy costs', Schwartz Center for Economic Policy Analysis, The New School, 21 April 2014, available at: http://www.economicpolicyresearch.org/index.php/the-worldly-philosopher/1446-the-digital-revolution-s-energy-costs

41. Swishing, http://swishing.com

42. Rifkin, J. (2014) *The Zero Marginal Cost Society*. New York: Palgrave Macmillan, p. 20.

43. Easterlin, R. (1974) 'Does economic growth improve the human lot? Some empirical evidence', in David, P. and Reder, M. (eds), *Nations and Households in Economic Growth: Essays in Honour of Moses Abramovitz.*, New York: Academic Press.

44. Stevenson, B. and Wolfers, J. (2008) *Economic Growth and Subjective Well-being: Reassessing the Easterlin Paradox*, National Bureau of Economic Research Paper no. 14282. http://www.nber.org/papers/w14282

45. Wolf, M. (2007), 'The dangers of living in a zero-sum world economy', *Financial Times*, 19 December 2007, available at: https://next.ft.com/content/0447f562-ad85-11dc-9386-0000779fd2ac

46. Rostow, W.W. (1960) *The Stages of Economic Growth: A Non-Communist Manifesto*. Cambridge: Cambridge University Press, p. 6.

47. Rogoff, K. (2012) 'Rethinking the growth imperative', *Project Syndicate*, 2 January 2012. http://www.project-syndicate.org/commentary/rethinking-the-growth-imperative

48. Polanyi, K. (2001) *The Great Transformation*. Boston: Beacon Press.

49. Marx, K. (1867) *Capital*, Vol. I, Part II, Chapter IV, available at: http://www.econlib.org/library/YPDBooks/Marx/mrxCpA4.html#Part II, Chapter 4

50. Aristotle (350 BCE) *Politics*, Book I, Part X, available at: http://classics.mit.edu/Aristotle/politics.1.one.html

51. Fullerton, J. (2012) 'Can financial reform fight climate change?' Interview on the Laura Flanders Show, 8 July 2012, available at: https://www.youtube.com/watch?v=NyVEK6A61Z8

52. Capital Institute (2015) *Evergreen Direct Investing: Co-creating the Regenerative Economy*. http://fieldguide.capitalinstitute.org/evergreen-direct-investing.html

53. Personal communication with John Fullerton, 23 June 2014.

54. Gessel, S. (1906) *The Natural Economic Order*, p. 121, available at: https://www.community-exchange.org/docs/Gesell/en/neo

55. Keynes, J.M. (1936) *The General Theory of Employment, Interest and Money*. London: Macmillan, Chapter 23.

56. Lietaer, B. (2001) *The Future of Money*. London: Century, pp. 247–248.

57. Lakoff, G. (2014) *The All New Don't Think of an Elephant*. White River Junction, VT: Chelsea Green.

58. Oxfam (2013), 'Tax on the "private" billions now stashed away in havens enough to end extreme world poverty twice over', 22 May 2013. https://www.oxfam.org/en/pressroom/pressreleases/2013-05-22/tax-private-billions-now-stashed-away-havens-enough-end-extreme

59. Tax Justice Network (2015) 'The scale of Base Erosion and Profit Shifting' (BEPS). http://www.taxjustice.net/scaleBEPS/

60. Global Alliance for Tax Justice, http://www.globaltaxjustice.org

61. Keynes, J.M. (1931) 'Economic possibilities for our grandchildren' in *Essays in Persuasion*, London: Rupert Hart-Davis, p. 5, available at: http://www.econ.yale.edu/smith/econ116a/keynes1.pdf

62. Coote, A., Franklin, J. and Simms, A. (2010) '21 hours: why a shorter working week can help us all flourish in the 21st century' London: New Economics Foundation.

63. Coote, A. (2012) 'The 21 Hour Work Week', TEDxGhent. https://www.youtube.com/watch?v=1IMYV31tZZ8

64. Smith, S. and Rothbaum, J. (2013) *Cooperatives in a Global Economy: Key Economic Issues, Recent Trends, and Potential for Development*. Institute for International Economic Policy Working Paper Series, George Washington University IIEP–WP–2013–6. https://www.gwu.edu/~iiep/assets/docs/papers/Smith_Rothbaum_IIEPWP2013-6.pdf

65. Kennedy, P. (1989) *The Rise and Fall of World Powers*. New York: Vintage Books.

66. C40 Cities Climate Leadership Group, http://www.c40.org

67. Rogoff, K. (2012) 'Rethinking the growth imperative', *Project Syndicate*, 2 January 2012. http://www.project-syndicate.org/commentary/rethinking-the-growth-imperative

68. Berger, J. (1972) *Ways of Seeing*. London: Penguin, p. 131.

69. Wolf, M. 'The dangers of living in a zero sum world', *Financial Times*, 19 December 2007.

70. Wallich, H. (1972) 'Zero growth', *Newsweek*, 24 January 1972, p. 62.

71. Brightman, R. (1993) *Grateful Prey: Rock Cree Human–Animal Relationships*. Berkeley: University of California Press, pp. 249–251.

72. Phillips, A. (2009) 'Insatiable creatures', *Guardian*, 8 August 2009, available at: https://www.theguardian.com/books/2009/aug/08/excess-adam-phillips

73. Gerhardt, S. (2010) *The Selfish Society: How We All Forgot to Love One Another and Made Money Instead*. London: Simon & Schuster, pp. 32–33.

74. Aked, J. et al. (2008) *Five Ways to Wellbeing: The Evidence*. London: New Economics Foundation.

We Are All Economists Now

1. Leach, M., Raworth, K. and Rockström, J. (2013) *Between Social and Planetary Boundaries: Navigating Pathways in the Safe and Just Space for Humanity*, World Social Science Report, Paris: UNESCO.

2. Mill, J.S. (1873) *Autobiography*. London: Penguin 1989 edn, pp. 178–179.

3. Keynes, J.M. (1924) 'Alfred Marshall, 1842–1924', *The Economic Journal*, 34: 135, p. 322.

4. Stiglitz, J. (2012) 'Questioning the value of economics'. Video interview with World Business of Ideas. www.wobi.com/wbftv/joseph-stiglitz-questioning-value-economics

5. Personal communication with Yuan Yang, 15 June 2016.

BIBLIOGRAPHY

Abramovitz, M. (1956) 'Resource and output trends in the United States since 1870', *American Economic Review*, 46: 2, pp. 5–23.

Acemoglu, D. and Robinson, J. (2013) *Why Nations Fail: The Origins of Power, Prosperity and Poverty*. London: Profile Books.

Aked, J. et al. (2008) *Five Ways to Wellbeing: The Evidence*. London: New Economics Foundation.

Alperovitz, G. (2015) *What Then Must We Do?* White River Junction, VT: Chelsea Green.

Anderson, K. and Bows, A. (2011) 'Beyond "dangerous" climate change: emissions scenarios for a new world', *Philosophical Transactions of the Royal Society A*, 369, pp. 20–44.

Arendt, H. (1973) *Origins of Totalitarianism*. New York: Harcourt Brace Jovanovich.

Aristotle (350 BCE), *Politics*, http://classics.mit.edu/Aristotle/politics.1.one.html

Arndt, H. (1978) *The Rise and Fall of Economic Growth*. Chicago: University of Chicago Press.

Arrow, K. and Debreu, G. (1954) 'Existence of an equilibrium for a competitive economy', *Econometrica* 22, pp. 265–290.

Ayers, J. et al. (2013) 'Do celebrity cancer diagnoses promote primary cancer prevention?', *Preventive Medicine* 58, pp. 81–84.

Ayres, I., Raseman, S. and Shih, A. (2009) *Evidence from Two Large Field Experiments that Peer Comparison Can Reduce Residential Energy Usage*. National Bureau of Economic Research, Working Paper 15386.

Ayres. R. and Ayres, E. (2010) *Crossing the Energy Divide: Moving From Fossil Fuel Dependence to a Clean Energy Future*. New Jersey: Wharton School Publishing.

Ayres, R. and Warr, B. (2009) *The Economic Growth Engine*. Cheltenham: Edward Elgar.

Bacon, F. (1620) *Novum Organon*. http://www.constitution.org/bacon/nov_org.htm

Banerjee, A. et al. (2015) *Debunking the Stereotype of the Lazy Welfare Recipient: Evidence From Cash Transfer Programs Worldwide*. HKS Working Paper no. 76.

Barnes, P. (2006) *Capitalism 3.0: A Guide to Reclaiming the Commons*. Berkeley: Berrett-Koehler.

Barrera-Osorio, F. et al. (2011) 'Improving the design of conditional transfer programs: evidence from a randomized education experiment in Colombia', *American Economic Journal: Applied Economics*, 3: 2, pp. 167–195.

Bauer, M. et al. (2012) 'Cueing consumerism: situational materialism undermines personal and social well-being', *Psychological Science* 23, pp. 517–523.

Bauwens, M. (2012) *Blueprint for P2P Society: The Partner State and Ethical Society.*, http://www.shareable.net/blog/blueprint-for-p2p-society-the-partner-state-ethical-economy

Beaman, L. et al. (2012) 'Female leadership raises aspirations and educational attainment for girls: a policy experiment in India', *Science* 335: 6068, pp. 582–586.

Beckerman, W. (1972) *In Defense of Economic Growth*. London: Jonathan Cape.

Begg, D., Fischer, S. and Dornbusch, R. (1987) *Economics*. Maidenhead: McGraw-Hill.

Beinhocker, E. (2007) *The Origin of Wealth*. London: Random House.

Beinhocker, E. (2012) 'New economics, policy and politics', in Dolphin, T. and Nash, D. (eds), *Complex New World*. London: Institute for Public Policy Research.

Benes, J. and Kumhof, M. (2012) *The Chicago Plan Revisited*, IMF Working Paper 12/202.

Benyus, J. (2015) 'The generous city', *Architectural Design* 85: 4, pp. 120–121.

Berger, A. and Loutre, M. F. (2002) 'An exceptionally long interglacial ahead?' *Science* 297, p. 1287.

Berger, J. (1972) *Ways of Seeing*, London: Penguin.

Bernays, E. (2005) *Propaganda*. New York: Ig Publishing.

Bjorkman, M. and Svensson, J. (2009) 'Power to the people: evidence from a randomized field experiment on community-based monitoring in Uganda', *Quarterly Journal of Economics* 124: 2, pp. 735–769.

Block, F. and Somers, M. (2014) *The Power of Market Fundamentalism: Karl Polanyi's Critique*. London: Harvard University Press.

Bolderdijk, J. et al. (2012) 'Comparing the effectiveness of monetary versus moral motives in environmental campaigning', *Nature Climate Change*, 3, pp. 413–416.

Bonaiuti, M. (2014) *The Great Transition*. London: Routledge.

Bowen, A. and Hepburn, C. (2012) 'Prosperity With Growth: Economic Growth, Climate Change and Environmental Limits', Centre for Climate Change Economic and Policy Working Paper no. 109

Bowles, S. and Gintis, H. (2011) *A Cooperative Species: Human Reciprocity and Its Evolution*. Princeton: Princeton University Press.

Box, G. and Draper, N. (1987) *Empirical Model Building and Response Surfaces*. New York: John Wiley & Sons.

Boyce, J. K. et al. (1999) 'Power distribution, the environment, and public health: a state-level analysis', *Ecological Economics* 29: 127–140.

Braungart, M. and McDonough, W. (2009) *Cradle to Cradle: Re-making the Way We Make Things*. London: Vintage Books.

Brightman, R. (1993) *Grateful Prey: Rock Cree Human–Animal Relationships*. Berkeley: University of California Press.

Brynjolfsson, E. and McAfee, A. (2015) 'Will humans go the way of horses?' *Foreign Affairs*, July/August 2015.

Chancel, L. and Piketty, T. (2015) *Carbon and Inequality: From Kyoto to Paris*. Paris: Paris School of Economics.

Chang, H.J. (2010) *23 Things They Don't Tell You About Capitalism*. London: Allen Lane.

Chapin, F. S. III, Kofinas, G. P. and Folke, C. (eds), *Principles of Ecosystem Stewardship: Resilience-Based Natural Resource Management in a Changing World*. New York: Springer.

Christianson, S. (2012) *100 Diagrams that Changed the World*. London: Salamander Books.

Cingano, F. (2014) *Trends in Income Inequality and its Impact on Economic Growth*. OECD Social, Employment and Migration Working Papers, no. 163, OECD Publishing.

Colander, D. (2000) 'New Millennium Economics: how did it get this way, and what way is it?, *Journal of Economic Perspectives* 14: 1, pp. 121–132.

Cole, M. (2015) *Is South Africa Operating in a Safe and Just Space? Using the doughnut model to explore environmental sustainability and social justice*. Oxford: Oxfam GB.

Coote, A. and Franklin, J. (2013) *Time On Our Side: Why We All Need a Shorter Working Week*. London: New Economics Foundation.

Coote, A. and Goodwin. N. (2010) *The Great Transition: Social Justice and the Core Economy*. nef working paper 1, London: New Economics Foundation.

Coote, A., Franklin, J. and Simms, A. (2010) *21 Hours: Why a shorter working week can help us all flourish in the 21st century*. London: New Economics Foundation.

Crawford, K. et al. (2014) *Demolition or Refurbishment of Social Housing? A Review of the Evidence*. London: UCL Urban Lab and Engineering Exchange.

Crompton, T. and Kasser, T. (2009) *Meeting Environmental Challenges: The Role of Human Identity*. Surrey: WWF.

Daly, H. (1990) 'Toward some operational principles of sustainable development', *Ecological Economics*, 2, pp. 1–6.

Daly, H. (1992) *Steady State Economics*. London: Earthscan.

Daly, H. (1996) *Beyond Growth*. Boston: Beacon Press.

Daly, H. and Farley, J. (2011) *Ecological Economics*. Washington: Island Press.

Dearing, J. et al. (2014) 'Safe and just operating spaces for regional social-ecological systems', *Global Environmental Change*, 28, pp. 227–238.

DeMartino, G. (2011) *The Economist's Oath*. Oxford: Oxford University Press.

Devas, C. S. (1883) *Groundwork of Economics*. Longmans, Green and Company.

Diamond, J. (2002) 'Evolution, consequences and future of plant and animal domestication', *Nature* 418, pp. 700–717.

Diamond, J. (2005) *Collapse: How Societies Choose to Fail or Survive*. London: Penguin.

Dorling, D. (2013) *Population 10 Billion*. London: Constable.

Easterlin, R. (1974) 'Does economic growth improve the human lot? Some empirical evidence', in David, P. and Reder, M. (eds), *Nations and Households in Economic Growth: Essays in Honour of Moses Abramovitz*. New York: Academic Press.

Eisenstein, C. (2011) *Sacred Economics: Money, Gift and Society in the Age of Transition*. Berkeley: Evolver Books.

Ellen McArthur Foundation (2012) *Towards the Circular Economy*. Isle of Wight, Ellen McArthur Foundation.

Epstein, J. and Axtell, R. (1996) *Growing Artificial Societies*. Washington, DC: Brookings Institution Press; Cambridge, MA: MIT Press.

Fälth, A. and Blackden, M. (2009) *Unpaid Care Work*, UNDP Policy Brief on Gender Equality and Poverty Reduction, Issue 01, New York: UNDP.

Fama, E. (1970) 'Efficient capital markets: a review of theory and empirical work', *Journal of Finance* 25: 2, pp. 383–417.

Ferguson, T. (1995) *Golden Rule: The Investment Theory of Party Competition and the Logic of Money-Driven Political Systems*. London: University of Chicago Press.

Ferraro, F., Pfeffer, J. and Sutton, R. (2005) 'Economics language and assumptions: how theories can become self-fulfilling', *Academy of Management Review* 30: 1, pp. 8–24.

Fioramenti, L. (2013) *Gross Domestic Product: The Politics Behind the World's Most Powerful Number.* London: Zed Books.

Folbre, N. (1994) *Who Pays for the Kids?* London: Routledge.

Folke, C. et al. (2011) 'Reconnecting to the biosphere', *AMBIO* 40, p. 719.

Frank, B. and Schulze, G. G. (2000) 'Does economics make citizens corrupt?' *Journal of Economic Behavior and Organization* 43, pp. 101–113.

Frank, R. 1988. *Passions within Reason.* New York: W.W. Norton.

Frank, R., Gilovich, T. and Regan, D. (1993) 'Does studying economics inhibit cooperation?' *Journal of Economic Perspectives*, 7: 2, pp. 159–171.

Friedman, B. (2006) *The Moral Consequence of Economic Growth.* New York: Vintage Books.

Friedman, M. (1962) *Capitalism and Freedom.* Chicago: University of Chicago Press.

Friedman, M. (1966) *Essays in Positive Economics*, Chicago: University of Chicago Press.

Friedman, M. (1970) 'The social responsibility of business is to increase its profits', *New York Times Magazine*, 13 September 1970.

Fullerton, J. (2015) *Regenerative Capitalism: How Universal Principles and Patterns Will Shape Our New Economy.* Greenwich, CT: Capital Institute

Gaffney, M. and Harrison, F. (1994) *The Corruption of Economics*, London: Shepheard-Walwyn.

Gal, O. (2012) 'Understanding global ruptures: a complexity perspective on the emerging middle crisis', in Dolphin, T. and Nash, D. (eds), *Complex New World.* London: Institute of Public Policy Research.

García-Amado, L. R., Ruiz Pérez, M. and Barrasa García, S. (2013) 'Motivation for conservation: assessing integrated conservation and development projects and payments for environmental services in La Sepultura Biosphere Reserve, Chiapas, Mexico', *Ecological Economics* 89, pp. 92–100.

George, H. (1879) *Progress and Poverty.* New York: The Modern Library.

Gerhardt, S. (2010) *The Selfish Society: How We All Forgot to Love One Another and Made Money Instead.* London: Simon & Schuster.

Gertler, P., Martinez, S. and Rubio-Codina, M. (2006) *Investing Cash Transfers to Raise Long-term Living Standards*, World Bank Policy Research Working Paper no. 3994, Washington, DC: World Bank.

Gesell, S. (1906) *The Natural Economic Order*, https://www.community-exchange.org/docs/Gesell/en/neo/

Giraud, Y. (2010) 'The changing place of visual representation in economics: Paul Samuelson between principle and strategy, 1941–1955', *Journal of the History of Economic Thought*, 32: pp. 175–197.

Gneezy, U. and Rustichini, A. (2000) 'A fine is a price', *Journal of Legal Studies*, 29, pp. 1–17.

Goerner, S. et al. (2009) 'Quantifying economic sustainability: implications for free-enterprise theory, policy and practice', *Ecological Economics* 69, pp. 76–81.

Goffmann, E. (1974) *Frame Analysis: An Essay on the Organization of Experience.* New York: Harper & Row.

Goodall, C. (2012) *Sustainability.* London: Hodder & Stoughton.

Goodwin, N. et al. (2009) *Microeconomics in Context.* New York: Routledge.

Gordon, R. (2014) *The Demise of US Economic Growth: Restatement, Rebuttals and Reflections.* NBER Working Paper no. 19895, February 2014.

Green, T. (2012) 'Introductory economics textbooks: what do they teach about sustainability?', *International Journal of Pluralism and Economics Education*, 3: 2, pp. 189–223.

Grossman, G. and Krueger, A. (1995) 'Economic growth and the environment', *Quarterly Journal of Economics*, 110: 2, pp. 353–377.

Gudynas, E. (2011) 'Buen Vivir: today's tomorrow', *Development* 54: 4, pp. 441–447.

Hardin, G. (1968) 'The tragedy of the commons', *Science* 162: 3859, pp. 1243–1248.

Hardoon, D., Fuentes, R. and Ayele, S. (2016) *An Economy for the 1%: how privilege and power in the economy drive extreme inequality and how this can be stopped.* Oxfam Briefing Paper 210, Oxford: Oxfam International.

Harford, T. (2013) *The Undercover Economist Strikes Back*, London: Little, Brown.

Heilbroner, R. (1970) 'Ecological Armageddon', *New York Review of Books*, 23 April.

Helbing, D. (2013) 'Economics 2.0: the natural step towards a self-regulating, participatory market society', *Evolutionary and Institutional Economics Review*, 10: 1, pp. 3–41.

Henrich, J. et al. (2001) 'In search of Homo Economicus: behavioral experiments in 15 small-scale societies', *Economics and Social Behavior*, 91: 2, pp. 73–78.

Henrich, J., Heine, S. and Norenzayan, A. (2010) 'The weirdest people in the world?', *Behavioural and Brain Sciences* 33: 2/3, pp. 61–83.

Hernandez, J. (2015) 'The new global corporate law', in *The State of Power 2015*, Amsterdam: The Transnational Institute.

Holland, T. et al. (2009) 'Inequality predicts biodiversity loss', *Conservation Biology* 23: 5, pp. 1304–1313.

Hudson, M. and Bezemer, D. (2012) 'Incorporating the rentier sectors into a financial model', *World Economic Review* 1, pp. 1–12.

ICRICT (2015) Declaration of the Independent Commissions for the Reform of International Corporate Taxation. http://www.icrict.org

Institute of Mechanical Engineers (2013) *Global Food: Waste Not, Want Not*. London: Institute of Mechanical Engineers.

International Cooperative Alliance (2014) *World Cooperative Monitor*. Geneva: ICA.

International Labour Organisation (2014) *Global Wage Report*. Geneva: ILO.

International Labour Organisation (2015) *Global Employment Trends for Youth 2015*. Geneva: ILO.

IPCC (2013) *Climate Change 2013: The Physical Science Basis. Contributions of Working Group I to the Fifth Assessment Report of the Intergovernmental Panel on Climate Change*, Cambridge: Cambridge University Press.

Islam, N. (2015) *Inequality and Environmental Sustainability*. United Nations Department for Economic and Social Affairs Working Paper no. 145. ST/ESA/2015/DWP/145.

Jackson, T. (2009) *Prosperity without Growth*. London: Earthscan.

Jensen, K., Vaish, A. and Schmidt, M. (2014) 'The emergence of human prosociality: aligning with others through feelings, concerns, and norms', *Frontiers in Psychology* 5, p. 822.

Jevons, W. S. (1871) *The Theory of Political Economy*, Library of Economics and Liberty, http://www.econlib.org/library/YPDBooks/Jevons/jvnPE.html

Kagel, J. and Roth, A. (1995) *The Handbook of Experimental Economics*. Princeton, NJ: Princeton University Press.

Keen, S. (2011) *Debunking Economics*. London: Zed Books.

Kelly, M. (2012) *Owning our Future: The Emerging Ownership Revolution*. San Francisco: Berrett-Koehler.

Kennedy, P. (1989) *The Rise and Fall of World Powers*. New York: Vintage Books.

Kerr, J. et al. (2012) 'Prosocial behavior and incentives: evidence from field experiments in rural Mexico and Tanzania', *Ecological Economics* 73, pp. 220–227.

Keynes, J. M. (1923) 'A Tract on Monetary Reform', in *The Collected Writings of John Maynard Keynes*, Vol. 4, 1977 edn. London: Palgrave Macmillan.

Keynes, J. M. (1924) 'Alfred Marshall, 1842–1924', *The Economic Journal*, 34: 135, pp. 311–372.

Keynes, J. M. (1931) 'Economic possibilities for our grandchildren', in *Essays in Persuasion*. London: Rupert Hart-Davis.

Keynes, J. M. (1936) *The General Theory of Employment, Interest and Money*. London: Macmillan.

Keynes, J. M. (1945) *First Annual Report of the Arts Council (1945–46)*, London: Arts Council.

Klein, N. (2007) *The Shock Doctrine*. London: Penguin.

Knight, F. (1999) *Selected Essays by Frank H. Knight, Volume 2*. Chicago: University of Chicago Press.

Kringelbach, M. (2008) *The Pleasure Center: Trust Your Animal Instincts*. Oxford: Oxford University Press.

Kuhn, T. (1962) *The Structure of Scientific Revolutions*. London: University of Chicago Press.

Kumhof, M. and Rancière, R. (2010) *Inequality, Leverage and Crises*. IMF Working Paper, WP/10/268, Washington, DC: IMF.

Kuznets, S. (1955) 'Economic growth and income inequality', *American Economic Review*, 45: 1, pp. 1–28.

Lacy, P. and Rutqvist, J. (2015) *Waste to Wealth: the circular economy advantage*. New York: Palgrave Macmillan.

Lakner, C. and Milanovic, B. (2015) 'Global income distribution: from the fall of the Berlin Wall to the Great Recession', *World Bank Economic Review*, 1–30.

Lakoff, G. (2014) *The All New Don't Think of an Elephant*. White River Junction, VT: Chelsea Green Publishing.

Lakoff, G. and Johnson, M. (1980) *Metaphors We Live By*. Chicago: University of Chicago Press.

Leach, M., Raworth, K. and Rockström, J. (2013) *Between Social and Planetary Boundaries: Navigating Pathways in the Safe and Just Space for Humanity*, World Social Science Report. Paris: UNESCO.

Leopold, A. (1989) *A Sand County Almanac*. New York: Oxford University Press.

Lewis, J. et al. (2005) *Citizens or Consumers? What the Media Tell Us About Political Participation*. Maidenhead: Open University Press.

Lewis, W. A. (1976) 'Development and distribution', in Cairncross, A. and Puri, M. (eds), *Employment, Income Distribution, and Development Strategy: Problems of the Developing Countries*. New York: Holmes & Meier, pp. 26–42.

Lietaer, B. (2001) *The Future of Money*. London: Century.

Lipsey, R. (1989) *An Introduction to Positive Economics*. London: Weidenfeld & Nicolson.

Liu, E. and Hanauer, N. (2011) *The Gardens of Democracy*. Seattle: Sasquatch Books.

Lucas, R. (2004) *The Industrial Revolution: Past and Future*. 2003 Annual Report Essay, The Federal Reserve Bank of Minneapolis.

Lyle, J. T. (1994) *Regenerative Design for Sustainable Development*. New York: John Wiley & Sons.

MacKenzie, D. and Millo, Y. (2003) 'Constructing a market, performing a theory: the historical sociology of a financial derivatives exchange', *American Journal of Sociology* 109: 1, pp. 107–145.

Mali, T. (2002) *What Learning Leaves*. Newtown, CT: Hanover Press.

Mankiw, G. (2012) *Principles of Economics*, 6th edn. Delhi: Cengage Learning.

Marçal, K. (2015) *Who Cooked Adam Smith's Dinner?* London: Portobello.

Marewzki, J. and Gigerenzer, G. (2012), 'Heuristic decision making in medicine', *Dialogues in Clinical Neuroscience*, 14: 1, pp. 77–89.

Marshall, A. (1890) *Principles of Economics*. London: Macmillan.

Marx, K. (1867) *Capital, Volume 1.* http://www.econlib.org/library/YPDBooks/Marx/mrxCpA.html

Max-Neef, M. (1991) *Human Scale Development*. New York: Apex Press.

Mazzucato, M. (2013) *The Entrepreneurial State*. London: Anthem Press.

Mazzucato, M., Semieniuk, G. and Watson, J. (2015) *What Will It Take to Get Us a Green Revolution?* SPRU Policy Paper, University of Sussex.

Meadows, D. (1998) *Indicators and Information Systems for Sustainable Development*. Vermont: The Sustainability Institute.

Meadows, D. (2008) *Thinking In Systems: A Primer*. White River Junction, VT: Chelsea Green.

Meadows, D. et al. (1972) *The Limits to Growth*. New York: Universe Books.

Meadows, D. et al. (2005) *Limits to Growth: The 30-Year Update*. London: Earthscan.

Michaels, F. S. (2011) *Monoculture: How One Story Is Changing Everything*. Canada: Red Clover Press.

Mill, J. S. (1844) *Essays on Some Unsettled Questions of Political Economy*, http://www.econlib.org/library/Mill/mlUQP5.html

Mill, J. S. (1848) *Principles of Political Economy*, http://www.econlib.org/library/Mill/mlP.html

Mill, J. S. (1873) *Autobiography*, 1989 edn. London: Penguin.

Minsky, H. (1977) 'The Financial Instability Hypothesis: an interpretation of Keynes and an alternative to Standard Theory', *Challenge*, March–April 1977, pp. 20–27.

Mishel, L. and Shierholz, H. (2013) *A Decade of Flat Wages*. EPI Briefing Paper no. 365, Washington, DC: Economic Policy Institute.

Molinsky, A., Grant, A. and Margolis, J. (2012) 'The bedside manner of homo economicus: how and why priming an economic schema reduces compassion', *Organizational Behavior and Human Decision Processes* 119: 1, pp. 27–37.

Montgomery, S. (2015), *The Soul of an Octopus*. London: Simon & Schuster.

Morgan, M. (2012) *The World in the Model*. Cambridge: Cambridge University Press.

Murphy, D. J. (2014) 'The implications of the declining energy return on investment of oil production', *Philosophical Transactions of the Royal Society A* 372.

Murphy, R. and Hines, C. (2010) 'Green quantitative easing: paying for the economy we need', Norfolk: Finance for the Future.

Murphy, S., Burch, D. and Clapp, J. (2012) *Cereal Secrets: the world's largest grain traders and global agriculture*, Oxfam Research Reports, Oxford: Oxfam International.

OECD (2014) *Policy Challenges for the Next 50 Years*, OECD Economic policy paper no. 9. Paris: OECD.

Ormerod, P. (2012) 'Networks and the need for a new approach to policy-making', in Dolphin, T. and Nash, D. (eds), *Complex New World*. London: IPPR.

Ostrom, E. (1999) 'Coping with tragedies of the commons', *Annual Review of Political Science* 2, pp. 493–535.

Ostrom, E. (2009) 'A general framework for analyzing sustainability of social-ecological systems', *Science* 325: 5939, pp. 419–422.

Ostrom, E., Janssen. M., and Anderies, J. (2007) 'Going beyond panaceas', *Proceedings of the National Academy of Sciences* 104: 39, pp. 15176–15178.

Ostry, J. D. et al. (2014) Redistribution, inequality and growth. IMF Staff discussion note, February 2014.

Palfrey, S. and Stern, T. (2007) *Shakespeare in Parts*. Oxford: Oxford University Press.

Parker, R. (2002) *Reflections on the Great Depression*. Cheltenham: Edward Elgar.

Pearce, F. (2016) *Common Ground: securing land rights and safeguarding the earth*. Oxford: Oxfam International.

Pearce, J. (2015) 'Quantifying the value of open source hardware development', *Modern Economy*, 6, pp. 1–11.

Pearce, J. (2012) 'The case for open source appropriate technology', *Environment, Development and Sustainability*, 14: 3.

Pearce, J. et al. (2012) 'A new model for enabling innovation in appropriate technology for sustainable development', *Sustainability: Science, Practice and Policy*, 8: 2, pp. 42–53.

Persky, J. (1992) 'Retrospectives: Pareto's law', *Journal of Economic Perspectives* 6: 2, pp. 181–192.

Piketty, T. (2014) *Capital in the Twenty-First Century*. Cambridge, MA: Harvard University Press.

Pizzigati, S. (2004) *Greed and Good*. New York: Apex Press.

Polanyi, K. (2001) *The Great Transformation*. Boston: Beacon Press.

Pop-Eleches, C. et al. (2011) 'Mobile phone technologies improve adherence to antiretroviral treatment in resource-limited settings: a randomized controlled trial of text message reminders', *AIDS* 25: 6, pp. 825–834.

Putnam, R. (2000) *Bowling Alone: The Collapse and Revival of American Community*. New York: Simon & Schuster.

Raworth, K. (2002) *Trading Away Our Rights: women workers in global supply chains*. Oxford: Oxfam International.

Raworth, K. (2012) *A Safe and Just Space for Humanity: can we live within the doughnut?* Oxfam Discussion Paper. Oxford: Oxfam International.

Razavi, S. (2007), *The Political and Social Economy of Care in a Development Context*. Gender and Development Programme Paper no. 3. Geneva: United Nations Research Institute for Social Development.

Ricardo, D. (1817) *On the Principles of Political Economy and Taxation*, http://www.econlib.org/library/Ricardo/ricP.html

Rifkin, J. (2014) *The Zero Marginal Cost Society*. New York: Palgrave Macmillan.

Robbins, L. (1932) *Essay on the Nature and Significance of Economic Science*. London: Macmillan.

Robinson, J. (1962) *Essays in the Theory of Economic Growth*. London: Macmillan.

Rockström, J. et al. (2009) 'A safe operating space for humanity', *Nature*, 461: 472–475.

Rode, J., Gómez-Baggethun, E. and Krause, T. (2015), 'Motivation crowding by economic incentives in conservation policy: a review of the empirical evidence', *Ecological Economics* 117, pp. 270–282.

Rodriguez, L. and Dimitrova, D. (2011) 'The levels of visual framing', *Journal of Visual Literacy* 30: 1, pp. 48–65.

Rogers, E. (1962) *Diffusion of Innovations*. New York: The Free Press.

Rostow, W. W. (1960), *The Stages of Economic Growth: A Non-Communist Manifesto*. Cambridge: Cambridge University Press.

Ruskin, J. (1860) *Unto This Last*, https://archive.org/details/untothislast00rusk

Ryan-Collins, J. et al. (2012) *Where Does Money Come From?* London: New Economics Foundation.

Ryan-Collins, J. et al. (2013) *Strategic Quantitative Easing: Stimulating Investment to Rebalance the Economy*. London: New Economics Foundation.

Ryan, R. and Deci, E. (1999) 'Intrinsic and extrinsic motivations: classic definitions and new directions', *Contemporary Educational Psychology* 25: 54–67.

Salganik, M., Sheridan Dodds, P. and Watts, D. (2006) 'Experimental study of inequality and unpredictability in an Artificial Cultural Market', *Science* 311, pp. 854–856.

Samuelson, P. (1948) *Economics: An Introductory Analysis* (1st edn). New York: McGraw-Hill.

Samuelson, P. (1964) *Economics* (6th edn). New York: McGraw-Hill.

Samuelson, P. (1980) *Economics* (11th edn). New York: McGraw-Hill.

Samuelson, P. (1997) 'Credo of a lucky textbook author', *Journal of Economic Perspectives* 11: 2, pp. 153–160.

Sandel, M. (2012) *What Money Can't Buy: The Moral Limits of Markets.* London: Allen Lane.

Sayers, M. (2015) *The UK Doughnut: a framework for environmental sustainability and social justice.* Oxford: Oxfam GB.

Sayers, M. (2015) *The Welsh Doughnut: a framework for environmental sustainability and social justice.* Oxford: Oxfam GB.

Sayers, M. and Trebeck, K. (2014) *The Scottish Doughnut: a safe and just operating space for Scotland.* Oxford: Oxfam GB.

Schabas, M. (1995) 'John Stuart Mill and concepts of nature', *Dialogue*, 34: 3, pp. 447–466.

Schumacher, E. F. (1973) *Small Is Beautiful*, London: Blond & Briggs.

Schumpeter, J. (1942) *Capitalism, Socialism and Democracy.* New York: Harper & Row.

Schumpeter, J. (1954) *History of Economic Analysis.* London: Allen & Unwin.

Schwartz, S. (1994) 'Are there universal aspects in the structure and content of human values?', *Journal of Social Issues* 50: 4, pp. 19–45.

Secretariat of the Convention on Biological Diversity (2012) *Cities and Biodiversity Outlook*, Montreal.

Seery, E. and Caistor Arendar, A. (2014) *Even It Up: time to end extreme inequality.* Oxford: Oxfam International.

Sen, A. (1999) *Development as Freedom.* New York: Alfred A. Knopf.

Simon, J. and Kahn, H. (1984) *The Resourceful Earth: A Response to Global 2000.* Oxford: Basil Blackwell.

Smith, A. (1759) *The Theory of Moral Sentiments*, http://www.econlib.org/library/Smith/smMS.html

Smith, A. (1776) *An Inquiry into the Nature and Causes of the Wealth of Nations.* 1994 edn, New York: Modern Library.

Smith, S. and Rothbaum, J. (2013) *Cooperatives in a Global Economy: Key Economic Issues, Recent Trends, and Potential for Development.* Institute for International Economic Policy Working Paper Series, George Washington University IIEP–WP–2013–6.

Solow, R. (1957) 'Technical change and the aggregate production function', *Review of Economics and Statistics* 39: 3, pp. 312–320.

Solow, R. (2008) 'The state of macroeconomics', *Journal of Economic Perspectives* 22: 1, pp. 243–249.

Spiegel, H. W. (1987) 'Jacob Viner (1892–1970)', in Eatwell, J., Milgate, M. and Newman, P. (eds) (1987) *The New Palgrave: a dictionary of economics*, Vol. IV. London: Macmillan.

Sraffa, P. (1926) 'The laws of returns under competitive conditions', *Economic Journal* 36: 144, pp. 535–550.

Sraffa, P. (1951) *Works and Correspondence of David Ricardo, Volume I.* Cambridge: Cambridge University Press.

Stedman Jones, D. (2012) *Masters of the Universe: Hayek, Friedman and the Birth of Neoliberal Politics.* Oxford: Princeton University Press.

Steffen,W. et al. (2011) 'The Anthropocene: from global change to planetary stewardship', *AMBIO* 40: 739–761.

Steffen, W. et al. (2015) 'The trajectory of the Anthropocene: The Great Acceleration', *Anthropocene Review* 2: 1, pp. 81–98.

Steffen, W. et al. (2015b) 'Planetary boundaries: guiding human development on a changing planet', Science, 347: 6223

Sterman, J. D. (2002) 'All models are wrong: reflections on becoming a systems scientist', *System Dynamics Review* 18: 4, pp. 501–531.

Sterman, J. D. (2000) *Business Dynamics: Systems Thinking and Modeling for a Complex World.* New York: McGraw-Hill.

Sterman, J. D.(2012) 'Sustaining sustainability: creating a systems science in a fragmented academy and polarized world', in Weinstein, M. P. and Turner, R. E. (eds), *Sustainability Science: The Emerging Paradigm and the Urban Environment.* New York: Springer Science.

Steuart, J. (1767) *An Inquiry into the Principles of Political Economy*, https://www.marxists.org/reference/subject/economics/steuart/

Stevenson, B. and Wolfers, J. (2008) *Economic Growth and Subjective Well-being: Reassessing the Easterlin Paradox,* National Bureau of Economic Research Working Paper no. 14282.

Stiglitz, J. E. (2011) 'Of the 1%, for the 1%, by the 1%', *Vanity Fair,* May 2011.

Stiglitz, J. E. (2012) *The Price of Inequality.* London: Allen Lane.

Stiglitz, J. E., Sen, A. and Fitoussi, J-P. (2009) *Report of the Commission on the Measurement of Economic Performance and Social Progress*, Paris.

Summers, L. (2016) 'The age of secular stagnation', *Foreign Affairs*, 15 February 2016.

Sumner, A. (2012) *From Deprivation to Distribution: Is Global Poverty Becoming a Matter of National Inequality?* IDS Working Paper no. 394, Sussex: Institute of Development Studies.

Thaler, R. and Sunstein, C. (2009) *Nudge: Improving Decisions About Health, Wealth and Happiness.* London: Penguin.

Thompson, E. P. (1964) *The Making of the English Working Class.* New York: Random House.

Thorpe, S., Fize, D. and Marlot, C. (1996) 'Speed of processing in the human visual system', *Nature* 381: 6582, pp. 520–522.

Titmuss, R. (1971) *The Gift Relationship: From Human Blood to Social Policy.* New York: Pantheon Books.

Torras, M. and Boyce, J. K. (1998) 'Income, inequality, and pollution: a reassessment of the environmental Kuznets curve', *Ecological Economics* 25, pp. 147–160.

Trades Union Congress (2012) *The Great Wages Grab.* London: TUC.

UNDP (2015) *Human Development Report 2015.* New York: United Nations.

UNEP (2016) *Global Material Flows and Resource Productivity: A Report of the International Resource Panel*, Paris: United Nations Environment Programme.

United Nations (2015) *World Population Prospects: The 2015 Revision.* New York: United Nations.

Veblen, T. (1898), 'Why is economics not an evolutionary science?' *Quarterly Journal of Economics*, 12: 4, pp. 373–397.

Wald, D. et al. (2014) 'Randomized trial of text messaging on adherence to cardiovascular preventive treatment, *Plos ONE* 9 (12)

Walras, L. (1874) *Elements of Pure Economics,* 1954 edn, London: George Allen & Unwin.

Wang, L., Malhotra, D. and Murnighan, K. (2011), 'Economics education and greed', *Academy of Management Learning and Education*, 10: 4, pp. 643–660.

Ward, B. and Dubos, R. (1973) *Only One Earth.* London: Penguin Books.

Weaver, W. (1948) 'Science and complexity' *American Scientist*, 36, pp. 536–544.

Webster, K. (2015) *The Circular Economy: A Wealth of Flows*. Isle of Wight: Ellen McArthur Foundation.

Wiedmann, T. O. et al. (2015) 'The material footprint of nations', *Proceedings of the National Academy of Sciences*, 112: 20, pp. 6271–6276.

Wijkman, A. and Skanberg, K. (2015) *The Circular Economy and Benefits for Society*. Zurich: Club of Rome.

Wilkinson, R. and Pickett, K. (2009) *The Spirit Level*. London: Penguin.

World Bank (1978) *World Development Report*. Washington, DC: World Bank.

World Economic Forum (2016) *The Future of Jobs*. Geneva: World Economic Forum.

ACKNOWLEDGEMENTS

This book comes out of 25 years of learning, unlearning, and relearning economics and there are many people I would like to thank because they have inspired me on that long journey. My first thanks are to my economics tutors Andrew Graham, Frances Stewart, Wilfred Beckerman and David Vines, without whose inspirational teaching I would never have been drawn to thinking like an economist in the first place. I am extremely grateful, in turn, to the students I have had the privilege to teach, especially those at Oxford University's Environmental Change Institute and at Schumacher College. It is largely thanks to their creativity and openness to new ways of thinking that I have such confidence in the planetary household managers of the future.

Many of the ideas in this book have grown out of Doughnut discussions that I have had in a range of countries over the past five years, with Oxfam colleagues, university students, Occupy protestors, corporate executives, UN negotiators, community groups, government policymakers, NGOs, academics and scientists. Thank you all – and particular thanks to Oxfam for giving me the opportunity to create the Doughnut in the first place.

My superb literary agents Maggie Hanbury, Robin Straus and Harriet Poland have all given me outstanding support from the

351

get-go. I am also profoundly grateful to my editors Nigel Wilcockson at Penguin Random House and Joni Praded at Chelsea Green for their excellent and incisive suggestions and advice; to my copy-editor, Beth Humphries, and to Rowan Borchers at Penguin Random House, who helped guide the book through its production stages. Thank you to Joss Saunders at Oxfam, Marla Guttman and Laura Crowley at Reed Smith, and to John Fullerton and Nora Bouhaddada at Capital Institute, who all provided expert technical support and advice. My especial thanks to Diane Ives and the Kendeda Fund for generously backing this book and its ideas: your support has been invaluable.

I am extremely grateful to Alan Doran, Carl Gombrich, Andrew Graham, George Monbiot and Garry Peterson for reading and giv-ing excellent comments on drafts of the whole text. Special thanks also to Richard King for outstanding data analysis, Marcia Mihotich for the beautiful graphics, and Christian Guthier for the iconic Doughnut images.

I received insightful comments, ideas and suggestions for the book from many generous people, including Adam Alagiah, Myles Allen, Graham Bannock, Alex Cobham, Sarah Cornell, Anna Cowen, Ian Fitzpatrick, Josh Floyd, Antonio Hill, Erik Gómez-Baggethun, Tony Greenham, Hugh Griffith, Emily Jones, William Kamkwamba, Finn Lewis, Bernard Lietaer, Nick Lloyd, Eric Lonergan, André Maia Chagas, George Marshall, Clive Menzies, Forrest Metz, Asher Miller, Tom Murphy, Cathy O'Neill, Rob Patterson, Joshua Pearce, Johan Rockström, Emma Smith, Niki Sporrong, Robin Stafford, Will Steffen, Joss Tantram, Ken Webster, Tommy Wiedmann, Rachel Wilshaw and John Ziniades. A big thank-you especially to Janine Benyus, Sam Muirhead and Yuan Yang for the inspiring conversations that we had in interviews for this book.

I greatly appreciate the support I have had from many colleagues and friends, among them Sasha Abramsky, Al-Hassan Adam, Steve

Bass, Sarah Best, Sumi Dhanarajan, Konstantin Dierks, Joshua Farley, Flora Gathorne-Hardy, Maja Göpel, Alissa Goodman, Duncan Green, Thalia Kidder, Sarah Knott, Diana Liverman, Ruth Mayne, Eka Morgan, Annalise Moser, Tim O'Riordan, Angelique Orr, Trista Patterson, Pete Shepherd, Claire Shine, Kitty Stewart, Julia Tilford, Tom Thornton, Katherine Trebeck, Aris Vrettos, Kevin Watkins, Stewart Wallis, Tim Weiskel, Anders Wijkman and Rebecca Wrigley. In the toughest of writing times, five people gave me outstanding advice: my deepest thanks to Phil Bloomer, Alan Buckley, Jo Confino, Julian Masters and Jo de Waal.

In years of exploring new economic thinking I have been inspired by many thinkers whose writing gave me those Aha! moments from which there is no turning back: thank you Michel Bauwens, Eric Beinhocker, John Berger, Janine Benyus, David Bollier, Ha-Joon Chang, Robert Costanza, Herman Daly, Diane Elson, Nancy Folbre, John Fullerton, Yann Giraud, Sally Goerner, Tim Jackson, Steve Keen, Marjorie Kelly, George Lakoff, Bernard Lietaer, Hunter Lovins, Manfred Max-Neef, Donella Meadows, Mary Mellor, Elinor Ostrom, Jeremy Rifkin, Johan Rockström, Amartya Sen, Juliet Schor, Fritz Schumacher, Will Steffen, John Sterman, Arron Stibbe and Ken Webster.

I am deeply grateful to my parents, Jenny and Ricky Raworth, and to my sister Sophie, for their unwavering support for my economic adventures.

Last and most, thank you to my partner in life Roman Krznaric, without whose love, conversation and co-parenting I would never have written this book. And to our children Siri and Cas who, like all children, deserve to thrive in a safe and just twenty-first century.

ABOUT THE AUTHOR

Kate Raworth is an economist focused on exploring the economic thinking needed to address the twenty-first century's social and ecological challenges. She teaches at Oxford University's Environmental Change Institute, where she is a senior visiting research associate. She is also a senior associate of the Cambridge Institute for Sustainability Leadership, and teaches on the Economics for Transition programme at Schumacher College.

Her internationally acclaimed idea of Doughnut Economics has been widely influential amongst sustainable development thinkers, progressive businesses and political activists, and she has presented its core ideas to audiences ranging from the UN General Assembly to the Occupy movement.

Over the past 20 years, Kate's career has taken her from working with micro-entrepreneurs in the villages of Zanzibar to co-authoring flagship reports for the United Nations Development Programme in New York, followed by a decade as Senior Researcher at Oxfam.

Named by the *Guardian* as 'one of the top ten tweeters on economic transformation', her media work includes articles and interviews for the *Financial Times*, the *Wall Street Journal*, the *New Statesman*, *CNN,* and *Al-Jazeera*. Her academic research has appeared in journals including *Nature Climate Change*,

Sustainability, Gender and Development, and the *Journal of Ethics and International Affairs*.

Kate has a BA in Politics, Philosophy and Economics, and an MSc in Economics for Development, both from Oxford University. She is a member of the Club of Rome and serves on several advisory boards, including the Stockholm School of Economics' Global Challenges programme, the University of Surrey's Centre for the Understanding of Sustainable Prosperity, and Oxford University's Environmental Change Institute.

www.kateraworth.com
www.facebook.com/doughnuteconomics
@kateraworth

INDEX

Page numbers in *italics* denote illustrations

PICTURE ACKNOWLEDGEMENTS

Illustrations are reproduced by kind permission of:

archive.org: 16. © Kyle Depew: 3. © Mark Segal/Panoramic Images, Chicago: 101. © McGraw-Hill Education: 20. Dreamstime: 174 (© Roman Yatsnya). Getty Images: 18 (© Yale Joel/The LIFE Picture Collection), 157 (© Hulton Archive/Stringer), 203 (© Lucas Oleniuk), 225 above (© urbancow), 225 below (© Matt Champlin), 270 (© Kurt Hutton/Stringer). LSE Library: 65. New York Public Library: 179. Wikimedia Commons: 14.

Diagrams designed by:

Christian Guthier: 11, 44, 51. Marcia Mihotich: 26–27, 39, 47, 54, 64, 71, 96, 108, 127, 132, 140, 168, 207, 212, 220, 247, 251, 259.